P9-DUU-119

Afropessimism

ALSO BY FRANK B. WILDERSON III

Incognegro: A Memoir of Exile and Apartheid

Red, White & Black:
Cinema and the Structure of U.S. Antagonisms

Afropessimism

FRANK B. WILDERSON III

LIVERIGHT PUBLISHING CORPORATION

A DIVISION OF W. W. NORTON & COMPANY

INDEPENDENT PUBLISHERS SINCE 1923

Copyright © 2020 by Frank B. Wilderson III

All rights reserved
Printed in the United States of America
First Edition

Excerpts from "Close-Up: Fugitivity and the Filmic Imagination: Social Death and Narrative Aporia in *12 Years a Slave*" reprinted with kind permission of *Black Camera, An International Film Journal* (Indiana University Press). Excerpts from "The Black in the Cul-de-Sac: Afro-Pessimism as the Crisis of Critical Theory" reprinted with kind permission of the *Journal of Contemporary Thought*. Excerpts from "Without Priors" reprinted from *The Big No* with kind permission of University of Minnesota Press. Excerpts from "The Black Liberation Army and the Paradox of Political Engagement" reprinted with kind permission of Campus Verlag. Excerpts from "Afro-Pessimism and the End of the Redemption" reprinted with kind permission of the *Occupied Times*. Excerpts from "The Prison Slave as Hegemony's (Silent) Scandal" reprinted with kind permission of *Social Justice*. Excerpts from "The Vengeance of Vertigo: Aphasia and Abjection in the Political Trials of Black Insurgents" reprinted with kind permission of *InTensions* (York University).

For information about permission to reproduce selections from this book, write to Permissions, Liveright Publishing Corporation, a division of W. W. Norton & Company, Inc., 500 Fifth Avenue, New York, NY 10110

For information about special discounts for bulk purchases, please contact W. W. Norton Special Sales at specialsales@wwnorton.com or 800-233-4830

Manufacturing by Lake Book Manufacturing
Book design by Daniel Lagin
Production manager: Lauren Abbate

ISBN 978-1-63149-614-1   **33614081687302**

Liveright Publishing Corporation, 500 Fifth Avenue, New York, N.Y. 10110
www.wwnorton.com

W. W. Norton & Company Ltd., 15 Carlisle Street, London W1D 3BS

1 2 3 4 5 6 7 8 9 0

To Anita Wilkins, for your love.

To Drs. Ida-Lorraine and Frank B. Wilderson, Jr.,
for molding my mind.

To Assata Shakur and Winnie Mandela, for everything.

CONTENTS

ACKNOWLEDGMENTS

In 2013/2014 I spent eleven months at the University of Bremen, Germany, as an Alexander von Humboldt Experienced Research Fellow. In Germany, I started writing an academic monograph that explained how and why Human capacity (the power to be a subject of relations) is violently parasitic on Black flesh; why Orlando Patterson's brilliant delineation of slavery needed to be abstracted in a way that showed how the Human is not an organic entity but a construct; a construct that requires its *Other* in order to be legible; and why the Human Other is Black. I was, and am, deeply indebted to the works of key thinkers who have also grappled with this highly controversial claim: Saidiya Hartman, Zakiyyah Iman Jackson, Joy James, David Marriott, Jared Sexton, Hortense Spillers, and Sylvia Wynter. I took them to Germany the way a zealot takes his Bible abroad. The idea for a book that would become a cross between creative nonfiction and critical theory came to me toward the end of my time in Bremen. For eight months my labors had been torn between a novel I was writing and the monograph I was funded to write. Without the freedom from teaching and administration, coupled with the library resources at my disposal, and the intellectuals, activists, and artists I communed with, I might not ever have considered embarking upon a book that weaves the abstract thinking of critical theory with blood-and-guts stories of life as it's lived: the hybrid seed you hold in your hands. In addition, UC Irvine's Humanities Commons gave me a publication support grant that helped me in the home stretch.

Bob Weil, editor-in-chief and publishing director of Liveright, is someone steeped in knowledge of the Black literary tradition, from having edited some of the most influential Black writers of the twentieth and twenty-first centuries. Not only did he bring laughter and friendship to our encounters, but he brought a unique improvisational literary vision needed to help me reconcile diverging characteristics of theory and storytelling, a project that many other editors might have found too daunting to attempt. Gabriel S. Kachuck, Bob's editorial assistant, is a jack-of-all-trades who has yet to meet a problem he can't solve. My thanks also to Amy Medeiros and Dave Cole, for the fine project editing and copyediting work they did. Peter Miller, Liveright's director of publicity, and Cordelia Calvert, publicity manager, worked tirelessly with Liz Cole of Evil Twin Booking and Gretchen Crary of February Media to launch a remarkable media-and-appearances campaign.

My agent, Charlotte Gusay, and her interns Sophie Gu, Julia Murray, and Richie Stone were invaluable in the help they provided me during the production of the book proposal and in pitching the book to editors.

Special thanks to Jocelyn Burrell, Adam Fitzgerald, Fred Moten, Claudia Rankine, and Alexei Setian, whose friendship, support, advice, and critique go far beyond what I can acknowledge here. In addition, there are many activists, scholars, artists, and traditional healers who have also supported and encouraged me throughout the writing of this book:

ACKNOWLEDGMENTS

Alexis Hernandez Abreu, Babalawo Raudemar Hernandez Abreu, Babalawo Noël Amherd, Sampada Aranke, Franco Barchiesi, Jed Bickman, James Bliss, Heinrich Böhmke, Wellington Bowler, Sebastiaan Boersma, Nicholas Brady, Sabine Broeck, Gregory L. Caldwell, LaShonda Carter, Christopher Chamberlin, Matthieu Chapman, Bridget Cooks, Cecilio M. Cooper, Huey Copeland, Ben Crossan, Jerome Dent, Patrice Douglass, Paula von Gleich, Che Gossett, Venus Green, Sora Han, Zakia Henderson-Brown, Athi Mongezeleli Joja, Carsten Junker, Peter Kent-Stoll, Ellen Louis, Prathna Lor, Marronage of Denmark (especially Mikas Lang and Yannick Nehemiah), Danae Martinez, Kerstin Mertens, Andile Mngxitama, Jalil Abdul Muntaqim, David Mura, John Murillo, Athinangamso Esther Nkopo, Linette Park, Rajagopalan Radhakrishnan, Omar Ricks, Myriam Sauer, Hannibal Shakur, Sara-Maria Sorentino, Samira Spatzek, Kai Thomas, Selamawit D. Terrefe, João Costa Vargas, Parisa Vaziri, Carol Vaubel, Kassian Vaubel, Sebastian Weier, Jaye Austin Williams, Wind Dell Woods, and Mlondi Zondi.

Finally, with love and gratitude I extend my appreciation to my wife, Anita Wilkins, who counseled me to "make the problem your subject" during those frustrating moments when seemingly insurmountable problems of writing haunted my forward momentum. More than that, she shared this intellectual journey with me in late-night discussions on the challenges Afropessimism presents to storytelling when the narrator is a Slave.

Afropessimism

I

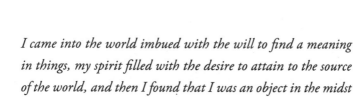

I came into the world imbued with the will to find a meaning in things, my spirit filled with the desire to attain to the source of the world, and then I found that I was an object in the midst of other objects.

FRANTZ FANON

I'm prized most as a vector through which others can accomplish themselves.

CECILIO M. COOPER

CHAPTER ONE

For Halloween I Washed My Face

1

A psychotic episode is no picnic, especially if you know you can't call it madness because madness assumes a change in the weather, a season of sanity.

I was moaning. Sobbing. The crisp disposable sheet that lined the gurney rasped as I shifted. I sat up when they came into the room. No one was going to strap me down. But I didn't climb down for fear of giving them cause. In the glare of fluorescence, they—the doctor and the nurse—were white as dust. The gurney rattled as I shook and cried. They didn't approach. They didn't call for help, not for themselves nor for me, a monstrous aphasic too black for care. That's how I saw them see me. And my urge to save them from me eclipsed my desire to be cured. But I couldn't speak. Not even to tell them that I wanted to protect them from me.

Cluster bombs spiked in my heart. I clutched my chest and cried out. Did they take a step back? Is it your heart? the doctor asked. I wanted to laugh. The funny thing about a mouth is that it needs to close as well as open if a word is to be made. Mine wouldn't close; if it closed, I knew it wouldn't open. The hinges of my jaws made moans or howls but not words. I thought, *How funny is that?* I answered him in the words of a bird as its throat is slit.

You keep clutching your chest, he said. Are you having a sharp pain, somewhere in the region of the heart? I nodded my head. Tell me more, he said. But I felt my lips twisting grotesquely; I didn't want to start sobbing again. He told me to take my time. The nurse nodded gravely, as though she were peering at a pug-nosed puppy in a cage. I had an urge to answer her gaze with a pug-nosed-puppy bark. As this urge grew, her sadness deepened. My bark and her sad, saucer eyes were headed for a collision. *Ruff! Ruff! Gimme a biscuit!* My head was splitting and so were my sides, but not in the same register of emotion. Sir Belly-Laugh rose up from my torso and met Mr. Why-the-Fuck-Am-I-Alive, who had fallen through my raging skull and landed in my throat. The sadness drained from the nurse's eyes. She was her frightened self again. The puppy-love had morphed into her need for self-preservation from this hulking black mass with matted, uncombed hair, and orbs of fireworks bursting from holes where the eyes should be.

The doctor sat on a stool, with one foot on the lower rung, one foot on the floor. But the nurse remained standing. He massaged a luxuriant eyebrow with his index finger and waited. Laughter is good, he said. Why don't you tell us what's so funny? I wanted to say, Would it be all right if I barked? I realized, however, that I would seem crazier if I asked his permission to bark than if I showed some initiative and simply barked without making a big deal of it. I fell through the chasm of laughter and tears.

No one had taken me to the student health center. I got there on my own. As I sat on the gurney, sobbing, fearing the fear of the world in the doctor's and nurse's eyes, I could only answer one of their questions (Is someone with you?) by shaking of my head. How did you get here? Who brought you? Tears scarred my face in reply. Did you drive? one of them said. I shook my head. They noticed car keys in my hand.

They still hadn't taken my pulse or my blood pressure. The doctor told me to rest. He said they would return momentarily.

When they left, the fluorescent lights pierced my eyes like daggers of ice that hung from mansions in the winters of my childhood. I didn't trust my sense of balance enough to slide off the gurney and turn off the lights. I had no wish to lie facedown with only this crinkling, disposable sheet between the front of my body and a cold mattress, which rebuked me like a dry cough when I moved. So I remained on my back. Roses exploded as my eyelids closed against the glare.

Had I been shaving this morning when I snapped? I wore a beard, so no, I had not been shaving. But I knew it had started in the mirror. I was washing my face when a stanza of poetry came to me. It started with a sensation of heat on my face and tightness in my chest. The way I often felt as a child on those mornings when I couldn't face the taunting day at a White grammar school set back from the dappled waters of a long lake spotted with willow trees. My flesh hummed as though my shirt were made of insects and the skin on my back shifted as it did when my mother closed the door behind me each morning. The memory of that frightened little boy who had answered to my name groaned in my ears like the echo of oarlocks on a calm, deserted sea. I pulled the oars for the shore, where every grief of my childhood waited.

I'm a middle-aged graduate student, I told the image that the mirror had ruined. I. Have. Got. It. Together. But the jag of pain in my chest wouldn't listen. It wanted to remember and hear that poem that, a moment ago, had flown in and out of my mind.

I knew that I had to get out before I died all alone of a heart attack in my bathroom. Walking seemed to make me want to faint.

The apartment was small, just a bathroom, then a bedroom, a kitchen, and a living room. In each room I found something for my hand to hold—the closet door, the stove, the back of a kitchen chair, the rows of living room bookshelves that ended at the front door. The front door closed behind me.

I was overcome with vertigo, as I looked down those seven steps, as though I were looking into a deep ravine. The urge to faint and the urge to vomit went to blows in my body. Bad karma, I thought, through wet, blurry eyes. I thought I would pass out. My Honda Civic dozed at the curb like a small blue lizard. My keys scratched the wrought-iron railing as I stumbled down. *We're going trick-or-treating*, I thought with a laugh, *we've washed our face and we're wearing our school clothes*. A beast with insane rage struggled to burst through my skin in a shower of blood and bile. I wanted to cry. One palm pressed against the window. One set of fingers fumbled with the keys.

"Help me, somebody," I sobbed into my neck, hoping no White person would hear. "Please, somebody help me."

Now, lying on the gurney, I recalled the threads of silver puke spooling onto the hood of my car. Then, without knowing how or why, I was on a bus in downtown Berkeley. I saw myself seeing myself through the eyes of passengers on the bus, as I slumped to one side and softly sobbed. *Make them feel safe*, I had thought to myself, even though I had never felt more at risk. I would think it again when the nurse and the doctor first came into this white sepulchre where I lay. Make them feel safe, the cardinal rule of Negro diplomacy.

Now, alone in the clinic, trombones of light blistered my eyes and the room grew cold. But if I closed them a string of past lives skidded down my skull like a train that had jumped the rails above a ravine. Each cascading car was a carriage of time. The engine was the time of *now*, the time of this moment on the gurney. Then came tumbling down a carriage of time that carried my life in apartheid South Africa, where Mandela's promises flickered and choked like the last gasps of lampposts. All that bloodshed for a flag-and-anthem nation, the mist of mythology, and tough love from his cronies who rebuked the so-called ultra-left with, "Now, comrades, you must understand that you cannot eat your principles." The next car that shot down the cliff face was the 1980s: a first-class compartment of nerves and ulcers. I was a newly minted college graduate who thought pain, like anything else in this life, could be traded on the floor of the exchange. For eight years, between graduating from Dartmouth and immigrating to South Africa to fight against apartheid, I worked as a retail stockbroker. The first Black stockbroker in Minnesota, I was told by the sales manager who so proudly hired me.

2

Those eight years all but ruined my health. The side of my face twitched and shuddered at will. An ulcer singed the lining of my stomach. My internist wasn't the first person to make this prognosis. Jasmine, a secretary at Merrill Lynch's head office on Wall Street, whom I'd met one summer during a month of training, had also told me that I didn't belong in that profession. She was right and I knew it at the time, but money is a great motivator; now I stood a good chance of spending all that money on long-term care if I didn't do something fast.

"You're not a capitalist," my internist told me. "You don't have the gut for it."

"I want money. I *need* money."

"You drink eight cups of coffee a day. Your cheek blinks like a Morse code lamp. You should wait till your ulcer is the size of my pinkie, is that what you should do?"

I tried to slow down, which meant my sales slowed down, and

soon it became clear that I should quit before the sales manager embarrassed me and ushered me out. I took a job as a waiter at an exclusive lakeside beach club—which did not admit Jews until the late 1960s and didn't have its first Black member until the mid-1970s. The clientele ran the gamut from Dan Aykroyd and Jim Belushi, whose entourage left the interior of the ballroom in need of, to say the least, repair, to the old blue-blood families that had tried to keep my parents out of the neighborhood in 1962. One day I walked into the ballroom balancing a large tray of nine Caesar salads on my shoulder. The tray wobbled and almost fell when I saw the faces at the table I'd been sent to. They were colleagues—former colleagues—from the broker-age firm I had left two months ago. I slowly got hold of the lie I'd told them when I left. "Tired of working for the man, fellas. Going to try my hand as a private dealmaker, with a little financial planning on the side." One by one I laid their salads down. My name sputtered out of their mouths, "*Frank?*"—a question tucked into a gasp. I quit a week later—which made no sense, they had seen me, the lie was laid bare—and went to work for less pay at an art museum.

I worked as a guard at the Walker Art Center overlooking down-town Minneapolis and I licked my wounds from the Calhoun Beach Club and eight ethically bankrupt years as a stockbroker. The First Intifada had just begun in Palestine and I had a dear friend from Ramallah who was also a guard at the museum. His name was Sameer Bishara. He was a photographer who studied at the Minneapolis Insti-tute of Art. We shared the same politics: revolutionary; and star sign: Aries. Two people who were often wrong but never in doubt. "If we were in an airplane," Sameer once told me, "and we crashed in the desert and a survivors detail was formed, some people would be tasked with finding water, it would be the job of others to forage for food and firewood, and we would need a team to build a shelter from what could be salvaged from the crash. But you, Frank, you would be the one sitting back giving us orders." I didn't spoil the satisfaction he got from the dig by telling him he had mapped onto me traits that were just as applicable to him.

Most of the guards were either artists or writers or students. But only Sameer shared my politics of insurrection. We bonded early and kept our distance from the others. I told him of my college dreams of going to Zimbabwe and fighting for ZANU/ZAPU or to New York to join Assata Shakur and the Black Liberation Army. Sameer longed to return to Ramallah in order to make what he thought would be a more meaningful contribution to the intifada than the talks he gave to moist-eyed Minnesota liberals. He was twenty-five. I was thirty-one. In five years, I would be the same age Frantz Fanon was when he died in the custody of the Central Intelligence Agency. By the time Fanon died, in 1961, he had fled Martinique, his native land, joined De Gaulle's army, and had been wounded fighting the Nazis. He had also completed his internship in psychiatry and medicine, joined the FLN in the Algerian revolution, and penned four books on revolution and psychoanalysis. I had five years to catch him—a bar set high by my shame-demon. Hubris at low places was where I lived. Much the same was true for Sameer. What a waste, he told me, photographing Scandinavians and loons when he felt he should be back home making bombs. We had different shoulders but they bore the same chip. I was convinced of this one morning when he came to work smiling, despite the fact that his right eye was slightly bulbous and closed.

"Last night," he informed me, "a friend of mine from Palestine and I met these two gorgeous women. White, of course," he added under his breath, and I didn't bother to question the "of course," because I wasn't sure that he wasn't wrong. That "White" means beauty goes without saying is the message one is fed all of one's life. To protest to the contrary is like saying, *It's not about money,* after you've been shortchanged.

Sameer said that he and his friend could have taken them home if three rich Kuwaitis hadn't sauntered into the lounge. When one of the Kuwaitis made a move on the woman Sameer was talking to, Sameer told him, in a kind way, to go back to his booth.

The man scoffed, "You don't even have your own country."

But he went back. As the night wore on the Kuwaitis sent champagne to Sameer's table. Then all three of them approached. They offered to take the women to an exclusive after-party at a penthouse suite in the suburb of Edina.

"Just you two," the Kuwaiti Sameer had sent packing said, "not these stateless ones."

Since the Kuwaitis numbered three and Sameer and his friend numbered two, the Kuwaitis accepted Sameer's offer to discuss the "details" of the after-party in the parking lot.

The teeth of the time clock pierced Sameer's time card. I followed suit, as he donned the blue museum blazer that we all wore. We walked together to the main gallery. As I continued walking, to take up my position on the mezzanine level, he smiled and whispered, "We beat those Kuwaitis until we were tired."

It wasn't as much bucked horns locked over the pride of possession of two forbidden females that sparked the dustup in the parking lot—though that was surely part of it. What seared the flesh on his skin the most was the Kuwaitis' ridicule of Sameer's statelessness. I thought I had the same loss too; because I thought my suffering was analogous to his. I was not an Afropessimist then.

"I would have beaten them too," I said.

A high, grassy knoll abutted the building that housed the Walker Art Center. The knoll is gone now, scalped clean as a root canal to make room for a restaurant. But when it was still a hill, Sameer and I would take our lunch there. In springtime, when the cold broke and the sky cleared, the hilltop commanded a sweeping view of white swans tracing Loring Park Lake. Distant cars in downtown streets sparkled like sequins in the sun. And from that knoll you could see the Basilica of Saint Mary's copper dome corroded by melted snow and driving rain to a blue-green brilliance that made me think ruin was the only true object of love. The knoll was also a vantage point from which death in the making would be seen. Just below it was the Bottleneck, an intersection where three streets converged into one, a place where some of the most horrifying collisions occurred. As a tween reading spy novels, I used to imagine the Bottleneck as a stretch of the German Autobahn where John le Carré's ill-fated spy, Alec Leamas, saw two young children waving cheerfully from the window of a small car; and the next moment saw it smashed between two large lorries. That hill was where Sameer told me about his cousin who was killed in Ramallah—blown up while making a bomb. But he wasn't a suicide bomber. It was an accident. Sameer blamed himself, the way that survivors often do, no matter how near or far in space and time they are from their dead. He survived by being here and not there.

My friend spoke openly as we watched the world below us rush by without even looking up to pay its respects. At one point Sameer spoke of being stopped and searched at Israeli checkpoints. He spoke in a manner that seemed not to require my presence. I hadn't seen this level of concentration and detachment in him before. That was fine. He was grieving.

"The shameful and humiliating way the soldiers run their hands up and down your body," he said. Then he added, "But the shame and humiliation runs even deeper if the Israeli soldier is an Ethiopian Jew."

The earth gave way. The thought that my place in the unconscious of Palestinians fighting for their freedom was the same *dishonorable* place I occupied in the minds of Whites in America and Israel chilled me. I gathered enough wits about me to tell him that his feelings were odd, seeing how Palestinians were at war with Israelis, and White

Israelis at that. How was it that the people who stole his land and slaughtered his relatives were somehow *less* of a threat in his imagination than Black Jews, often implements of Israeli madness, who sometimes do their dirty work? What, I wondered silently, was it about Black people (about *me*) that made us so fungible we could be tossed like a salad in the minds of oppressors and the oppressed?

I was faced with the realization that in the collective unconscious, Palestinian insurgents have more in common with the Israeli state and civil society than they do with Black people. What they share is a largely unconscious consensus that Blackness is a locus of abjection to be instrumentalized on a whim. At one moment Blackness is a disfigured and disfiguring phobic phenomenon; at another moment Blackness is a sentient implement to be joyously deployed for reasons and agendas that have little to do with Black liberation. There I sat, yearning, in solidarity with my Palestinian friend's yearning, for the full restoration of Palestinian sovereignty; mourning, in solidarity with my friend's mourning, over the loss of his insurgent cousin; yearning, that is, for the historical and political *redemption* of what I thought was a violated commons to which *we both belonged*—when, all of a sudden, my friend reached down into the unconscious of his people and slapped me upside the head with a wet gym shoe: the startling realization that not only was I barred, ab initio, from the denouement of historical and political redemption, but that the borders of redemption are policed by Whites and non-Whites alike, *even as they kill each other.*

It's worse than that. I, as a Black person (if *person, subject, being* are appropriate, since *Human* is not), am both barred from the denouement of social and historical redemption and *needed* if redemption is to attain any form of coherence. Without the articulation of a common negrophobogenesis that relays between Israel and Palestine, the narrative coherence of their bloody conflict would evaporate. My friend's and his fellow Palestinians' negrophobogenesis is the bed-rock, the concrete slabs upon which any edifice of Human articula-tion (whether love or war) is built. Degraded humanity (Palestinians) can be frisked by exalted humanity (Ashkenazi Jews) and the walls of reason remain standing (notwithstanding the universal indignity of stop-and-frisk). But if the soldier is an Ethiopian Jew . . .

Pain gripped my chest. Sameer and I were antagonists, not because as friends we were mismatched, and not because our politics were incompatible; but because the imago of the Black is "responsible for all the conflicts that may arise." For the libidinal economy that positions the Black imago as a phobogenic object saturates the collec-tive unconscious; it usurps me as an instrument *for*, though never a beneficiary *of*, every nation's woes; even two nations at war.

I was no Afropessimist in 1988. In other words, I saw myself as a degraded Human, saw my plight as analogous to the plight of the Palestinians, the Native American, and the working class. Now I understood that analogy was a ruse. I was the foil of Humanity. Humanity looked to me when it was unsure of itself. I let Humanity say, with a sigh of existential relief, "At least we're not him." To quote Saidiya Hartman, "The slave is neither civic man nor free worker but excluded from the narrative of 'we the people' that effects the linkage of the modern individual and the state . . . The everyday practices of the enslaved occur in the default of the political, in the absence of the rights of man or the assurances of the self-possessed individual, and perhaps even without a 'person,' in the usual meaning of the term."

Black people *embody* (which is different from saying are always willing or allowed to express) a meta-aporia for political thought and action.

For most critical theorists writing after 1968, the word *aporia* is used to designate a contradiction in a text or theoretical undertaking. For example, Jacques Derrida suggests an aporia indicates "a point of undecidability, which locates the site at which the text most obviously undermines its own rhetorical structure, dismantles, or deconstructs itself." But when I say that Black people embody a meta-aporia for political thought and action, the addition of the prefix *meta-* goes beyond what Derrida and the poststructuralists meant—it raises the level of abstraction and, in so doing, raises the stakes.

In epistemology, a branch of philosophy concerned with the theory of knowledge, the prefix *meta-* is used to mean *about (its own category)*. Metadata, for example, are data about data (who has produced them, when, what format the data are in, and so on). In linguistics, a grammar is considered as being expressed in a metalanguage, language operating on a higher level of abstraction to describe properties of the plain language (and not itself). Metadiscussion is a discussion about *discussion* (not any one particular topic *of* discussion but *discussion itself*). In computer science, a theoretical software engineer might be engaged in the pursuit of metaprogramming (i.e., writing programs that manipulate programs).

Afropessimism, then, is less of a theory and more of a *metatheory*: a critical project that, by deploying Blackness as a lens of interpretation, interrogates the unspoken, assumptive logic of Marxism, postcolonialism, psychoanalysis, and feminism through rigorous theoretical consideration of their *properties and assumptive logic*, such as their foundations, methods, form, and utility; and it does so, again, on a higher level of abstraction than the discourse and methods of the theories it interrogates. Again, Afropessimism is, in the main, more of a metatheory than a theory. It is pessimistic about the claims theories of liberation make when these theories try to explain Black suffering or when they analogize Black suffering with the suffering of other oppressed beings. It does this by unearthing and exposing the meta-aporias, strewn like land mines in what these theories of so-called universal liberation hold to be true.

If, as Afropessimism argues, *Blacks are not Human subjects, but are instead structurally inert props, implements for the execution of White and non-Black fantasies and sadomasochistic pleasures*, then this also means that, at a higher level of abstraction, the claims of universal humanity that the above theories all subscribe to are hobbled by a meta-aporia: a contradiction that manifests whenever one looks seriously at the structure of Black suffering in comparison to the presumed universal structure of all sentient beings. Again, Black people *embody* a meta-aporia for political thought and action—Black people are the wrench in the works.

Blacks do not function as political subjects; instead, our flesh and energies are instrumentalized for postcolonial, immigrant, feminist, LGBTQ, transgender, and workers' agendas. These so-called allies are never *authorized* by Black agendas predicated on Black ethical dilemmas. A Black radical agenda is terrifying to most people on the Left—think Bernie Sanders—because it emanates from a condition of suffering for which there is no imaginable strategy for redress—no narrative of social, political, or national redemption. This crisis, no, this catastrophe, this realization that I am a sentient being who can't use words like "*being*" or "*person*" to describe myself without the scare quotes and the threat of raised eyebrows from anyone within earshot, was crippling.

I was convinced that if a story of Palestinian redemption could be told . . . its denouement would culminate in the return of the land, *a spatial, cartographic redemption*; and if a story of class redemption could be told . . . its denouement would culminate in the restoration of the working day so that one stopped working when surplus values were relegated to the dustbin of history, *a temporal redemption*; in other words, since postcolonial and working-class redemption were possible, then there must be a story to be told through which one could redeem the time and place of Black subjugation. I was wrong.

FRANK B. WILDERSON III

I had not dug deep enough to see that though Blacks suffer the time and space subjugation of cartographic deracination and the hydraulics of the capitalist working day, we also suffer as the hosts of Human parasites, though they themselves might be the hosts of parasitic capital and colonialism. I had looked to theory (first as a creative writer, and only much later as a critical theorist) to help me find/create the story of Black liberation—Black political redemption. What I found instead was that redemption, *as a narrative mode*, was a parasite that fed upon me for its coherence. Everything meaningful in my life had been housed under the umbrellas called "critical theory" and "radical politics." The parasites had been capital, colonialism, patriarchy, homophobia. And now it was clear that I had missed the boat. My parasites were Humans, all Humans—the haves as well as the have-nots.

If critical theory and radical politics are to rid themselves of the parasitism that they heretofore have had in common with radical and progressive movements on the Left, that is, if we are to engage, rather than disavow, the difference between *Humans* who suffer through an "economy of disposability" and *Blacks* who suffer by way of "social death," then we must come to grips with how the redemption of the subaltern (a narrative, for example, of Palestinian *plenitude*, *loss*, and *restoration*) is made possible by the (re)instantiation of a regime of violence that bars Black people from the narrative of redemption. This requires (a) an understanding of the difference between loss and absence, and (b) an understanding of how the narrative of subaltern loss stands on the rubble of Black absence.

Sameer and I didn't share a universal, postcolonial grammar of suffering. Sameer's loss is tangible, *land*. The paradigm of *his* dispossession elaborates capitalism and the colony. When it is not tangible it is at least coherent, as in the loss of *labor power*. But how does one describe the loss that makes the world if all that can be said of loss is locked within the world? How does one narrate the loss of loss? What is the "difference between . . . something to save . . . [and nothing] to lose"? Sameer forced me to face the depth of my isolation in ways I had wanted to avoid; a deep pit from which neither postcolonial theory, nor Marxism, nor a gender politics of unflinching feminism could rescue me.

Why is anti-Black violence not a form of racist hatred but the *genome* of Human renewal; a therapeutic balm that the Human race needs to know and heal itself? Why must the world reproduce this violence, this social death, so that social life can regenerate Humans and prevent them from suffering the catastrophe of psychic incoherence— absence? Why must the world find its nourishment in Black flesh?

3

When the doctor and the nurse returned, I was finally able to speak. They asked what had brought this on. I told them it was the stress of graduate school. The best way to deal with an interrogation is to weave a bit of truth into your lie. I couldn't tell them I had suddenly realized what it meant to be an Afropessimist; that my breakdown was brought on by a breakthrough, one in which I finally understood why I was too black for care. They asked me about my current medications, in order to know whether the medications that they might prescribe would clash with whatever I was on. Like a bat darting through a cave, my mind echolocated for the answers. But no torch cast its light on the medication I took; instead, I discovered the forgotten lines of my poem.

for Halloween I washed my
face and wore my
school clothes   went door to
door as a nightmare.

CHAPTER TWO

Juice from a Neck Bone

1

At the age of eleven, I lay at night alone in the dark on the floor of our living room listening to Gregorian chants, phonograph recordings of my mother's cantorum, the choir of which she was a member at the Basilica of Saint Mary, in downtown Minneapolis. Alone in the dark, I saw myself ten years in the future, draped in a white cassock, followed down the cold stone aisle by two altar boys. Traced with incense was the cool cathedral air. It was humid in Minnesota that summer of 1967. The Summer of Love on the California coast was a moist, mosquito-harassed season in the Land of Ten Thousand Lakes. But it was cool on the floor, so I would lie shirtless on the carpet, and surrender my skin to the sonorous sounds, wake upon wake of mounting waves through which I tunneled and imagined myself as a priest. *Sanctuary.*

I was no Afropessimist at the age of eleven and my knowledge of what gave me so much anxiety was bereft of a critical race vocabulary. But I knew I was Black; not because smells of filé powder and smoked sausage thickening in a gumbo roux wafted from my house and no other in the neighborhood, but because we were the only ones they called Negroes. I would not be Black until the following year, 1968, when I turned twelve. In the dark, at eleven, lying on the living room floor, I knew I was a Negro not due to my cultural elements but because it was my source of shame; a shame not shared by the neighbors. The Gregorian chants trembled in my chest, extending the darkness in long, hollow catacombs that stretched through me and out the other side where I saw myself in the future, a future where I was revered by my parishioners, instead of shunned, as I was in first grade by a little girl who wouldn't hold my hand for fear that my soot would stain her. In the sound tunnel of my future, the children and my teachers genuflected when I passed, they stood and knelt on my command, they confessed their sins to me before being worthy of the body of Christ. *Bless me, Father, for I have sinned. I wouldn't hold his hand because his soot would rub off on me. Bless me, Father, for I have sinned. I called him a monkey when he climbed up the rope in gym class. Bless me, Father, for I have sinned. Between my teeth and my upper lip, I wedged my tongue and scratched my armpits when he climbed down. Bless me, Father, for we have sinned. We laughed. Bless me, Father, for we have sinned. We pressed his face in the snow. Bless me, Father, for I have sinned. I called him "friend" and brought him home to my mother's curiosity. How does it feel, she asked, to be a Negro? Bless me, Father, for I have sinned. I made him face the class and lead us in the Pledge of Allegiance.*

My chest, my arms, and the cabernet carpet soaked their confessions like a field of wheat repeating the sound of rain. When my aunts and uncles came up from New Orleans, or from the sweet, pungent soil forty miles upriver, they'd ask me if I wanted the light turned on. Children down South didn't brood in the dark. No, Aunt Joyce, I want the dark. You relaxing, ba-by? Yes, I would answer, I'm relaxing; when what I really meant was, I'm composing my hymn of redemption.

I was at rest, but I wasn't relaxing. Relaxation is a state of being in the present, living scenes of the present. As a boy I seldom lived in the present. It hurt too much to be in the present. When I occurred to myself I was myself in the future. The present was the penance, what I had to pay for my soot. I dreamed that the present would pass one day. But I arrived each year to find that the present had already packed its bags on the road to meet me. It was standing in the lobby with my room key. Even as I lay on the floor of our living room and took confessions from sinners of the present in their incarnation as supplicants of tomorrow, I knew, in some deep place beneath the chants, that the present would always be waiting for me: At the end of that summer, sixth grade would be no different than the slow, acid drip of years gone by; another year of seeing myself through the eyes of others: *Our young Negro neighbor. The Wilderson boy. Cleaner than you might expect. Polite. Well-spoken. Fresh-smelling. Too quick to fight. Behind in spelling. Ahead in spelling. Reads above his grade level. Late with his math homework. Ashy legs. Gorilla lips. Been known to wet the bed.*

That Christmas past, my teacher recommended that I repeat the fifth grade. In the fourth grade, they said I was so smart I could skip fifth grade; my parents, however, did not like the idea of kids skipping grades. Then, in the fifth grade, I began to wet the bed more often and my mind shut down. I couldn't, or wouldn't, get up in the morning. Months passed without one assignment being turned in. That summer as I listened to Gregorian chants I marveled at how I made it out of fifth grade. In March I had gone to my teacher and asked for all the assignments I hadn't turned in.

She said, "How about everything since October?"

Over Easter break, I closed the door to my room and completed six months' worth of math and reading assignments in one week. I dumped them on her desk in April. She graded them all and gave me all A's and B's. It took her a week to grade them and she scolded me for giving her such a fright all year. I took my praise by proxy.

Had I been White, my athleticism and my charm would have made me popular. My friends would have been popular too. But my friends were from the land of misfit toys. Liam Gundersen couldn't distinguish between the threat of a bear and the threat of a butterfly. He hyperventilated and bit his arm when someone raised a hand to him. His father and mother came from Norway and had been tortured in a Japanese internment camp when they were missionaries in China. The children on the playground got their kicks whenever Liam bit his arms. He was the youngest of thirteen, who were grown and gone. His brothers had left behind novels by Graham Greene, John le Carré, and Ian Fleming. Liam and I spent long hours reading them in his attic. In the three years from eleven through thirteen I spent in Liam's attic, I didn't understand those books as well as Liam did; nor could I translate the smattering of French words that Graham Greene dropped on the page like spare change. But Liam could. Oskar Nilsen's dad was a chiropractor, which meant "witch doctor" in the rich, White enclave of Kenwood, where parents were executives, bankers, architects, attorneys, doctors, and statesmen like Senator, soon-to-be Vice President Walter Mondale, and Mark Dayton, a politician whose family owned Target and B. Dalton Bookseller. Then there was Elgar Davenport, who was short and stout and looked at the world through Coke-bottle glasses and a left eye that wandered as if lost. Elgar was a quiet embarrassment to his mother, who was blond, trim, and sporty and always walked ahead of him. Elgar had red hair and freckles. Mr. Davenport drove a red Corvette and "played the market" for a job. I thought it would be cool if my father bought a sports car in my color; but then, as quickly as it came into my mind, the downside followed. The downside of owning a sports car in my color was something I felt without having words for. But knowledge is often deeper than words.

Elgar Davenport, Liam Gundersen, Oskar Nilsen, and I were playing secret agent on the grounds of a dark stone mansion across the street from my house. The house had an elevator and ten bedrooms, I was told, though in the sixteen years I lived across the street from it I was never inside. It changed hands: at one point a wealthy family with almost as many kids as bedrooms (though they were too young to be my playmates); at another time, Senator Mark Dayton. It was his family home away from Washington; and they would live there until he became governor and moved to the governor's mansion in St. Paul. We played secret agent on the far grounds, away from the main building, near a one-bedroom carriage house at the end of the wide gravel drive. The mansion served its purpose; it was vital to the mise-en-scène of our spy games. Sometimes it was the Soviet Embassy in a dark wooden corner of Washington, D.C. Sometimes it was a SMERSH center for the training of assassins who were being prepared to kill James Bond. Our spy games were more Salvador Dalí than Ian Fleming. For example, a low wire fence ran along one end of the property separating the backyard of a smaller mansion from the Dayton home. We called this wire fence the Berlin Wall, without making any geographical adjustments, such as relocating the mansion from Washington, D.C., to Berlin. The surrealists in us ruled over cartographic realists.

If we didn't draw straws we'd end up being four boys playing CIA agents and no Communists. One sour day, Elgar and I drew Soviet spy straws. Liam and Oskar were the good guys. The game involved two witless Soviets running and screaming at two witless Americans who also ran and screamed as they tried to hurdle the low wire fence of the Berlin Wall and get back to Checkpoint Charlie before the Soviets caught them.

Elgar and I crouched behind the carriage house at the end of the gravel drive. The Americans would come from somewhere up near the mansion but we didn't know which side of the mansion. Normally, one of the boys who played the good guys would be the decoy, the one who would come out from a tree on the side of the mansion and run at breakneck speed toward a far end of the fence while the other boy waited until both Soviets had been drawn away. Then he would try to make his escape. Elgar and I peered out from behind the carriage house waiting for the two American spies. We curled our thumbs and forefingers and held them to our eyes as binoculars.

"Hey," Elgar whispered.

"Yeah," I whispered back.

"My mom told me to ask you, how do you feel being a Negro?"

"I dunno," I said, not as softly.

"How come?"

"Pretty good . . . I guess."

"Here they come!"

Oskar and Liam were on the move! We caught Liam, but Oskar made it to Checkpoint Charlie in the McDermotts' backyard.

The next time I saw Elgar, he told me his mom didn't like my answer. I was worried. I asked him if she was mad. No, he told me. I asked him was he sure? Sure, I'm sure, he said, she wants you to come to lunch. I said okay, but I'd have to ask my mom.

Celina Davenport was visibly taller than her husband, Elgar Sr. She didn't have red hair like Elgar Jr. or Elgar Sr. Before we sat down to lunch, she brought me to the living room and she showed me the mantel with her tennis trophies from a college she said was one of the "Seven Sisters" back East where they didn't have any boys. In her husky dry-martini voice, she said the place had her climbing the walls.

"Elgar knows how I climbed the walls," she said, mussing his hair.

She led us to the kitchen. I was so uptight about being there, and I didn't know *why*, that I was only half listening to her, which meant I only half understood what she meant. But I had been taught that when you don't know what to say to someone, rather than let uncomfortable dead air pass between you, you ask them a question. So I asked her why she wanted to climb the walls. She looked at me as though I'd asked her if they ate cat food for dinner. Then she laughed and called her maid, Mrs. Szymanski, to serve lunch. We ate in the kitchen, Celina Davenport, Elgar, and me. Mrs. Szymanski set a platter of sandwiches on the table and poured lemonade for Elgar and me. Mrs. Davenport drank lemonade too, but with a splash of gin. As covertly as I could, I lifted one edge of the bread to have a look. I wasn't covert enough.

"Something wrong with the sandwich, Frankie?" Mrs. Davenport asked me.

"He doesn't like that name, Mom."

"What name do you like, hon?"

"Frank," I said, trying not to sound cross, like Elgar.

"Your mother calls you Frankie, when she calls you to come inside."

This startled me, because I didn't know she knew my mother. I knew she knew *of* my mother, but the Davenports had signed a petition of five hundred households to keep us out of Kenwood; and most of the neighbors never spoke to my mother. I didn't say anything.

She asked again. "What's wrong with the sandwich . . . Frank?"

"Nothing, Mrs. Davenport."

"Tell me, I won't be offended if you don't like my sandwiches."

The irony of this statement slipped past me at the time, because they weren't *her* sandwiches, Mrs. Szymanski made them.

"I wanted to see where the meat was so I could move it to the middle."

This tickled Elgar's mom. "It's an Italian sandwich: provolone, spinach, and tomatoes, all with a little pesto. You'll bloat if you eat meat in this heat."

"That's what my mom says," I said. "She makes these sometimes."

"Does she, now?" Mrs. Davenport nodded and lit a Pall Mall. "Don't torture yourself. You don't have to eat it," she said.

This was a momentary reprieve from a death sentence, until I remembered my mother told me to be on my best behavior. I took a generous bite. Nausea toyed with my intestines as I tried to swallow. The mayonnaise, the rubbery cheese, and the acidic tomatoes, all combined with that touch of pesto, struggled down my esophagus in doughy, half-chewed wads.

Then Celina Davenport asked the question Elgar had asked me at the carriage house by the Berlin Wall. In a chair directly opposite to me she sipped her lemonade and gin, took another drag of her cigarette, and looked directly at me as she waited for me to answer.

I stopped eating. ("I would never hire a man who salts his food before eating." One of my father's axioms. "It means don't act or speak in haste, Frankie. If you don't know the answer, *think*, take a moment to figure out what's being asked.") I took in the room. Her lace curtains billowing in the breeze through the kitchen windows; her polished green gas range with gold antique knobs; her Frigidaire that gleamed like Marvel Comics' Silver Surfer, with an ice maker in the door, along with a water dispenser so that ice and water could be dispensed without having to open the appliance, something I had never seen before; her white pleated tennis skirt, white sneakers, her well-toned legs, and the way she waited without blinking. *She stares like an East German border guard. The wrong answer, and you won't make it back. She's not just a pretty tennis lady and those aren't just pretty tennis shoes; there are razor blades in the toes of her shoes and she will kick you in the shin if you forget what Dad said and speak in haste.*

"*Mom*," said Elgar, "I already told you what he said."

"I can't trust you to bring the right change home, Elgar. 'Pretty good. I guess'? Elgar, that's how *you* talk. *His* father's an educator."

"I meant to say more," I apologized.

"Of course you did. Elgar didn't give you the chance."

She looked pleased. I wanted her to stay that way. Every spy knows how to keep the guards smiling.

I told her it was nice to be a Negro. She blew yet another thin cyclone of smoke. She didn't look pleased. So I told her Negroes get to do cool stuff.

"Like what?" she said, more alert.

I was stumped, so I told her about Masongate Resort on Gull Lake, near Brainerd, Minnesota. I said our family and a bunch of other Negro families spend a week there every August, fishing, boating, swimming, and waterskiing. She knew of Masongate Resort, but something in my story didn't gel with what she knew of it. She asked me if I was confusing Masongate Resort with someplace else.

She stood up and leaned on the counter, with her back to the window. She lit another cigarette with the first and flicked the stub of the first one out the window.

"What would Smokey the Bear say?" Elgar asked with alarm.

"You'll make someone a good wife one day, Elgar," she said, but she was looking at me.

The first and only time she took her eyes off me was when she used her lighter to light her first cigarette. Now she took her eyes off me again and exhaled to the side. When she looked at me again there was still no warmth in her face.

I was lying and she knew it. We didn't stay at Masongate Resort; we stayed at Twilight Loon Cabins, two miles away from Masongate, on the side of the lake with marshes where sandy beaches should be. A part of the lake where there were no speedboats, no grand lodge with nightly entertainment, no water sports like Jet Skiing, no elegant restaurant serving walleyed pike and roast potatoes. Instead of Mason-gate's lush, air-conditioned rooms, Twilight Loon Cabins had self-catering cabins with screen doors in need of paint, and the sounds of their closing slapped across the lake. The grounds lights were so far apart that at night you needed a flashlight to walk from one cabin to the next. It was only the previous year, 1966, that the four Negro families had begun taking the kids up to Masongate to have dinner and enjoy the activities there. We didn't stay there, however, and something told me Mrs. Davenport knew. She doused the new cigarette under the tap.

"Elgar Sr. doesn't think the Twins will make the World Series this year," she said, as though she were talking to someone who wasn't in the room. She ran a glass of water from the tap and drank some of it. "Where's his home team spirit?"

2

Goops of mayonnaise, cheese, tomatoes, and raw nerves, all combined with the new sensation of pesto, sloshed in my stomach as I bundled up the hill from Elgar's house to mine. As I came up the back porch stairs I could hear a Dinah Washington song on the radio. S&H Green Stamps and a booklet to paste them in lay on the kitchen table, next to a textbook on statistics for students of psychology. Mom was taking a break from studying and pasting stamps into the book.

"So?" she said.

"There's no meat in her sandwiches."

Mom laughed and turned the radio down.

"We're *in* Minnesota," she said, "but we're not *of* Minnesota. Bull Connor could save money on dogs if he'd had that woman's food."

"Mom?"

"Yes?"

"Nothing."

"What is it?"

"How do you feel?"

"I *feel* like I should be on my veranda with a mint julep, fanning myself instead of breaking my brain over statistics or licking S&H Green Stamps."

I hadn't moved.

"Why do you ask?" She was seated; just the right height to look me in the eye.

"So I know what to say next time."

"What next time?"

"Next time Mrs. Davenport asks me how it feels to be a Negro."

"No!" Her face was a violent wish. "No, she *didn't*." She pressed her palms on the table as though she were about to stand up and go knock Mrs. Davenport out. *And then what?* she must have thought, because she didn't stand. *And then what?*

She was learning something valuable about White upper-crust Northerners, something that she would not have imagined possible before she moved to Kenwood: how one can fight a war by proxy through someone else's child. She knew now how it must feel to be killed by a guided missile. What kind of woman would hurt you through your child? "*The good, the beautiful, and the true*," was a Du Boisian axiom that my mother cherished. "Those must be our aspirations. And it starts with how you treat people." *This long-range messing with my mind, and my son your guided missile*; if that's what she thought when I came home, then she also would have reminded the Celina Davenport deep inside her skull how she makes Elgar and all the children in this neighborhood feel at home when she's with them; how she scoops the ice-cream cones for them always with a half scoop extra; how she makes red, white, and blue gunboat hats for the kids on the Fourth of July, and lights their sparklers as they walk up the hill on parade. *But you twist my son's stomach into knots.*

One night when I was older and almost living on my own, I came home late and quietly. Mother was alone in the dark, in front of a fire. Dad was stretched out on the sofa, asleep. The soft glow in the fireplace was the only light. She was sticking needles into little stuffed-cloth dolls, naming them with the names of two of her White coworkers. "And this one," she said deliciously, as she stabbed the doll, "I leave shaking with the palsy." I smiled and went up to bed, without her knowing I had seen her. *She's sane*, I thought, as I climbed into bed. *After all she's been through, she's sane.*

3
—

The next time we played secret agent at the mansion across the street, I drew a Soviet straw.

"*Again?*" I complained.

Liam Gundersen was a Soviet agent with me; Elgar and Oskar were MI6 agents. I caught Elgar at the Berlin Wall and locked him in the guardhouse with its imaginary walls of air. I dashed along the fence to help Liam catch Oskar before he crossed into West Berlin. I hadn't gotten far when I heard Elgar yell.

"I escaped!"

His short, stout body rolled over the fence.

I yelled back, "You're caught; you have to stay in the guardhouse!"

He yelled, "You didn't handcuff me!"

He was over the fence now, dashing through the McDermotts' backyard, on his way to the Tysons' backyard. I was livid.

"Don't run, fuckface!"

His red hair flounced in the wind. He turned his freckled face around and laughed.

My foot nudged something solid on the ground next to the fence. It was a plastic bottle of emerald-colored Palmolive dish soap. I bent down and picked it up. Its heft in my hand was substantial because it was nearly full. I gripped the bottle by its neck. I felt my arm sling back. Then it slung forward. End over end the green bottle whirled, now a tomahawk, now a wand, as it shot toward the sun; the high-noon light prismed in the green liquid, until the bottle disappeared in the jaws of the sun. I closed my eyes so as not to go blind.

Plop! Splat!

Elgar's knees buckled. He was facedown in the McDermotts' backyard.

We raced to his side. Green dish soap oozed into the grass from a crack in the plastic bottle. Blood oozed from the back of Elgar's skull. A temple of his Coke-bottle glasses was torn from its hinge and lay beside his head on the ground.

But the word *blood* took a few moments to find me. At first what I saw on the back of his skull was a cowlick, a red tuft of hair gone awry. Then I saw it as a small spurt of water like the spurt of water from the fountain outside of Mrs. Anderson's room that was so small your lips touched the faucet when you drank.

Liam and Oskar ran for help.

I stood there, the sun beating down upon my neck, my eyes beating down upon Elgar as he bled. It would be wrong to say that I meant to hurt him. But now that he was hurt, I didn't want to help him. I knew that I *should* want to help him; but that was knowledge stripped of desire, and it voiced itself in the second and third persons—*You should want to help him*, or *The Wilderson boy should want to help him.* Voices up the back stairs and a little to the left of what I really felt.

The tiny gurgle of blood from the soft spot in the back of his head died within seconds, but I stood there waiting for the tiny geyser's return. *Elgar Davenport bleeds. If Elgar bleeds, his mother bleeds.* Until that point, people around me in Kenwood seemed bloodless and eternal.

(Three years later, in the spring of 1970, when we lived in Berkeley, a Black Panther handed me Frantz Fanon's *The Wretched of the Earth* in a study session that he and others held for junior high kids. That night I read what I could of "Concerning Violence," where Fanon wrote about the moment that the native of Algeria sees the French settler bleed, that moment when the Algerian "finds out that the settler's skin is not of any more value than a native's skin; and it must be said that this discovery shakes the world in a very necessary manner," and I thought of that day with Elgar.)

I felt a twinge between my legs. The same twinge of bliss I felt at night when, half asleep and half awake, I wet the bed; the pleasure of release that could last until I felt the wet spot.

When the paramedics parsed the story, one said to the other, "Landed on the fontanel."

"Explains the bleeding." His partner nodded.

On the three-count they hoisted Elgar onto the gurney. One of them said Elgar was lucky his fontanel wasn't as soft as a baby's, or the injury would have been far worse. Elgar's eyes were open but he didn't say anything. The first paramedic shook his head.

"What are the chances?"

"One in a million."

"Not even."

When I saw Mrs. Davenport pleading with the paramedics to let her ride in the ambulance, I knew my parents would beat me. But they didn't beat me. They were too dazed, their arms too limp and useless to lift something as heavy as a belt. Not only was I not spanked, but my parents didn't even punish me. The next day they were still shaken, but not enough to keep them from differing over how Elgar's injury should be explained to me.

My father, who knew Latin and who had taught speed reading to corporate executives to earn money while he earned his Ph.D., talked to me like I was one of his graduate students.

"A space in the skull where ossification is not complete, Frankie, and the natural sutures haven't been formed."

"The baby's soft spot," Mom said, sighing.

"Talking goo-goo, ga-ga won't improve his vocabulary, Ida-Lorraine." Dad frowned.

She said we'd have to go over to the Davenports' house together. But before we did, she wanted me to tell them, again, what had happened. They sat side by side on the sofa in the living room. I stood before them. I told them everything all over again. How Elgar was captured at the Berlin Wall. How Elgar broke the rules when he left the guardhouse. How I reached down and snagged a dish soap bottle by the neck.

"And I threw it. Not *at* him, Mom. I just threw it."

My dad had quit smoking cigarettes several years ago. He was trying to give up his pipe. It was unlit. With his mouth closed over it, he gnawed its stem gently. He looked at me as though I were one of the children in the psych ward he once managed, a mixture of admiration and horror.

"Twenty yards or more and you cracked his fontanel." Dad almost smiled. His voice was strange, as though he were talking about someone who had broken a track-and-field record.

I looked at my mother. "I didn't mean it, Mom." Then I sobbed.

She held me. "I know. I know," she said. "You're a good boy. I know how bad you felt."

When she said this, I recalled how my first bursts of feelings had not been kin to remorse. But how could I tell her and still be a "good boy"?

Mom baked a casserole with extra ground beef and extra cheese.

I told her, "Mrs. Davenport doesn't serve heavy food." I said it three times; and each time Mom told me, "It's the thought that counts." Mom said this without looking at me. Looking back, I wonder if the "thought that counts" had more to do with Mrs. Davenport's interrogation of me and less to do with my attack on her son; or perhaps the two were inextricably bound. Instead of slapping you into next week I baked a meal you can choke on. Bon appétit!

Mom and I walked down the hill to the Davenports'. Elgar was still in the hospital under observation, but Mrs. Davenport said he was fine. I told Mr. and Mrs. Davenport how sorry I was, which was true. But there was another truth that couldn't be spoken, not even to my parents. What, I wondered, between regret and desire, would come of this duel in the heart?

4

I survived the next year, 1968, on quotations from film stars, espionage novels, and, by the end of August, quotations from Chairman Mao. A monk with malachite beads, I clenched the words of others. But of my graceless lurch through that White grammar school, was it Stevenson or Poe or another wine-and-revolver scribe I pledged to memory and took to my mother?

"'Before a man dies he must write a book, love a woman, and kill a man.'"

She eyed me as though I were a parcel intended for the neighbors. "You mean, 'What does it mean'?" she asked.

"No. I mean is it true." We were alone. Windows in the living room were open. The drapes shuddered softly, refusing to say why she looked away.

In 1968, something cracked inside of me. I still lay in the dark on the living room floor listening to music, as I did the summer before when I was eleven. But Gregorian chants had been replaced by the music and the voice of Curtis Mayfield, urging me to be "a winner" of "the good black earth." The first time I heard Curtis Mayfield sing, "No more tears do we cry / And we have finally dried our eyes," I wept. I thought if I listened long and hard enough, Curtis Mayfield's voice would strain, clear and fierce, through the phonograph needle and shield me from a hell people said I was blessed to inhabit. ("There are boys in the ghetto who don't have it this good.")

As the year began, the Tet Offensive laid siege to our living room. Just before midnight, our living room crackled with white noise as my parents, thinking they were alone, searched for a signal on the radio in the hi-fi. Sometimes I hid on the front staircase and tried to get a glimpse of them through the spindles of the balustrade. They often sat on the floor; I could see their outstretched legs. I didn't dare go below the first landing for fear of being spotted, and the first landing was close enough for me to hear the radio and wait for my uncle's name in the call of the dead.

The music stopped. The DJ announced that the station would soon be signing off; but first the nightly bulletin from Vietnam.

"A mechanized infantry convoy from the Second Brigade, U.S. Fourth Infantry Division was ambushed two miles northwest of Plei Mrong in Kon Tum Province. Convoy security elements returned the enemy fire while Army helicopter gunships and artillery supported the action. A UH-1 helicopter was hit by enemy ground fire and crashed in the area, wounding all five persons on board."

Then the roll call came. At this point, the clink of ice in my mother's cola stopped. The bones of my father dried in my bones. They didn't move. They seemed not to breathe. The only living thing was the radio.

"Tuesday, August twenty-ninth." The announcer paused. Was he sipping water? Was his right hand on the mic and his left hand cupped over a cough? "Two hundred forty-two servicemen have died in combat this week. We close this broadcast as we close every evening, with the names of those who have fallen today, followed by a sampling of the messages our listeners have left on our answering machine. The views and opinions do not reflect the views and opinions of the management here at WGBH, nor the views and opinions of the stations that broadcast this show.

"Specialist William C. Gearing, twenty-two, East Lansing, Michigan.

"Lance Corporal Joseph L. Rhodes, twenty-two, Memphis, Tennessee.

"Captain Michael C. Volheim, twenty, Hayward, California.

"Private First Class Craig E. Yates, eighteen, Sparta, Michigan.

"Private First Class Ramon L. Vazquez, twenty-one, Puerto Nuevo, Puerto Rico.

"Private First Class Calvin R. Patrick, eighteen, Houston, Texas."

After the announcer read the names, his voice continued in its bedside manner, as though tucking the dead soldiers into bed.

"Now," he said soothingly, "a selection of your voices from our parent studio."

A small beep, as he pressed a button to play the messages from the station's answering machine.

A woman with a coal-town twang thanked the station for telling her of her son's death two days before the Marines came knocking at her door. It meant she didn't crumple to the floor when they came. She had done that already, in private. Her neighbor down the way had slumped on her porch at those two Marines' feet. "It's a shame," she said, "they're not allowed to hold you or pick you up off the floor. Thank you for sparing me that indignity."

A man from Tulia, Texas, demanded the station stop reading the names on the air. "You are supporting the anti-war demonstrators, who are traitors to this nation."

A girl from Seattle said two nights ago she heard the name of someone who'd graduated last year from her high school. "He scored the winning touchdown when we won homecoming. We think we should cancel the homecoming parade this year and hold a candle-light vigil instead. Please advise."

A woman from Ohio said, "I'm a White woman, but I always wonder how many Southern Black boys lay claim to the names you read each night. What did they die for? Tar-paper shacks, malnutrition, degradation, and no jobs? Please, somebody tell me."

I heard the clink of ice as my mother dared to sip her cola again.

"Your brother's alive," she said softly.

My father said, "Yes, another day of life."

I heard them saying their Our Fathers together, and I knew they were on their knees.

One of Dad's students fled to Canada to dodge the draft. The Canadians took him in, no questions asked. I wondered if they'd take me in, no questions asked, if I fled my war in Kenwood.

I turned twelve in April, the same day Congress passed the Fair Housing Act and seven days after the murder of Martin Luther King. I watched the riots on television with my grandmother, a New Orleans Catholic who had taught second grade and at one time played piano with the Preservation Hall Jazz Band. Grandmother Jules loved all kinds of sports. Her husband, 2-2 Jules (named for his ability to strike out a batter every time the call was two balls and two strikes) turned down an invitation to join the Negro National League and worked the rails as a porter, and then as a plasterer when the Great Depression came. But he was dead in 1968. When Grandmother Jules came north to visit us, she spent time with me and my father watching baseball, football, and basketball, and never hunted for antiques with my mother, her daughter. She loved pickled pigs' feet and a beer called Hamm's, which was brewed across the river in St. Paul.

The murder of Martin Luther King and the Tet Offensive changed my family's relationship to radio and TV. My parents listened for my uncle's name in the nightly broadcasts of casualties. My grandmother and I watched the riots.

One night her feet shot up from the easy chair and damn near knocked her beer and pigs' feet off the TV dinner tray. As I steadied the table, she laughed like I'd never seen her laugh before.

"Go ahead, son!" she cried.

I'd heard her say this many times over, whenever Tony Oliva made a base hit, or when Gale Sayers ran for a touchdown. But neither Oliva nor Sayers were on the screen. I caught her joy and laughed out loud too. A knot loosened in my chest, a phantom tumor that had been there since first grade. We were watching the riots, and my grandmother laughed my pain away. If I said that for the past six years I'd hated the vast majority of students and half the teachers at my school, I would be lying; it was never that straightforward. But it would be accurate to say that I was never at ease in their presence; and since their faces were with me even when I was not with them, it would also be true to say that I was seldom, if ever, at ease.

"Go ahead, son!"

She wasn't talking to me, she was talking to the man on the screen; but, at that moment, she and I were triangulated with that man on the screen. And I felt loved.

I'd like to say the city on the screen was Cleveland, but it could have been Detroit; D.C.; Cincinnati; Chicago; Kansas City; Baltimore; Pittsburgh; Trenton, New Jersey; or Wilmington, Delaware. It could have been anywhere and everywhere. No fires were visible, but smoke plumed over ruined buildings. Skid marks scarred the street where a shirtless man with a do-rag snapped around his conk nosed a shopping cart down the boulevard. Grandmother Jules laughed like her chest was full of carbonation. I knew there and then that for me the priesthood was dead. I was going to grow up to be a looter and make my grandma proud.

Our racket roused the killjoy giants who owned the house. My mother came downstairs and told her mother not to say such things. I saw my mother in silhouette framed by the living room's sliding French doors, with light from the dining room at her back. She was graceful even when she was still. She and Dad modeled in fashion shows that the Boulé and the Links, two of the Black middle-class social groups to which they belonged, put on. The whole room hushed when the two of them came down the catwalk. Mom's friends said she looked like Donyale Luna, who took the world by storm in 1966 when she became the first Black woman to grace the cover of *Vogue*. And I struggled to see how the blood in my mother's light skin and slender body was the same blood that ran through my grandmother, who was short and dark, sucked juice from a neck bone, and stomped the damper pedal when she played the piano. At the age of thirty-six, my mother stood in the threshold, framed by her reproach, and spoke to her sixty-three-year-old mother as though their ages were reversed. My grandmother and I looked at her like two kids caught being naughty.

"Don't say that, Mother. Next thing you know he'll be saying that at school. He's wayward enough as it is."

When we turned back to the television, the man with the conk, the do-rag, and the shopping cart was gone. Mom went upstairs and we went back to our antics.

"Why are we mad?" I asked my grandmother as we gazed at the plumes of smoke rising from the flat roofs.

"Because we ain't got no jobs?" I said, giggling and looking cautiously at the French doors for signs of my mother and her citation for "ain'ts."

"No," grandmother replied, "it's not about jobs."

"Because we ain't got no hot water?"

"It's not about water, child."

"Because we live in the ghetto."

"Frankie, *you're* not in the ghetto," she said with a chuckle, "and *you're* mad." (How she knew that was a mystery to me, for I don't recall ever telling her what went on at school.)

Then, on the count of three, we said, "We're mad at the world!"

From the top of the staircase we heard, "Mother, *please!*"

It would, though, be a stretch to say that my grandmother was an Afropessimist. But Afropessimism isn't a church to pray at, or a party to be voted in and out of office. Afropessimism is Black people at their best. "Mad at the world" is Black folks at their best. Afropessimism gives us the freedom to say out loud what we would otherwise whisper or deny: that no Blacks are in the world, but, by the same token, there is no world without Blacks. The violence perpetrated against us is not a form of discrimination; it is a necessary violence; a health tonic for everyone who is not Black; an ensemble of sadistic rituals and captivity that could only happen to people who are not Black if they broke this or that "law." This kind of violence can happen to a sentient being in one of two circumstances: a person has broken the law, which is to say, cracked out of turn given the rules that govern; or the person is a slave, which is to say, no prerequisites are required for an act of brutality to be incurred. There is no antagonism like the antagonism between Black people and the world. This antagonism is the essence of what Orlando Patterson calls "social death," or "deathliness" in the words of David Marriott. It is the knowledge and experience of day-to-day events in which the world tells you you are needed, needed as the destination for its aggressivity and renewal.

The antagonism between the postcolonial subject and the settler (the Sand Creek massacre, or the Palestinian Nakba) cannot—and should not—be analogized with the violence of social death: that is the violence of slavery, which did not end in 1865 for the simple reason that slavery did not end in 1865. Slavery is a relational dynamic—not an event and certainly not a place in space like the South; just as colonialism is a relational dynamic—and that relational dynamic can continue to exist once the settler has left or ceded governmental power. And these two relations are secured by radically different structures of violence. Afropessimism offers an analytic lens that labors as a corrective to Humanist assumptive logics. It provides a theoretical apparatus that allows Black people to *not* have to be burdened by the ruse of analogy—because analogy *mystifies*, rather than clarifies, Black suffering. Analogy mystifies Black peoples' relationship to other people of color. Afropessimism labors to throw this mystification into relief—without fear of the faults and fissures that are revealed in the process.

Grandmother Jules would turn in her grave to know I thought of her as an Afropessimist. She was a Catholic woman whose confessions never lapsed. But once she retired, her speech was relieved of the ruse of analogy, which meant she could let herself say that we weren't mad for the reasons people who suffered class oppression, gender discrimination, or colonial domination were mad. Their anger had grounding wires internal to the world. We were the world's grounding wire. We were the targets of rage that would otherwise be turned in on itself. Black people were the living, breathing contradistinction to life itself. And when we were too old (like Grandmother Jules) or were too young (like me) to know what my mother knew, we refused the ruse of analogy and let our rage speak its truth: Human life is dependent on Black death for its existence and for its coherence. Blackness and Slaveness are inextricably bound in such a way that whereas Slaveness can be separated from Blackness, Blackness cannot exist as other than Slaveness. There is no world without Blacks, yet there are no Blacks who are in the world. You had to be young or you had to be old for this Eucharist to touch your lips.

A schism soon wedged between my parents and me. I had more contempt than compassion for them. My mother was finishing her Ph.D. and, sometime during this period, she worked as a public school administrator for the Minneapolis public schools. My father was a professor and associate dean at the University of Minnesota. Both of my parents were psychologists who, in addition to laboring as academics during the day, held down a private practice; and they threw themselves into MLK's dream of racial equality and Lyndon Johnson's dream of a Great Society. This meant that they lent their skills as grant writers to grassroots initiatives, and hosted endless social and political gatherings in our large living room, where a patchwork of people who might not have otherwise met (university administrators, liberal businessmen, urban planners, activists, and students) came together to jump-start job training centers in the Black community, outreach programs for Native Americans, mental health programs for people without means.

In 1968, the year the Fair Housing Act was passed, my parents went door-to-door in Kenwood handing out leaflets that explained the act in such a way that, they hoped, would not be threatening and would encourage the same people who worked so hard to keep them out of Kenwood to welcome one or two other Black families with open arms. They conducted several Fair Housing workshops in the homes of wealthy Kenwoodites and asked them to drive the wooden stakes of FAIR HOUSING signs in their lawns. It soon became clear that the demographic of these workshops were White women whose husbands were away at the office. The housewives loved my dad and tolerated my mother, even though they both were beautiful. Dad was over six feet tall. In marble foyers he removed his full-length leather coat where underneath he wore cuff-linked shirts and suits that looked tailored. He looked them in the eye when he spoke, and they smiled at him and nodded like supplicants. When it was my mother's turn to speak, their attention waned, and the tinkling of demitasse cups and saucers salted the air.

Mom had tried to throw herself into the times as best she could. To this end, she had bought an Afro wig and wore it. At the end of each workshop, it was time for the big ask: "How many of you would like to take the FAIR HOUSING signs we have in the car and place them on your lawn"? A woman raised her hand. Bypassing the issue at hand, she asked my father if he had ever done any modeling. If not, she continued, she knew a man who knew a man who ran an agency.

With a clenched smile, Mom tried to steer the conversation back to fair housing. Another woman raised her hand to concur that Dad would be such a handsome model. Then yet another shot up her hand to add that as much as *she* would like to place one of the signs on her lawn, her husband would not approve. Mom left the room. Bypassing the model suggestion, Dad told them that he and Mom would be happy to return to anyone's house for a one-on-one with anyone's husband. Mom watched them from the foyer, where she sat on the bottom step of the stairs. She removed the Afro wig from her head and placed it on the step beside her.

5

The year 1968 was also when the American Indian Movement was founded in South Minneapolis, only three miles from Kenwood.

Overnight, issues of Native American sovereignty and the demands of AIM were part of the University of Minnesota landscape. Dad was running a program on a reservation several miles outside of the city; it was a joint program with the tribal government. The board meetings were held with urban Indians, tribal leaders from the reservation, and Dad, in South Minneapolis. As with the fair housing workshops, my parents let me go to these meetings. At once, it became clear that the people on the reservation did not want to adhere to some of the requirements of the University of Minnesota, which funded the project. Politically, I thought Dad's institutional interests were wrong, and the indigenous peoples' interests were right. I thought the university should turn over its resources to the Native Americans without insisting that they account for how they spent the money.

The room was packed. All twenty of the seats at the large conference table were taken. Another fifteen to twenty Native Americans stood against the wall and sat in the deep windowsills. Jeers and insults were hurled at my dad whenever he tried to speak, but he never jeered back. There was an affective charge in the room that had more to do with my dad as a Black person than with him being a representative of the university. At one point, a Native man with whom I shared a windowsill seat lurched forward.

"We don't want you, a *nigger man*, telling us what to do!" The crowded walls detonated with applause.

What I couldn't see then, and had no interest in seeing then, was that the wealthy White housewives in the fair housing workshops shared the same psychic space as the Indians in the underserved neighborhoods of South Minneapolis, despite the fact that the women who attended my parents' workshops lived in a part of town as divorced from the streets where AIM was launched as Atlantis is divorced from Mars. To be sure, the myth of Manifest Destiny, upon which these

White women were weaned from childhood, was inextricably bound to the near-annihilation of Indigenous life. It would be wrong to say that the White women of Kenwood and the Indigenous man seated in the windowsill beside me, who called my dad a "nigger," prayed at the same church. But in the final instance, both their worlds were sustained by a need to distinguish themselves from the same alien embodiment. In the plush drawing rooms of Kenwood, the women fed their Negrophilia on my father's flesh, and pushed my mother to one side. In the tribal meeting hall, the Indians had no use for either of my parents: *Whether we are White and wealthy or Red and poor, we don't want a nigger telling us what to do.* The White women expressed their refusal to be authorized by Blackness through their unconscious Negrophilia ("Have you ever been a model, Professor Wilderson?"), coupled with a need to remove my mother from scene of their fantasy. The Native Americans expressed their refusal through their unconscious Negrophobia ("We don't want you, a *nigger man*, telling us what to do!"). The force of both White and Indigenous affect spoke with one voice: a chorus of libidinal economy. In the collective unconscious of Indigenous imagining, the specter of Blackness was a greater threat than the settler institution that had dispatched a Black professor to do its dirty work.

My father looked up from the table. He maintained eye contact with the Native man seated next to me, while the room exploded in his ears, but he did not show anger; and pain appeared in his eyes only after his eyes met mine, with their approval for the voices that jeered him. A father stared into the jeering eyes of his son. I took pleasure in his pain, because his ruin made me a part of a community. By jeering this "nigger" I was one with the "we."

Afterward, my father and I sat in the car for several minutes. The key was in the ignition, unturned. He didn't speak to me. My father never showed rage or pain in public and I was now as much a member of the public as the Indians who drove him from that room. I could see the expansion and contraction of his chest. He let out a long, slow breath.

"Why not just give them what they want? It's their land. It's their money," I said.

He sighed. He sparked the ignition. He put the car in gear. I was too young to know how anti-Blackness is driving the quest for sovereignty as much as it drives the desire to get rid of the settler. And he was too numb to explain. The Native Americans were speaking as sovereigns to one who was not. The essential problem is not in the name they called my dad, that is to say, the essential problem is not in the performance of their antagonistic feelings, but in the *structure* of an antagonistic relationship between Indigenous people with something to salvage and a Black person with nothing to lose.

My parents carried their rage like vials of nitroglycerin packed in straw. Unlike me, they knew the fallout of Black rage. My parents knew, and taught the people who were being gunned down and the students who fled to Canada to avoid the draft. And they knew that they themselves were being watched by the FBI. I, knowing little of the anvil that weighed on them, thought they were simply sellouts. I thought they held their tongues when their White colleagues made racist statements because they didn't care about the revolution that was raging around them. Slowly, after years of being at odds with them, my view of them changed when I went into academia and was hit, firsthand, with what Jared Sexton calls "the hidden structure of violence that underwrites so many violent acts, whether spectacular or mundane."

Dissemblance had been a survival tool, an implement they used to stay alive and put food on our table. They knew that Black intellectuals could push the envelope only as far as their non-Black interlocutors were willing to accommodate. They also knew that they needed to know the limits of what their White colleagues and interlocutors could handle, especially if those interlocutors didn't know where their own breaking point was. My parents had to know on their behalf. "Imagine the black man the white man wants you to be . . . and be him (or, at least, mime him)," David Marriott writes in his treatise on lynching. "[O]ur unconscious . . . is given over to that work of second-guessing, of dare and double dare. There's no place here for what the black man wants, or for a black unconscious driven by its own desire and aggression."

I watched the world put my parents' desire on lockdown, while I marveled at my grandmother and her jailbreak conversation. Black desire is a runaway crime. America no longer needed Grandmother for nurturing, for confirmation, for a woman to blame as the nation split at the seams—the way it still needed my mother. "I am a marked woman," Hortense Spillers writes, "but not everybody knows my name. 'Peaches' and 'Brown Sugar,' 'Sapphire' and 'Earth Mother,' 'Aunty,' 'Granny,' 'God's Holy Fool,' a 'Miss Ebony First,' or 'Black Woman at the Podium': I describe a locus of confounded identities, a meeting ground of investments and privations in the national treasury of rhetorical wealth. My country needs me and if I were not here, I would have to be invented."

America was finished with my grandmother as its invention. She was free to kick back and kill them, if only in her dreams, or with me, when we watched the riots in 1968. But America was not finished with my mother, a thirty-six-year-old Black woman in her prime. Just three years earlier, in 1965, Daniel Moynihan had named the imago of my mother as the source of a destructive vein in "ghetto culture," and in the Black family. She didn't enter a room as a woman with a Ph.D. She entered as the foremost reason men feel castrated; as a drag, greater than anti-Blackness, on the Black man's dream of a far horizon. My outbursts of joy at the sight of a looter would only confirm what the world already knew about her. For Moynihan, I was a monster of my mother's making.

6
―

We went to Seattle that summer, a summer sabbatical for my father, a summer of research for my mother. Not a day went by when I wasn't surly. When a bishop came to catechism class on a cool Wednesday evening and asked the scrum of twelve- and thirteen-year-old girls and boys to part that week with their allowance and donate to his mission in Africa, I raised my hand. As in my catechism classes in Minneapolis, I was the only black face in the room. Sister Mary Alvin beamed. The bishop nodded with pious encouragement. A nod I knew well from six years in an all-White grammar school back home in Minneapolis: Look, the Negro boy is going to speak. See how politely he raised his hand.

"Did the Africans ask you to come over?" I blurted.

The bishop looked at Sister Mary Alvin. Then the bishop looked at me.

"The Holy Spirit needs no invitation. One must, of course, repent and be baptized."

I told the bishop my thirty-five cents was going for a Snickers bar. He could have my allowance next week if he flew to Africa and came back with a letter from the Africans stating that they wanted him there.

News of this reached home before I did, where a spanking was waiting for me.

It became apparent to all that I excelled in sports, and my parents must have thought that the sheer exertion of football and baseball would sweat the surliness from my pores. On her way to the University of Washington, Mom would drop me off at a community center. It was more of a boys' club. I don't recall my younger sister going with me, nor do I see any girls in my mind's eye when those days return to memory. I can only surmise that she and my father thought that it would do me good to be around what I had never been around in my neighborhood, a group of Black men (boys, really, but unless you were in love with your dentist you wouldn't call them boys). It was here that I came close to what I had only seen on television with my grandmother. Not only did I come to understand that "surly" was not a personality deficiency of mine and mine alone, but was instead a communal inheritance, as was rage, and strong laughter at all the things that made most White people sad; but I also learned about the Black Panthers at this "boys' club." I heard the full-throttle speech of thoughts I had harbored as wishes without words; such as, "I'm three seconds off a honky's ass!"

The first time I heard those words spoken at the community center in Seattle, I laughed out loud. How could one word bring so much joy? *Honky!* It tickled me for days. *I'm three seconds off dat honky's ass!* I knew that my parents would not be tickled if they heard it from my lips; that *I'm three seconds off dat honky's ass* wasn't what they had in mind when they decided Seattle would be the place where I'd meet young Black men as role models. I was clever enough to know that that phrase could land me at a White community center for the rest of our summer in Seattle. But I couldn't help myself. Not since my grandmother's "Go ahead, son!" had I been so inspired by words!

To the far corner of our backyard I would go just to hear all the different ways I could make those few words sing. I'd sing them deep and mellow, in Barry White's baritone voice. I'd sing them like Aretha insisting on R-E-S-P-E-C-T. I'd sing them falsetto like Eddie Kendricks breaking glass with his voice. Alone in the backyard, I'd go toe-to-toe with the honky-tree, let it know, "Big don't mean bad. I'm three seconds of your honky-tree ass!"

Mom came to the back porch. I don't know how long she had been standing there. All she heard was the sound of my laughter. All she saw was that I was talking to a tree. In her mental-health voice, she asked if I was all right. Oh yeah, copacetic, I said. (*'Bout to beat the bark off this here honky-tree, that's all.*) And I would have to hold my gut to keep it from busting open. Glad to see you smiling, son, she would call out to me before going back inside.

There was one "honky" that wasn't a tree. He ran the principally Black community center in Seattle. His name was Reg, but we seldom called him by his name (except to his face), which made perfect sense because we weren't talking to his name. Reg had the ambience of a large but fit and bearded cop I saw on several occasions when I later lived in South Africa; a man who went to Black watering holes, called shebeens, in Soweto and bought the Africans beers. He had tortured some of them and, when it was over, made them turn the meat on the barbecue grill. He would sit down at the picnic table with them to show them that there was nothing personal in the way he had tortured them. Reg thrust his chin out when he spoke—either to praise the younger boys like me or caution the older ones. Whether in motion or at rest, he fired short, instinctive breaths between his words. He hastened from the playground, through the parking lot and gym, with the sangfroid of a man who rules.

A dustup went down in the parking lot under a rainless sky. I was inside the community center playing dodgeball when someone yelled, "The shit is on!" What was the shit and why was it on? Everyone who raced for the door seemed to know. I was the only one who had no clue. I knew—*everyone* knew—the hazy contours of why it had happened. The whole world of the center revolved around Reg's rules. Reg decided who could have the basketballs and who couldn't. Reg chose the activities for the week. Reg put a demerit by your name in his book if you cracked out of turn, or just spoke too loud. Three demerits and you couldn't come back for a week. He'd given Luke, a boy of seventeen, his third demerit. Reg wanted Luke to step off the property. I knew that much when I rushed outside because they had been inside when Reg gave Luke his third warning. Luke had let Reg lead him to the parking lot. But he had stopped, as though he'd changed his mind, and turned to go back inside. Reg's hand was at Luke's elbow, steering him away. A crowd began to collect around them. I minnowed my way through the crush of man-childs who wanted Luke to get their licks in for them.

"Touch me again," I heard Luke say.

Luke and Reg were toe-to-toe. I watched with astonishment as Reg inched closer. Reg was a man of at least twenty-five and he looked like he lifted weights, whereas Luke had the build of a small forward on a high school basketball team.

Reg said, "The rules apply to everyone, even to me."

To which Luke said, "Touch me again, alright."

Luke slipped his hand into his pocket. Reg's expression indicated that he knew exactly what would happen if Luke's hand reappeared and how much the outcome was desired not only by Luke but by all the boys around. And Reg seemed to know that his desperate courage would be devoured if he made one false move. Reg stared at us for a moment and he came nearer to tears or an apology than I had ever seen him come.

I was aware of how short I was compared to the others, most of whom, proper teenagers, were older than me. I had to look up to see who was speaking when someone cussed Reg, or told Luke to get busy. Birds strafed the sun like a fist of pepper in the last good eye of God. Luke looked like he was tickling his thigh from inside his pants pocket. Reg's voice was cracking, but he couldn't stop reciting the rules. I heard the click of Luke's switchblade before I saw its straight, stiff gleam.

Mom used to joke that in the part of New Orleans where she grew up you could get stabbed over a peanut butter sandwich. Even though she laughed when she said this, the glint in her eyes (and my father's "*sure-nuff*") convinced me she knew what she was on about. I, however, had never seen a stabbing, blood drawn with singular intent. (The blood I drew from Elgar Davenport was a result of the lack of wind and the pull of the earth, not the force of my intentions. The forward intent of Luke's switchblade bore scarce resemblance to a chance parabola of a dish soap bottle that arced and fell and split Elgar's head.)

"That's right, put your hands on me again."

Someone behind me said, "Bleed his ass."

Then someone to my left said it, "Bleed his ass."

Then a third someone sang it like a hymn.

Reg shook his head, more in prayer, it seemed, than defiance. He glanced up, but the clouds had run for cover.

I heard a woman's voice.

"No! No! You don't want to do this!" I knew that voice. Sometimes, in church, if I closed my eyes, it would thread the rich fabric of Gregorian chants and touch me in my pew. My mother had shoved her way to the front, pushing us all aside like wind in tall grass.

"You all don't want to do this," she kept repeating.

She stood between Reg and Luke. That is to say, between Reg and Luke's blade.

Someone in the crowd said, "Who's this lady?" And, before I could slink back into the center, another voice said, "Aw, that's L'il Man's mama."

She told Luke to take everyone inside. To my astonishment he closed his switchblade and obeyed. That wasn't the worst part. The worst part was that she made *me* wait in the parking lot with the honky while she went inside to speak with Luke. When she came out, she said only one word: "Come."

She bundled Reg into the front seat of her car. She made me sit in the back. As we drove away, Reg's cheek twitched. Sweat pasted his bangs to his forehead. My mother asked him what street he lived on and he told her. After that, no one spoke. We dropped him at his house and drove off without my being allowed to sit in the front seat.

I held her in contempt for the rest of the summer; and I held my father in even more contempt for saying she did the right thing. Now I know she wasn't trying to save Reg, so much as she was trying to save us from how short our futures would be cut if Reg got bled.

Like her, we had our whole, incarcerated lives ahead of us.

CHAPTER THREE

Hattie McDaniel Is Dead

1

This is a story I've never told before. Not to my brother or to my sisters. Not even to the women I've partnered with and married. Nearly forty years came and went before I could bring myself to say what happened to Stella, her daughter Malika, and me.

To go into it, I've always thought, would only cause embarrassment for me, a sudden need to be elsewhere, which is the natural response to a confession. Even now, I'll admit, the story makes me squirm; living with the shame of wanting out when I thought I could die. For years I've had to live with it, feeling this shame, trying to push it away. There have been times when I've tried to write about it in hopes that, through this act of remembrance, putting events down on paper, I could relieve the pressure on my conscience.

Courage, I seemed to think, comes to revolutionaries in finite quantities, like an inheritance that you stash away, let it earn interest, and draw down on when the day of reckoning arrives. It was a comforting theory. It offered hope and grace to a fool.

I believed that when it was time for the get-down I would face the Man like BLA soldier Assata Shakur faced the Man on the New Jersey Turnpike when the state troopers shot her in the chest; that I would get busy like Jonathan P. Jackson got busy at the courthouse in Marin County, California.* If the stakes ever became high enough—if the revolution required my sacrifice—I would simply tap a secret reservoir of courage that had been accumulating inside of me from the age of twelve, when I read Eldridge Cleaver's *Soul on Ice*, and when my junior high and high school teachers were the doppelgängers of the defendants in political trials, like the Chicago Eight and the Panther 21.† Stella happened to be one of those doubles. We were together almost ten years, though we never married. She was thirty-eight when we met, I was twenty-two.

I thought it all started when I met Stella at the end of March 1978 just a week after Dartmouth College sent me home for leading Black students in a campaign in solidarity with the people who made the food and cleaned the toilets and lived outside of town. Apparently, some frat boys had complained to the administration that the people from the Appalachian Trail had facial and other deformities brought on by what some Dartmouth fraternity brothers called hillbilly inbreeding. Seeing those people from the Appalachian Trail eating in the same room with them gave them indigestion, the letter claimed. The

---

* Assata Shakur is a Black Liberation Army member the BLA liberated from prison in 1979. She was granted political asylum in Cuba. Since her escape, Shakur's life has been depicted in songs, documentaries, and various literary works.

† Chicago Eight: Eight anti–Vietnam War activists charged with conspiracy to cross state lines to incite violent demonstrations at the August 1968 Democratic National Convention in Chicago. Panther 21: Twenty-one members of the Harlem Chapter of the Black Panther Party were charged with one hundred fifty-six counts of "conspiracy" to blow up subway and police stations, five local department stores, six railroads, and the Bronx-based New York Botanical Garden. On May 12, 1971, they were acquitted of all one hundred fifty-six charges.

administration responded by ruling that the service workers in Thayer Dining Hall and the buildings and grounds workers must, from that moment on, eat during off-peak hours and only in antechambers of the dining room that would be set aside for them and them alone. I lobbied the nearly three hundred Black students on campus. This was a fascist decree, I argued, and we had to take action. But many others pointed out that the workers who came from nearby backwater towns like Lebanon, New Hampshire, and many two-store-and-one-saloon towns skirting the mountains flew the Confederate flag in some of the bars, and yelled, "Nigger," from speeding pickups when they drove past us. Once, there were three of us lost in the countryside in a time when not even Dick Tracy had GPS. We drove past low-roofed houses ranged along a forest road like matchsticks spilled on the floor. Every fourth or fifth car was a rusted carcass with cinder-block wheels. I was startled by the lack of hatred in the eyes of the children who stared at us as we drove by. When I turned in my seat and looked back at them, they were still staring, as though waiting for God to help them name what they had just seen. In the end, the Afro-American Society voted to launch a civil disobedience campaign aimed at forcing the administration to rescind its decree. During the campaign I was arrested and jailed. A dean waited for me outside the Hanover, New Hampshire courthouse. He handed me a two-page, single-spaced charge sheet. I told him the town had dropped all charges. He implored me to read the letter. "Your troubles with the town have just ended. But your troubles with Dartmouth College have just begun."

Two years prior, the FBI had tracked me to Trinidad. Like most intelligence files by the time they are declassified, mine is riddled with redactions like sprigs of buckshot etched on the flank of a deer. The name of the agent who tailed me to Trinidad in the winter of 1976, the winter of my sophomore year at Dartmouth College, has been redacted. Nor did he or she seem interested in what the not-quite-twenty-year-old young man he or she shadowed was studying. At the University of the West Indies he studied Caribbean theater. He did field research on Rada, a major family of loa (spirits) in Trinidad's incarnation of the West African religion Voudon. His third course was an independent study he designed himself, a fifty-page thesis paper he wrote on his experiences as a participant-researcher of the Communist Party in Trinidad. The FBI file referenced none this.

> During his stay in Trinidad, Wilderson was in contact with a member of the Trinidad and Tobago Puerto Rican Solidarity Committee, and he promised that individual he would attempt to make contacts in the United States for that organization to obtain literature for it, and to attempt to procure financial aid.
> Wilderson allegedly claimed to be a member of an unspecified revolutionary group in the United States. He was born on April 11, 1956, in the United States, is a student at Dartmouth College, possesses U.S. Passport No. F 2316717, and his mailing address is Hinman, Box 3983, Dartmouth College, Hanover, New Hampshire 03755.

This report was sent from "LEGAT, CARACAS," the legal attaché in Venezuela, to Clarence M. Kelley (Hoover's successor as Director of the FBI). According to official propaganda, "The FBI legal attaché works with the law enforcement and security agencies in their host country to coordinate investigations of interest to both countries. The role of legal attachés is primarily one of coordination, as they do not conduct foreign intelligence gathering or counterintelligence investigations." No explanation is given as to why the LEGAT for the FBI in Venezuela was running an asset in

Trinidad to spy on an American student; or what the nature of the joint operation between the U.S. and the host country (Trinidad or Venezuela?) might be. The report begins, "The confidential source abroad mentioned in the memorandum is." The redaction is nearly two lines long. In other words, more than a name is being withheld. It continues: "[Blank] requested to be informed if WILDERSON has come to the attention in the past for political extremist activities in the United States." Then, "The Bureau and the Boston Office are requested to advise if WILDERSON has come to prior attention in connection with security activities."

This, however, is *not* the story I had never been able to tell. That story I'm going to tell you now, but this FBI report complicates that story. It corrupts the causal links that had helped me make sense of the violence that Stella and I were subjected to, four years after I returned from Trinidad; two years after Dartmouth College had kicked me out for leading a civil disobedience campaign on behalf of workers who were White and, to our Black and lonely student minds, unrepentant racists.

The FBI file came in the middle of writing this chapter. It corrupted the causal logic of the events that make my hand quiver as I scratch these words with my pen. Before the file arrived, I thought that at last I can chart a point-to-point pilgrim's progress of the chain of events that drove Stella and me and Malika, her young daughter, from our home; events that left us no alternative but to send Malika away to live with relatives for her own safety; events that drove Stella and me from the state of Minnesota when we ran out of friends and sanctuaries. The FBI file came when I was finally steadfast in my conviction that what happened to us had to do with Stella's past, not hers and mine. I even blamed the break-in at my studio apartment, by two White men who wanted nothing of value, as collateral heat from Stella's lawsuit against the government.

2

It's a month before I turn twenty-four, and I've stolen my parents' car. They're in Moscow, Mom and Dad, or Peking, or maybe they're in Bremen or Belize, a two-month tour studying the pitfalls of Soviet mental health clinics, three weeks of consulting with Chinese special education administrators, a Ford Foundation study of German urban renewal, or a rescue mission for American students who smoked too much dope and were bounced into jail in Belize— I don't know because I don't live with them anymore. My fourteen-year-old brother gave me the details, but all that registered was the fact that their car was in their garage. Two years prior, in March 1978, I was, as mentioned, kicked out of Dartmouth College for leading an act of civil disobedience. It was the end of winter quarter in my senior year and I was three classes shy of my degree. To Stella and whoever else asked, I wore "indefinite suspension from Dartmouth College" like a combat medal. But no one knows how much I cried on that Greyhound back to Minneapolis. Before I left the room of the tribunal, with my pink slip giving me forty-eight hours to pack my dorm room and leave Hanover, the chair of the committee, a dean, acknowledged that the punishment was harsh but, he explained, a team of psychologists had been evaluating me since I had arrived at Dartmouth. I'd had four years, these phantoms of therapy whom I had never met concluded, to "inculcate the esprit de corps of an Ivy League institution"—the dean's exact words and the words, no doubt, of the psychologists. For four years I'd been under psychiatric care without ever meeting my caregivers. In this they were one with the FBI asset who had tracked me to Trinidad and reported to Boston and Caracas; all day, all night, angels watching over me.

3

Stella had changed from the woman she was nine years prior, when I saw her at the Armory on the University of Minnesota's campus. I was almost fifteen; she had been thirty-one for three months. It was March 1971, the same month and year as the break-in at the FBI office in Media, Pennsylvania, that would soon blow the lid off COINTEL-PRO. On that morning William Calley was convicted for the massacre of nearly five hundred Vietnamese civilians by Company C, in a village called My Lai. The massacre was in the forefront of Stella's mind as she stood by a bus and told anxious inductees they'd return from Vietnam wearing the tucked sleeve of a one-armed boy. Richard Nixon took, reassuringly, to the airwaves: "American troops are now in a defensive position . . . The offensive activities of search and destroy are now being undertaken by the South Vietnamese." The bombing of Cambodia was still under way and I was a shoplifter in Dinkytown two blocks away from the campus of the University of Minnesota.

The cold front had quickly crumbled and temperatures rose from the fifties to as high as seventy degrees. There was no ice or slush on the sidewalks. My friend Robert Stevenson Stone and I boosted rock albums and sold them to the hippies, at cut-rate prices. With the pavements dry we could outrun any cashier in Dinkytown.

The *E Plurbis Funk* albums by Grand Funk Railroad, I recall, were completely round and covered with a silver-like film to resemble a large coin. The back side of the cover of this album included a picture of Shea Stadium, to celebrate Grand Funk Railroad beating the Beatles' Shea Stadium attendance record by selling out in just seventy-two hours.

I stole three of them from a record store in Dinkytown, near a coffee shop where Bob Dylan used to play. Dinkytown was not a town or even a neighborhood, but simply two blocks of shops and eateries at the edge of the University of Minnesota. Our high school consisted of two buildings, one at each end of Dinkytown. Tucked behind the main gate of the university was Pike Hall, which had been the university Lab School for the children of professors. At the other end of Dinkytown was an uninspired brick building that had been Marshall Public High School for White working-class kids. The two schools merged in 1968 in a social experiment financed, in large part, by funds from LBJ's Great Society initiatives. The children of liberal mandarins were made to mingle with the children of flour mill and railway workers and, to give the experiment demographic integrity, Native Americans were bused in from the south side and Blacks were bused in from the north side, to the tune of four percent and nine or ten percent, respectively.

On my way to the record store, where five-finger discounts awaited, I walked through Dinkytown with my face turned, triumphantly, up to the first real warmth of sun.

Bob Stone was long and lanky, sort of like Al Green on stilts. We had been the same height when we started the ninth grade but over the Christmas break he grew like a plant in time-lapse photography. I was jealous of his height, so I told myself I had something better, a letter jacket with gold bars and felt stars for my *three* sports—football, ski jumping, and track and field—none of which Bob participated in because, though he could run, he wasn't athletic. I told Bob to boost only *E Plurbis Funk* albums. He said we could get more money for some Hendrix LPs. *"Band of Gypsies* won't fit under your shirt," I protested. But Bob wouldn't listen. He damn near got us busted.

We always entered the record store separately, and we each had our inherent diversions to offer. The clerks would look up and see my black face. I didn't have to look at them to feel the way their eyes narrowed on my face and my hair. A moment later, I could feel their gaze settle serenely on my letter jacket. *Sports keep him out of trouble.* Bob wasn't so lucky. He lived in the projects and he didn't have a sport. Whereas I lived in a mansion and had a sport for each season. So he didn't have a letter jacket, and the windbreaker his mother had not replaced since seventh grade looked like a nylon T-shirt.

He went in first. I normally came in second. From the window on the street I watched the clerk watch Bob's every move. When I arrived he focused on me. In the interstice of time when he would decide if I was a good Black, or just a Black, Bob would make his play and slip an album or two up under his windbreaker. I first saw Stella the same day Bob went off-script and switched from Grand Funk Railroad to Jimi Hendrix.

We'd been in the store five or six minutes. The clerk went back to reading *Ramparts*, that countercultural left-wing magazine of the period, and looking up once or twice to watch Bob, who had his back to him, as he fingered a crate of albums at the far end of the store. I had three *E Plurbis Funk* albums lined against my ribs and still had room for two more. I walked to the counter to buy some Zig-Zag rolling papers, hoping Bob could scram while I paid. But the dude at the till was a task-stacker. He counted my change with one eye and peered over my shoulder with the other.

It would've been a groove if not for the pointed breasts Bob had poking through his windbreaker—breasts he didn't have when he came in. "Watch the counter!" The man told me as he chased Bob out the store and down the block in the direction of campus.

The long, flaxen-haired cashier came back winded and sweaty, his cheeks the color of flamingos.

"You know him?"

I shook my head.

"Boosting ain't a hip thing, my brother. We're one tribe, man," the clerk said to me. And he thanked me for watching the cash register.

Bob and I met six blocks away at the ROTC armory on campus, a sandy brick fortress with ramparts at each end like rooks on a chessboard. Three chartered buses faced southeast on University Avenue in front of the armory. Five White men and three White women sat in the street, their backs to the bumper of the lead bus. They smoked cigarettes. They held two fingers up in the air. A crowd gathered along the sides of the buses. Bob said we should off-load our gear before the pigs came and vamped. "*Get they cash, man*, before they get they heads busted." Carbon monoxide puttered from the quiet tailpipe of one idling bus. A line of inductees filed down the steps of the armory and the crowd of protesters began to chant beneath a salmon-colored sky.

She was hard to miss, Stella. There weren't many Black men among the protesters and she was the only Black woman. She was in front and down the steps, close to the buses. The draftees were all down the stairs now. Bob and I climbed the stairs and looked down. It was the perfect place to be in case 5-0 vamped with their nightsticks. They would bust the protesters' heads by the buses, not ours as long as we stood on higher ground. "Hell, no, we won't go, we won't fight for Texaco!" yelled the crowd. Not Stella. She spoke to each inductee, *individually*, as they got on their bus. She asked them if they had a loved one she could contact if they died. She told another one, "The people you kill over there will always be in your head." An easy wind rustled the trees; a pair of large Bose 901 speakers in the window of the frat house across the street was playing "The Weight (Take a Load off, Fannie)." The lead singer's voice was high as a lusty wildcat, as stern as a Southern preacher, as depleted as a Rebel soldier going back to Turkey Scratch, Arkansas; a dirt farmer at the end of his day. The music kite whistled over the crowd of protesters and the line of young, vacant faces filing onto the buses. Stella thrust a *Life* photograph of Lieutenant Calley up to them as they passed her. I thought she was bulletproof.

"You're better than this," she told them.

A sergeant snatched the photograph from Stella. He tore it to shreds.

"Tell them," she said, pointing to the men looking out the window. "Turn around and tell them they'll come back with their sanity, as well as their arms and legs."

Bob stood next to me on the top step of the armory. He noticed how I marveled at her.

"That's too much woman for you," Bob said.

"The hell you say."

"And look how she's performing for these hippies."

"They aren't hippies. They're SDS—look, man, a couple of our teachers are here." Our school was a lab school, one building was on campus and the other building was on the other side of Dinkytown. Some of our teachers were graduate students going for their Ph.D.s in education. "The New Left and the hippies are on different tips. Do you actually *read* the *Ramparts* magazines I give you?"

"They're all the White unwashed to me. And she's playing to them."

I slipped the three albums out from under my jacket and said, "*We're* playing to the White unwashed, aren't we?"

"We're getting paid. She's getting used."

"The war's not a race issue. It's a class issue. It affects us all."

"I'm just saying I know her type."

"What type is that?"

"The type who into White boys. Not like it matters to you; the way you came up."

"How did I 'come up'?"

"Forget it, Frank."

"No, tell me. And which is it: She's too much woman for me or we're both the same kind of Oreo?"

"Go for what you know, Frank. She could burp you at night before you go to sleep."

As it happened, Stella, during my high school and college years, worked as a nurse until she broke her back. It never healed well enough for her to go back to nursing, so she went to work as an administrator in the College of Education, where my father was a dean during the Vietnam War. She managed the placement and affairs of graduate students who worked as teachers at the experimental ("lab") high school that Bob and I attended on campus. But in 1978, when we became lovers, she worked as an aid for elementary school teachers and collected welfare to cover the gap.

After that first meeting (or rather, *sighting*) at the armory, seven years would pass until we met again. And the seven years from the age of fifteen to the age of twenty-two were longer in my mind than the seven years she traveled from thirty-one to thirty-eight; which is to say, less time and fewer memories had passed in those seven years for Stella than they had for me. I had gone from ninth grade to the end of my senior year in college. Unlike me, she grew but did not grow up in those years. So, when she saw me again at a branch of the library near her house, in faded khaki pants tucked into Frye boots, an army surplus trench coat draped across the chair I wasn't using, and my hair cornrowed in neat lines along my scalp, she recognized me immediately. But I didn't know where I'd seen this beautiful woman with her wide-eyed daughter before. The next day, I hitchhiked from Minneapolis to Columbus, Ohio. After a month, I came back to Minneapolis and looked her up. By the end of the summer, we were in love.

We baked soufflés in her large cast-iron skillet. In the evening, after supper, when her daughter, Malika, went to bed, we would sit on her front porch and watch the sun redden, and I would read to her from a novel I was writing or she'd teach me how to listen to Miles. "The long pauses between notes," Stella said, just under the music. "Miles made silence part of his music. Small clusters of intention without sound," she said. She made me feel comfortable enough to read my fledgling prose to her. She closed her eyes as she listened.

"So much woe in your voice," she said. "You're the prince of darkness. You were born on a Wednesday. Am I right?"

Two bolts of silver-gray etched themselves on the front of her natural hair like low sparks of lightning rising above her eyes. Heads turned to watch her when she entered a room; and I felt a surge of manhood when they looked from her to me. That's right people, she's with *me*. At a distance, folks on campus would take her for Angela Davis, and I was honored as if through osmosis. But even when the mirage had melted they drank of her singular beauty, for even in leather sandals she was tall for a woman; she didn't powder her face or rouge her lips. She owed her flawless skin to the fact that she ate organically long before it was the fashion and that she had no truck with sugar. When I first saw those two lightning bolts in her hair, I thought she could take down the world. Some folks called her a troublemaker. I saw a Black woman who stood up for herself and anyone else who was being abused.

When she sat in her porch chair and watched people come and go across the courtyard of the apartment complex where she lived, Stella "smoked" a corncob pipe without ever lighting it, as my father had done when I was a kid. And it looked just like the one I saw my great-grandmother smoke when I was twelve years old, the one and only time I saw her. In fact, Stella had the same cleft at the bridge of her nose that I see on Grandma Harper when I conjure her. It chiseled both women's gaze. Stella would bring her flute to hear Frank Wess play, long after he left Count Basie's band. The club was small and half the people weren't listening to the music; so when the band took a break Stella took me to the stage and introduced me to him. Then she took out her flute, and Wess improvised with her for a moment or two. No way in hell was I going back to Dartmouth.

She saw how depressed I was about being kicked out of school. The stronger my putative pose of indifference, the more seismic my mood swings. I could be in a room with Malika and Stella and I might not say a word for five minutes, though words roiled in my head, loud as foghorns. Not only had Stella been a nurse, but she was an autodidact nutritionist. She was the first person to tell me how cancer might be cured by diet (something I learned, years later, was called the Gerson Method). She and Malika rarely ate meat and very little poultry. I can't remember one fried meal; and places like McDonald's, White Castle, and Burger King (where I had worked in Dinkytown when I first laid eyes on Stella) were off-limits. I ate a fair amount of chocolate bars in 1978, when we first got together. She made me uncomfortable, the way she watched me and said, "It's your funeral," with the shrug of her shoulders. When I finally moved in with her, she would snatch a Snickers bar out of my hand with, "Let's see what those *crimnals* are poisoning you with," turning a three syllable word into two. Then, as I looked on with forlorn loss, Stella would read aloud all the unpronounceable chemicals put into it by the Mars, Incorporated, a corporation that I, even as a young communist, saw as my friend who just wanted me enjoy a scrumptious nougat topped with caramel and peanuts enrobed in mouthwatering milk chocolate. I had never thought to read the ingredients, nor would I have thought they were "poison." But Stella insisted that the high-fructose corn syrup and the artificial flavoring were major contributors to my mood swings and depression. On New Year's Day 1979, she made a deal with me. Give up my Mars bars, my Snickers bars, my Three Musketeers for six weeks. She also wanted me to be a label sleuth with her in the store; by which she meant we would read the labels of everything we considered purchasing, from cereal to ketchup, and discard the products with more than seven grams of processed sugar or any amount of high-fructose corn syrup. If, after six weeks, I did not feel the fog lift from my brain, if the mood swings continued as before, then I could go back to my old reckless ways. Needless to say, Stella's wager worked. I had the kind of clarity of mind that I had not known in my two decades and change on the planet. I often wonder how I might have weathered the storm at Kenwood Elementary School had I known about sugar when I was a child. It wasn't just abstinence she wanted from me. Over those six weeks we read William Dufty's *Sugar Blues,* a book that argues that sugar was once the cocaine of the Western world, and is still as debilitating and addictive as nicotine.

In winter we made stovetop coffee in a saucepan of water and four tablespoons of fine-ground coffee floating on the surface. If we got to talking at the table and not paying attention, we would almost let it boil. It had to only *almost* boil for its rich roasted taste to keep from turning bitter. The year I made up my mind that I was never going back to Dartmouth, we lived five blocks from the campus. The war in Vietnam had ended three years before, and the campus didn't look anything like the place I knew in high school. When Saigon fell in 1975 the atmosphere thinned of the righteous indignation that had thickened the air. It made me melancholy and made Stella sort of a has-been. Gone were the incandescent barricades severing the university's Washington Avenue artery to downtown Minneapolis. Gone were the voices with their list of demands from the occupied windows of Morrill Hall. Gone were the lectures that were thrown out the window when classes and seminars were commandeered for "anti-imperialist" teach-ins. All that was a brief moment when the world was being remade, and Stella could arrive, unannounced, and she could rise and be applauded before she even spoke. But that moment was no more. The White Left had robbed her while licking her face. "One, two, three mini-Vietnams," she said with a laugh. "It wasn't about Vietnam. It was about the shit they hadn't worked out at home. Now they want to go home. That's what you can do if you're White in this country. You can be a tourist in your own movie." Stella wasn't wrong. Weather Underground fugitives were even turning themselves in to the police and doing unheard-of deals with prosecutors, while members of the Black Liberation Army were still being hunted and tortured if and when they were captured. At one sleepy New York precinct Weather Underground fugitives made the inconvenient error of trying to surrender in the afternoon on a Friday; they were told to come back on Monday and turn themselves in. "Imagine," Stella said, "if that was you and me turning ourselves in. Friday be *damned*. They would stay late, not to book us but to beat us; and be so deep in their pleasure when they got done that they'd forget to put in for the overtime."

One night in bed, I said that the two streaks of silver in her hair were beautiful, but I noted that a woman in her late thirties was too young to have gray hair. Did something happen to you, I asked her, something traumatic? I wanted her to trust me the way I trusted her.

"Stress," she said. Then she turned over and went to sleep.

Stella turned me on to the works of Toni Morrison and Alice Walker. Together we discovered Fuentes, Amado, and García Márquez. And though she was almost a generation older and grew up in the South, while I was born in the South but grew up in Minnesota, we shared the same way of being in our bodies, the same tonalities in our voices when we were with our White friends. We both knew how to make them feel at home. Our words were effortless and well chosen. They told us (not in words) how authentic they felt with us; how they were going to take themselves seriously from now on. The jazz was always soft when they came to our house. With our Black friends we discussed what worrisome burdens White people can be. But this duality had limits. Making our White friends feel safe in our presence made them think that we were somehow evolved in a way that the Black people they saw burning down the cities in the 1960s were not.

From 1978 until we fled our apartment in the spring of 1980, we hauled crates of apples and organic produce with our White friends at the Wedge, the city's first coop, with its unfinished floors and its funky bins of oatmeal, chia seeds, raw almonds, and stone-ground millet in bulk. They felt at home in our home, a sense of welcome they could never feel (even if it was extended to them) in the Black neighborhood on the Near North side of town. Our dwelling was the ground floor of a duplex in the center of a courtyard and drive that was ringed by a ramshackle horseshoe of wooden town house apartments just five blocks from campus. There's something about a campus community that makes you feel as though nothing catastrophic can happen to you there; as though the real world begins at the border. No lunch-bucket laborers stepping tired off the bus, no Deuce and a Quarters double-parked on the boulevard, no big hats and overcoats slung over one arm in basement nightclubs, no burst of sound in the street that stops the heart. Visiting our home was less strain on their nerves than adding ornaments from far-off places to their shelves. And they left with the feeling that they'd marched in Selma or hurled bricks during the riots on the Near North side.

But that wasn't enough for Josephine, who worked with nuclear fusion and nuclear waste in a lab at the university. I've long since forgotten if she was on the faculty or if she worked as a technician. This amnesia has kept me sane for almost forty years.

She lived above us. Before I came on the scene, Josephine and Stella had issues—mainly their disagreement over the ethics and safety of nuclear power. The Three Mile Island accident had happened on March 28, 1979, less than six months after I became a factor in Stella's and—by extension—Josephine's lives. But their heated debates over this issue, and even the way Stella's routine changed when we became lovers, were not the real cause of the meltdown between these two women. Stella was simply tired of playing Hattie

McDaniel to Vivien Leigh. "I've nursed her through her failed relationships; but she never seemed to care about what I was going through." Josephine seemed to think that the downstairs part of the house was simply an extension of the upstairs part, where she lived. It wasn't the unscheduled visits that annoyed Stella (and me) but the injury Josephine felt when Stella asked her to knock before coming inside, or to call first when "Frank is here." When she heard such words, you could set your watch by the sundial on her face: Guilt. Resentment. Aggression.

Malika, Stella, and I were in the back of the house eating dinner at the kitchen table. We heard the front door open and close. Josephine appeared in the threshold of the kitchen with bushels of lilacs in a straw basket. She had picked them in the courtyard, just for us. No doubt, in her mind the gift of flowers offset her violation of our space. But, looking back on it, all I see is the extension of the master's prerogative in the way Josephine treated Stella. There's a scene in the film *12 Years a Slave* in which the master, Edwin Epps, bursts into the slaves' cabin while they're in bed. He dances in the middle of their sleeping quarters and commands them to rise and make "merriment" in the big house with him. It has taken me forty years to understand how neither he nor Josephine had violated anyone's space. The cabin where they slept belonged to him as much as their flesh belonged to him. The regime of violence that made them his property and prosthetics of his desire made it impossible to see what he did as a violation. This is to say that I was wrong to think Josephine did something wrong.

At one time in history, Eastern Seaboard slaves had grown to believe in the elasticity of accumulation and fungibility; in other words, slaves on the Eastern Seaboard were *not* Afropessimists, in that they did not see themselves as, primarily, the objects of captivity; rather, they saw themselves as the subjects of hyper-exploitation; and, like me and Stella in 1980, slaves of the late eighteenth and nineteenth centuries on the Eastern Seaboard might have imagined that their dwellings were also their homes—and not the always and already home of Josephine and her race. They were in for a traumatic awaking when, starting in 1808:

> The westward movement of plantation culture [to Georgia, Alabama, Mississippi, and Louisiana]—whether it was driven by individual owners who accompanied their slaves or by professional slave traders—tore that society asunder, exiling hundreds of thousands from their birthplace and traumatizing those who remained. Families and sometimes whole communities dissolved under the pressure of this Second Great Migration.

In short, Josephine was *libidinally* within her "rights" on the day she barged in while we were eating dinner.

With as much poise as she could muster, Stella thanked Josephine, and said that the two of them should meet tomorrow for coffee.

"I thought you said you and Frank were busy tomorrow, Mom."

Stella eyed her daughter as if to say, Let's not do this now. Josephine was in no mood for discretion. In fact, Stella's poise rankled Josephine more than if she had jumped out of a bag.

"Why coffee all of a sudden?" Josephine said.

"To talk about boundaries."

"I thought you were a feminist," she told Stella, as she turned to go.

For almost forty years, I've wondered how this scene between Josephine and Stella played out in Malika's twelve-year-old mind. We weren't always the best parents, Stella and I. We never took time with Malika after these tense confrontations with someone like Josephine. This isn't entirely true. Stella always explained to her the underlying nature of racism, the monstrous violence ensconced within the mundane of microaggressions. But—and this I regret with all my heart—we never asked her how she processed these spectacles emotionally. We didn't know how she had been wounded, just as I had no idea as a young boy how Mrs. Davenport's words would later affect me.

Needless to say, the fact that I was only eleven years older than Malika didn't help our relationship. She and I had a hard time adjusting to one another. On more than one occasion she told me, "You're not my father." As a young girl she had a lot to contend with. Her biological father was Jewish, and though he seemed to have abandoned her, emotionally and financially, and though his family had disowned and disinherited him (until he divorced Stella), she carried with her the ensemble of dilemmas that seems to afflict mixed-race children into adulthood—a fear of slipping into the darkness of their Black side and without ever having ascended to the light of White redemption. And, for my part, I resented the fact that she was born with this crisis and I was not; a crisis in which I, as a dark-skinned person with no whiteness in my features, was the living, breathing image of the hell into which she could descend.

Stella told me how hard she had worked to teach her daughter about our culture and the lashes we endured for the rights most people don't even know they have. But it's slipping away, she said, sobbing, the longer I stay here the more it slips away.

As time went on I saw other things: how her breath quickened, as if she'd felt a sudden tightness in her chest, when she spoke of Urban Risers, one of LBJ's Great Society programs, and the lawsuit she had filed against it. She said she had proof of embezzlement, legal documents and audiotapes of board meetings that she had recorded herself.

"You're saying the federal government or someone at HEW* knew about all this?" I asked her.

I meant it as a question. She took it as a challenge. "You can ask my lawyer, Noam Davidov," she said, "if you don't believe me."

"You talk like you're used to being doubted."

"I'm a *Black* woman. What rock have you been under?"

Noam Davidov came to the house and said that after years of wrangling with the federal government he had secured a court date for her, November 13, 1980—which at this time was in less than a year. He also said he didn't have the resources—I remember very distinctly the word he used was "resources"—to help her. Then he looked my way and said, "Or you, until we go to court." He didn't mean "help," he meant "protect"; and by "resources," he seemed to be referring to protection. It was then that I would understand the gravity of Stella's lawsuit. The board members of Urban Risers whom she was accusing of graft and maybe even people in the government who ran interference for them or looked the other way could not afford for the recordings and documents Stella had amassed to be made public.

Noam's hair was curly, like Abbie Hoffman's. He was a movement lawyer; it was clear he earned more gratitude than money, with his brown corduroys, his unknotted necktie, and his stonewashed raincoat home from the wars.

In the early 1970s, Noam Davidov worked with the radical lawyer William Kunstler, as well as Mark Lane, and a group of researchers to represent the American Indian Movement (AIM) defendants in the Wounded Knee trial.† I didn't know Stella back then, but Stella and Noam had been lovers, and she attended every session of the trial. At

---

* Health, Education, and Welfare (also known as HEW) was a cabinet-level department of the United States government from 1953 until 1979.

† Attorney Mark Layne joined Kunstler's legal team in 1974.

the front door, she straightened the collar of his shabby raincoat. So now a dull, metallic jealousy began to gather at the back of my mind. She and Noam shared a history salted with victories, like the verdict in favor of the Native American defendants Noam had helped to secure. She and I had no history at all; and the history we were making, I feared (a fear that yokes me to this day), was unfolding as a story I would never want to tell. I wished I'd gone to the kitchen or turned my head to cough—to go back in time and orchestrate a random distraction to prevent me from the sight of her fingers straightening his collar. I wanted him to leave, but just as strongly, I wanted him to stay. I believed that he, not I, had the credentials to tell her to take the settlement and not go to trial. As much as my heart pained to see them speak so effortlessly together, even when they disagreed, as much as I wanted that to be over, it was clear that if anyone could change Stella's mind it was Noam, not me.

He made it plain that the government would settle with Stella out of court. Noam was absolutely sure Stella would get $100,000. She would have to hand over all of the tapes of the secret recordings she'd made when she was an employee of Urban Risers. She would have to relinquish financial documents she photocopied to prove corruption, and the secret audio recordings she made of Urban Risers meetings that might be incriminating of Kapalei Kenyatta, who had been the director of Urban Risers, or employees of the federal government with whom Kapalei Kenyatta worked. All of this would be sealed.

"There's one more thing. You'll have to sign a nondisclosure agreement giving your word you won't talk about the case. *Ever*," he emphasized. "You talk about this after they pay you, Stella, and they'll come after you."

"What if I don't settle out of court?"

"Then you're down for next November a week after the presidential elections [of 1980]. As your lawyer, I have to advise you—"

Stella scoffed.

"I've waited *years*; I can wait eleven months."

"Take a few days to think about it."

"You wouldn't settle if you were in my shoes, would you? You never settled with the government."

"I was never the litigant. And I'm not a single mom with financial challenges."

"Just say 'welfare,' Noam, it's only two syllables."

"Have you forgotten all the people who were murdered by government proxy during the Wounded Knee affair?" Then Noam turned to me. "What do you think?"

"You didn't answer my question," Stella interjected before I could speak.

"You can start over with that kind of money!"

"He said, still not answering the question," Stella rejoined.

"A trial could reveal Kapalei Kenyatta's connection to government officials who can't afford to be linked to someone like him. If you make it to the courthouse—"

"*If* I make it to the courthouse?"

I watched these two old lovers talk about death as though they were the heroine and hero of a film noir classic weighing their options against the mob. But as the conversation wound down and Stella had still refused the settlement, I knew it wasn't a film and I knew that I wasn't a spectator.

"If I settle out of court," Stella said, as Noam set his teacup down on the living room table and inched forward in the easy chair, "I'll never know who was behind all this. If it even makes it to the newspapers (and you're basically telling me that won't happen because the money buys my silence), based on the evidence so far they'd call it a another example of the kind of gangsterism and shady business dealings people associate with the ghetto in North Minneapolis, but not when they think of 3M Corporation in Maplewood, the regional banks downtown, or the Pillsbury Companies' assortment of businesses. The government will get away clean. A hundred thousand dollars is nothing for them to pay if it means they can avoid indictments up the food chain."

Noam stood up and said he understood. Stella had always been a fighter and he hadn't expected her to take the out-of-court settlement. As I watched them and listened, I had the feeling of being eleven years old, seated at a folding table with other children at Thanksgiving, catching fragments of what the adults said at the long old wood table in the center of the room. Noam picked up his vintage leather briefcase, scooped the files from the coffee table, and put them in.

"There's more to this than meets the eye," he said as he slung his raincoat on. It sloped to one side. A corner of his collar had folded under and he hadn't noticed. She rose and plucked it free. It was an act of tenderness and joy and, I hoped to God, not desire.

"Oh, Noam." She chuckled as she patted his lapel with her palm. For the past ninety minutes I had waited for an intimacy to pass between them. He smiled back. *They've done this a hundred times before*, I thought. I watched her watch him down the stairs.

Though I spent nights on end in the lower level of the duplex where Stella lived with Malika, I still had my own apartment when Noam came to Stella's house. It was November 1979. By the end of the year I would be on welfare. In fact, it was that November of 1979 that Stella and I saw our revolution die. It was the month we rejoiced at the news that Assata Shakur had been freed from a maximum-security prison by the Black Liberation Army. It was the month the Ku Klux Klan shot and killed Black demonstrators in Greensboro, North Carolina: just rode up to the picket line, got out of the car, and shot them at near point-blank range. November was the month we watched it on the news. The Klansmen opened their trunk. They fetched their weapons. They sprinted ten yards to the marchers. They opened fire. Five lay dead on the ground. That month, Stella and I had no idea that Assata would have to spend the rest of her life in Cuba, in exile. We had no idea that the film we saw would not be enough to convict the assailants; and we had no idea that by March of the coming year we'd be sleeping in my parents' car.

Several days after Noam left, days crowded with silence as Stella thought on what he had said, she called a man named Jamal. She told him she needed protection. There was silence on his end for three interminable beats.

"Protection from who?" Jamal asked her.

"The system," she said.

By the end of 1979, the number of people Stella knew who could hear "the system" without raising an eyebrow had dwindled. But Jamal used to say, just because you're not paranoid doesn't mean they're not after you. In 1968, when he and Stella and damn near everyone they knew believed in revolution, Jamal had gone up against the system and did a nickel of a ten-year stint in the Stillwater prison in Bayport, Minnesota. He wasn't someone who would raise an eyebrow when someone mentioned "the system."

As a result of Stella's call, Jamal and a brilliantly taciturn brother dropped by Stella's house one night when I wasn't there. Jamal said, Let's go for hamburgers, as he motioned to the ceiling light and the telephone, then he put his finger over his lips. Stella thought of White Castle as a temple where Satan killed you with sodium and trans fats, but this wasn't a night for insisting that Jamal sit down with her and pore over back issues of *Prevention* magazine.

In the booth at the White Castle restaurant on Thirty-Sixth Avenue and East Lake Street, Stella's daughter (who never missed anything) watched as the quiet brother looked around the restaurant, then nodded to Jamal. Malika saw Jamal unwrap his hamburger and put it on his lap. Then he fetched something from his pocket and wrapped it in the hamburger paper, which he passed to Stella. Later that night, Malika told me that she got up to go to the bathroom and found her mother sitting on the bed with an automatic handgun and a magazine of bullets. She watched her mother snap the clip into place, wrap it in an oilskin, and hide it in the closet, deep behind the shoes.

I was not yet driving a cab at that point. That would start when I moved in with Stella. I still worked as a waiter at Williams Café, but the restaurant was slow one night and I was sent home early. My studio was on the ground floor of an old brownstone six blocks from Lake of the Isles. The key worked but the door to my studio was chained from the inside. *How I could have done* that? I thought in self-rebuke. It took a moment for me to realize that, in point of fact, I could *not* have done that. Someone else did that. That someone was inside! I sprinted down the hall. I burst out the front door and dashed to where I could see my apartment window. The alley light lit them in silhouette. One leg curled out the window of my studio, then his torso, then the other leg. He stumbled and almost fell before he ran. Then the other one rolled out with the grace of a pole vaulter clearing the bar. His long hair flounced up and down in the low yellow light. Like a fool, I chased them halfway down the alley. Like an even bigger fool, I called the cops. When they arrived, even with the Murphy bed closed into the wall there was little space left, with one large cop by the sink and stove and me and his partner in the middle of the room. You have this wad of cash on you, or you left it here when you went to work? the one by the sink said to me, pointing to the money in the dish drainer (tip money that I carelessly left by the sink until I went to the bank). I told him I had left it there. Did you leave this Miranda camera here when you went to the restaurant? I nodded.

The cop by the sink was counting. "Eighty, eighty-five, ninety,

ninety-five dollars in cash. A camera worth, what, two C-notes? Three hundred bucks worth of stuff, just left here? You say someone—"

"Two people."

"You say two people climbed in, chained the door from the inside, and then, what, played bridge; had a cup of coffee? You see how it looks from where we stand."

"I have a right to privacy. That's what they stole."

They looked at me as though I had said I have a right to shingles.

My books had been taken from my bookshelf and arranged on the floor in neat orderly rows. The case to my typewriter was open and pages from a novel I was writing were spread on the desk.

"Whoever did this knew my schedule. They thought they had time—"

"Time for *what*?"

"You won't know that unless you investigate."

The cop by the sink nodded. "Investigate. Gotcha." Then he stooped and picked up two books from the floor. "I. F. Stone, *The Killings at Kent State: How Murder Went Unpunished*; Karl Marx, *The Communist Manifesto*." He placed them both back neatly on the floor.

"What are you reading this stuff for?"

Not surprisingly, I soon moved in with Stella and Malika and a gun in the closet that we didn't know how to use.

4

We had fallen back to sleep after making love when we heard someone enter Stella's apartment. We were naked under the sheets. It was half past nine in the morning. For a moment I thought, *This isn't happening.* Now I realize what struck such terror in me, that which I had no words for at the time. My mind flashed on the image of our throats being slit: *This isn't a robbery; they want to be heard; they want us to know they're here.* I jumped out of bed. My feet slapped the wood floor. I opened the closet where Stella kept the gun Jamal had given her. Stella wasn't alarmed. She told me it was Malika, who'd left earlier for school. "She must have forgotten something." The front door and living room were near Stella's bedroom. As she tugged into her clothes she called out through the door, "What'd you forget, Malika?" There was no answer. A chair scraped the floor. I started to get dressed as well, but Stella motioned for me to stay in the bedroom. "Let me talk to her before you come out." The voice that accosted Stella in the living room did not belong to Malika.

"Aren't you tired of this pattern, Stella, putting me in cold storage whenever you find someone new?"

It was *Josephine.* I couldn't believe it. After what Stella had told her just the other day about boundaries, this woman had the nerve to enter the apartment, *again*, without knocking!

"Get out," I heard Stella say.

"He's your *daughter's* age!"

I opened the bedroom door in time to see Stella grab Josephine and yank her toward the door.

"Hattie McDaniel is dead. You're not welcome anymore."

They were on the front porch now. Josephine didn't fight back, but nor was she cowed.

I stayed inside the screen door, not knowing what my role was or should be. Stella told Josephine, "You've been misled. I'm not here for your amusement; and your being a nuclear physicist at the University of Minnesota doesn't make you Scarlett O'Hara."

"Stella, we used to be there for each other."

Stella let out a shrill laugh. "That's what you call it, 'there for each other'? You're a parasite, no, a psychopath. You act like you own me."

The word "psychopath" inflamed Josephine's face. For nearly

forty years the expression on her face has boomeranged from the back of my brain at intervals beyond my control. I last saw it at the movies. The film was *12 Years a Slave*, and a woman in the film by the name of Mary Epps looked first at her husband and then at her husband's concubine, a slave named Patsey, with the same wild eyes and thin mouth as Josephine's. In the film, Mary Epps demands that her husband sell Patsey. But Edwin Epps tells her that he'd divorce her before he sold Patsey. This all takes place in the drawing room at midnight. Edwin Epps has forced his family's slaves to wake up (even though they must work in the fields in a few hours) and play music and dance for him in the drawing room. What's telling about this scene is the way Patsey functions as an object, *but not a subject*, for both Edwin and Mary.

"You will sell her!" Mary demands.

The slaves have stopped dancing. They are all in the same room with the couple that owns them but they are objects—not agents—of the discussion, even Patsey. Neither Edwin nor Mary ever turn to Patsey and say, in the case of Edwin, for example, Do you have a take on this mess?; or, in the case of Mary, How could you be so low as to steal my husband? Patsey has enough survival skills to stay silent. But this doesn't stop Mary Epps from bashing her in the eye with a large crystal whiskey decanter when Edwin Epps refuses to sell her. For his part, Edwin simply sighs as Patsey, lying on her back on the floor, clutching her eye, is dragged away by two of the other slaves. He yells at them; he commands Solomon and the other fiddlers to go on playing; he shouts at the others to show some merriment and dance; he says, "I will not have my mood spoiled."

I don't think Josephine was enraged because she had just been called a psychopath. I think she was enraged because Stella had dared to speak. Josephine's slave had spoken. Period. This has less to do with the actual word Stella used ("psychopath") and more to do with the fact that an object meant merely for the pleasure of possession had gazed back at a Human subject. Stella had cracked out of turn.* For years, Stella had suffered Josephine's presence and possessiveness diplomatically. In other words, Josephine had characterized *Stella's* behavior, freely, without restraint; but Stella had never returned the favor. It was the same pavane that Black women have danced with White women for centuries, where only the White woman could break the rules and take hold of the Black woman. Josephine was now furious.

She ran through a list of names, six of Stella's past lovers: a famous saxophonist who got his start in Minneapolis and now had good work in Chicago; a Pro Bowl linebacker, who had just been inducted into the NFL Hall of Fame; Noam Davidov, the civil rights lawyer who had been in the news during Wounded Knee; her ex-husband, Uri, whom Stella had helped make his mark as a counterculture photographer; a famous oil painter; and, of course, the man named Jamal, who couldn't decide, Josephine said, if he was a revolutionary or a heroin addict. Stella shoved her. Josephine didn't skip a beat as she stumbled down the stairs of the porch, saying, Now you're in there fucking a foster child. If I'm a psychopath, you're a pedophile.

Stella told Josephine that if she ever entered without knocking again, she, Stella, would treat it like breaking-and-entering. People from the surrounding walk-ups took note of the two women standing on the gravel drive. Josephine raised her voice so that they could all hear and said, Are you threatening me? First you assault me, now you're threatening me.

The manager of the complex was outside tinkering on his 1976 Harley-Davidson. I'd managed to avoid him up till now. His hair shagged down to his shoulders but up front he was practically bald. He wore a black leather jacket with markings and insignias I didn't

---

* We will see later how this is not the same as a non-Black subjugated person breaking the rules or the contract of their domination.

recognize, but he had friends with bikes and the same leather jackets with the same insignias that made my skin tremor when their engines rumbled outside our windows. His name, I had learned, was Cody, and I often saw him in the company of bikers. He wore shades both day and night; and from his belt hung a leather sheath with a blade that was blacksmithed from a railroad tie.

Josephine and Cody had never been friends. Josephine once told Stella he looked "like a rapist." And although Josephine and Cody were not that far apart in age, Josephine, with her close-cropped hair, her oversized handbag, her wooden clogs, and her black tights and shapeless tunics, bore no resemblance to the women I had seen on the back of his motorcycle. But the bond they formed against Stella in the courtyard that day was formed spontaneously and with the ease of mental telepathy. Cody's feet guided him to stand next to Josephine.

"We're not having threats made in the courtyard," he told Stella.

I went into the kitchen. I remember opening one of the drawers. The top drawer was for tableware. The middle drawer held soup ladles and kitchen knives. The bottom drawer held screwdrivers, hammers, and nails.

I ran down the porch steps and over to Stella's side. She had just called them both "xenophobes." All your two-dollar words and you're still on welfare, Josephine said, from behind her biker prince. Up until that moment I had lived twenty-three years on the planet under the false assumption that my greatest fear was the fear of death. But now, as I saw the Gothic patterns of death on Cody's jacket and the head of a rail spike that someone had forged into a knife, I knew that I was afraid of something much worse than death. A few folks from the other units ventured nearer now. They asked Cody and Josephine what was going on. It was then that it struck me: the thing I had never before been able to get hold of in words. I feared a death without meaning. A death without a story to it, a chain of events that would make sense to those who survived me, a clear and logical chain of events that anyone could read and, when they finished, lift their heads from the page and say, I can see why he died.

"It's under control," Cody told the people around us. Then, to Stella, "You need to go inside."

"You need to get out of Stella's face," I said. My palm was an oil slick; the hammer or knife I had grabbed in the kitchen kept slipping.

I don't recall how this confrontation drew to a close. I can see all four of us exchanging words and then, apparently, walking away from each other. I can see Josephine walking away, and she's inviting Cody up to her apartment for a beer. She'd never said boo to him before. I see me and Stella mounting the steps on the porch. I see what came after, because it didn't end there.

What went down between Stella and Josephine can't be reduced to a fight between neighbors. The antagonism between them was prefigured before they even met. In other words, the die was cast hundreds of years ago on the plantation. The fact that Josephine was, on a conscious level, oblivious to this antagonism doesn't diminish it. In fact, when driven by the force of one's unconscious one often plays out one's role with a deeper sense of commitment to maintaining the paradigm of despotic violence into which one has been stitched and stamped from the beginning. Stella, however, was a student of racial antagonisms. Her seeming obliviousness to the irreconcilability between her position in the world and Josephine's was not so much the labor of unconscious disavowal as, I would say, a tactical maneuver of the mind—one she'd designed for years in order to postpone, if not avoid altogether, the very moment at which she and Josephine had arrived: the moment in which the antagonism insisted upon a stage on which it could be played out in the open.

Stella, in other words, had spent years attempting to displace her reservations and discomfort over Josephine's behavior as a White person onto Josephine's commitment to nuclear energy. She wanted to make the conflict *sane*, by homing in on the contradiction between Josephine's liberal politics and her reactionary commitment to nuclear fusion. This is far more manageable for a Black person's mind than nightly ruminations on the ways in which my upstairs neighbor is my master and I am her slave. There's no hope for a redemptive narrative if that is the case. But this was a function of Stella's active intellectual labors; a mind game she played with herself to crowd into corners distant and dark her acute awareness not just of the power imbalance between her and Josephine, but of the rituals of terror and the regime of violence that allowed White women to see in her face what they needed to see. *You can live a lifetime as a White woman's mirror*, Stella once told me. She was the implement of Josephine's renewal and sense of herself. What happens when a tool talks back; when the mirror breaks itself?

It seemed like four days didn't go by without Stella needing to claim her right to privacy. Each time, Josephine seemed to harden—a chitin shell now surrounding her. When Stella called Josephine a xenophobe, Josephine looked like she'd been hit with a nasty gym shoe. There were three or four neighbors in the courtyard. They heard it too. They stopped. No one said anything. Josephine seemed to have lost the air of command she carried so effortlessly. The whole ordeal lasted all of thirty seconds, but it seemed like a three-year root canal. At last, Josephine said, "I don't know what that word means." The scientist had been bested by the welfare mother. If only it was that and that alone. Josephine seemed to quake. She stood perfectly still. She didn't bat an eye. But everyone could see the crags an earthquake of shame had torn through her pride. Stella made Josephine suffer, made her watch her mouth for the hint of a smile.

"Look it up," said Stella.

On a plantation Stella would have paid on the spot for her cheek-iness, and paid for it in flesh. Josephine would have had her horse-whipped in the middle of the courtyard. But this was the winter of 1979/1980, and it was Minnesota, not Mississippi—and Minne-sota, after all, was the land of progressives. A public whipping would embarrass Josephine and her liberal sense of ethics. And yet, rather than avoid Stella and let us live in peace, Josephine did all she could to set the stage, to *occasion and allow* the conditions that were guaranteed to lead to her humiliation. She was a masochist, yes; but she was also in charge of the masochistic encounter.

"Hattie McDaniel is dead," Stella had averred. She was saying she was sick and tired of being Josephine's tool; "a stage prop," as she put it, "for whatever sick shit is going on in your mind." These words indexed the regime of violence I alluded to earlier; a regime of violence that Josephine, as a White person, had at her disposal, whether or not she ever tapped into it.

For decades, I have tried to understand why Josephine (and later her two male accomplices, Cody and another man whom I had never seen before) took her satisfaction from our flesh; how it got to the point where our only options were to go upstairs and break her door down in an effort to find out why our skin was burning, or to flee our home, leave completely, drop a note in her mailbox, "We give up. You win."

We would not have been the first Black family to be run out of town. In 1921, in Tulsa, Oklahoma, Black Wall Street was burned to the ground, thirty-five people were massacred, eight hundred were hospitalized, Black businesses were bombed from the air. And picnic-lynching is not an oxymoron, but a blending of pleasures and psychic renewal.

When Stella said, "Hattie McDaniel is dead," she named herself as Josephine's slave. In the South, perhaps, such a naming wouldn't work in Stella's favor. If Josephine had been a Southerner she might have been immune to shame; and she might not have been Stella's "friend." But Josephine didn't see herself as a Southerner; she saw herself as an enlightened Northerner. What true-blood woman from the land of cotton would wear clogs and REI jackets and choose to live a mile from campus in a ramshackle block of flats where students lived cheek-by-jowl with a few graybeard relics from the New Left, middle-aged bohemians, and a few young, sanctified yuppies living on the cheap, trying to save enough money to cross the river and move downtown? The "Courts," as our complex was called, did not seem like the antebellum South. Yet, in some strange way, every single scene in America is played out on an antebellum stage. It's just that in the North it can take the actors some time to learn their lines and play their roles. Josephine didn't know how she'd been cast; the roles she and Stella had played for so long were only legible in her unconscious, until Stella said, "Hattie McDaniel is dead." The brilliance of recognition flashed in her eyes. The terror of lynchings, whippings, mutilations, and her people's violent consumption of the African continent unmasked itself as her birthright. An inheritance she did not have to ask for.

The tension between Josephine and Stella (and later between Cody and me) escalated into violence, violence that is hard to mold into narrative because violence in a narrative must have an explanation, a trigger, a contingent moment that makes it make sense. But anti-Black violence won't cooperate with narrative. The explanation bleeds out beyond the actors. It is immune to rational thinking and logical predictions. It is a force from which there is no sanctuary. It is rainproof to rebuke; for it comes as enforcement followed by the law. When violence *is* the law, and not the effect of its enforcement, it presents the rules of narrative with a crisis; because what we have is a situation that resists retelling, for the simple reason that narrative's causal principle, the ghost in the machine we call the causal logic (or "because principle") of the story, is missing. This is how a Black story is jinxed. There is no ghost in the machine; the reason for the violence is beyond the grasp of reason. There's nothing "universal" about it; therefore, the only way to make it intelligible is to leave out the parts that may only be accepted by another Black person, and even then discreetly.

What if you belonged to a race of people with a private army under the command of their fantasies? Reason would have to go to war with your regime of violence before your conditions would be ripe for you to reconsider the phantasms you had projected onto the world. Imagine the resources of a violent structure that can deputize the whims of an entire race. Slave narratives have tried to imagine this violence, but they have also turned away at crucial moments; moments when it becomes clear that without a causal logic, the story could fall apart. In cases such as these, the solution has been to disavow the inconvenient truths and get on with narrative. This is how Northerners "get along." We lived in the northernmost state on the Mississippi River, where calling people by their names (Josephine, Stella, Frank, Cody), while at the same time disavowing their positions within a regime of violence (master, slave), is required for the sake of racial harmony. But a thousand miles south as the crow flies, on that stretch of the Mississippi from Baton Rouge to New Orleans, the antagonisms have routinely been played out in the open.

If one asked Mary Epps why she bashed Patsey's eye with a whiskey decanter or why she goaded Edwin Epps into whipping Patsey within an inch of her life, as he eventually does, even she would try to find a reason—Patsey seduced my husband—which would fall apart the moment it was brought to her attention that Patsey lived without consent, without, that is, the right to accept or deny Edwin and Mary access to her body. As a slave Patsey has no right to sanctuary, sexual or otherwise. Edwin Epps might also feel compelled to make sense of the senseless mutilation: I whipped Patsey at the end of the film because she betrayed me; I think she slept with Solomon and she left the plantation without my permission. He would not be consciously lying. But, much like Josephine, who couldn't tap into the core of her relationship to Stella until Stella said, "Hattie McDaniel is dead," Edwin Epps would have forgotten the key word he spoke whenever he brutalized his slaves: "pleasure." "I am in my pleasure." Both Solomon Northrup's autobiography and the film Steve McQueen made from it are queasy about the way society's pleasure is subtended by anti-Black violence. They hold it up to us, only to disavow its depth. Josephine, with her annual subscription to *Ms.* magazine, her small donations to the Sierra Club, her no-nonsense clogs, and her green CARTER-MONDALE bumper sticker (A TESTED AND TRUSTWORTHY TEAM), was the spectator the film had in mind when it felt the need to lie. But Josephine was also a modern-day doppelgänger of Mary Epps and Edwin Epps combined.

The film tries to anchor the whippings that a Black woman receives in the rational explanations of jealousy and transgression. In other words, the narrative asks us to believe that the principal reason for so much mutilation of the flesh is contingent upon some inappropriate act, a transgression that can be named. We are told Mary Epps, the wife of a ruthless plantation owner, wants Patsey, a beautiful (of course, only the "beautiful" ones are wanted) and productive slave, beaten and sold because her husband creeps down from the mansion at night to rape Patsey (an act he, no doubt, sees as more amorous than violent). We are told that Solomon's back is opened with a paddle and a whip because he could not be disciplined or because he (and other slaves) did not pick his quota of cotton for the day. Jealousy and transgression put the audience at ease, release them from the horror of having to think of this violence as *pleasure* without purpose—like an act of love or a song in the heart or skipping down the street when no one is looking, all the things that sustain Human life but don't appear on the ledger. What if anti-Black violence could be counted among the things that make life *life*, without registering as profit or loss? What if jealousy and transgression are ruses, disguises that the real reasons for the violence hide behind? If no contingency triggers this violence, how can it fit in a story? How do we make sense of a prelogical phenomenon like anti-Black violence?

"I am in my pleasure."

In other words, the whippings are a life force: like a song, or good sex without a procreative aim. "Jouissance" is the word that comes to mind. A French word that means enjoyment, in terms both of rights and property, and of sexual orgasm. (The latter has a meaning partially lacking in the English word "enjoyment.") Jouissance compels the subject to constantly attempt to transgress the prohibitions imposed on his or her enjoyment, to go beyond the pleasure principle. Jouissance is an anchor tenant of psychoanalysis. But until the work of the critical theorists David Marriott, Jared Sexton, and Saidiya Hartman—that is to say, prior to an Afropessimist hijacking of psychoanalysis—devotees of Lacan and Freud had not made the link between jouissance and the regime of violence known as social death. This juxtaposition, unfortunately, takes place at a level of abstraction that is too high for narrative and the logic of storytelling. Unlike violence against the working class, which secures an economic order, or violence against non-Black women, which secures a patriarchal order, or violence against Native Americans, which secures a colonial order, the jouissance that constitutes the violence of anti-Blackness secures the order of life itself; sadism in service to the prolongation of life.

One thing that makes this sadism life-affirming and communal (as opposed to destructive and individual) is the fact that it is a family affair. In his book, Solomon Northup recalls episodes of Patsey's beatings with details that are crucial and missing from the film. "Mistress [Mary] Epps," he writes, "stood on the piazza *among her children* gazing on the scene with an air of heartless *satisfaction*."

The scene that Solomon Northup paints of Mary Epps standing on the piazza brings to mind the musings of Mary Boykin Chesnut, the most cited chronicler of the American Civil War, who wrote, "Our men live all in one house with their wives and their concubines, and the mulattoes one sees in every family exactly resemble the white children . . . All the time they seem to think themselves patterns, models of husbands and fathers." In the realm of the conscious mind, Mary Chesnut is as incensed by the licentious satisfaction White male slaveholders extract from Black women as Mary Epps is (in her conscious mind, as well). But Solomon Northup's psychoanalytic labor indexes how, in the realm of the unconscious mind, this "heartless satisfaction" is the currency of men like Edwin Epps *and their wives*; despite the fact that only the former can secure his satisfaction in the open. The point to be made is that this satisfaction is shared even if its expression is not.

Like her husband, Mary Epps is "in [her] pleasure"; and she is also with her children, who are in their pleasure as well. This generalization of satisfaction and pleasure, subtended by gratuitous violence against Black flesh, fans out from conventional sadism between sexual partners to a family gathering of adults and children of all ages, like the Eppses' son, a boy of ten or twelve who rides his pony out to the cotton fields and "without discrimination . . . applies the raw hide, urging slaves forward with shouts and occasional profanity." We would be wrong to think that the boy's "urging slaves forward" lends purpose and legibility to the violence—it does not. Like any other child, the boy is at play. He is in his pleasure. Each time he rides his little pony to the fields, he compels an old man named Uncle Abram to be his cheering squad, his chorus, to "laugh . . . and commend him for being a thorough-going boy."

Northup's book implies, without stating directly, why this generalization of sadism—brutality as the constituent element of family bonding—cannot be understood as being triggered by transgressions. It is as ubiquitous as the air he breathes. "It was rarely a day passed without more whippings . . . It is the literal, unvarnished truth, that the crack of the lash and the shrieking of slaves, can be heard from dark till bedtime . . ." Patsey and Solomon, unlike Stella and me, were living in a place and time when civil society and the Human were neither ashamed nor embarrassed by this. A thousand miles upriver and one hundred twenty six years later, Josephine was shocked by this inheritance, but it didn't take her long to recover, and to claim it.

Though the structure of Stella's "life" (or, better, the paradigm of social death, for the quotation marks are essential here) cannot be reconciled with the structure of Josephine's life (or the paradigm of social life), there *is* a connection. But this connection is parasitic and perverse—regardless of what the socially dead Black person (i.e., Stella and Patsey) or the socially alive Human (i.e., Josephine or Mary Epps) might *say* about their "relationship." It is parasitic because White and non-Black subjectivity cannot be imbued with the capacity for self-knowledge and intersubjective community without anti-Black violence; without, that is, the violence of social death. In other words, White people and their junior partners need anti-Black violence to know they're alive.* If Hattie McDaniel were to truly die, as Stella proclaimed, it would be tantamount to the death of a parasite's host.

---

* Junior partners are people who are Human but not White hetero males. For example, people of color and White women who are targets of White supremacy and patriarchy, respectively, and, simultaneously, the agents and beneficiaries of anti-Blackness. This category also includes LGBT people who are not Black and Indigenous communities. They are "partners" because, as with White hetero males, anti-Blackness is the genome of their paradigmatic positions and because they suffer at the hands of contingent violence rather than the gratuitous or naked violence of social death.

This is what makes social death something more surreal than the end of breath. It is, in the words of David Marriott, a deathliness that saturates life, not an embalming; a resource for Human renewal.

It is perverse for many reasons: one of which is the fact that as civil society matures (from 1853 to December 1979, when it all went south with Josephine)—and we move historically from the obvious technologies of chattel slavery to universal suffrage, the discourse of human rights, and the concept of universal access to civil society— the anti-Black violence necessary for the elaboration and maintenance of White (and non-Black) subjectivity gets repressed and becomes increasingly unavailable to conscious (as opposed to unconscious) speech. ("I judge people by the quality of their character," as Dr. King said, "and not the color of their skin"; or the commonly spoken, "At the end of the day, we're all Americans and we're in this together"— and other such malarkey of the conscious mind.) But the pageantries of naked and submissive Black flesh, pageantries of bleeding backs and buttocks, whip marks, amputations, and faces closed by horse bits, provide evidence of the role sadism plays in the constitution of White subjectivity, and *12 Years a Slave* makes this visible on the screen, despite its repression in the narrative of both the film and civil society writ large.

It is tempting and commonplace to reduce Mary and Edwin Epps's sadism to individual psychopathology. Or one might think that Edwin Epps is one of a group of exceptionally sadistic people who lived in an exceptionally sadistic time and place. But the film, and to an even greater extent the autobiography, *sees* (rather than *narrates*) sadism—the sexual perversion in which gratification is obtained by inflicting physical or mental pain on a love object—not as the individual pathology of a handful of people, but as a generalized condition; generalized in that pleasure, as a constituent element of communal life, cannot be disentangled from anti-Black violence.

Conventionally, the *object* of sadism can, tomorrow, become the *subject* of sadism. But the sadism that constitutes the spectacles of *12 Years a Slave*, and which constitutes early nineteenth century society, is not imbued with such reciprocity. The Slaves of social death cannot switch places and make Edwin Epps or his equally cruel wife the love objects of *their* collective sadism. If they did so in private (if Patsey beat Edwin or Mary in a private bedroom encounter, for example) it is because such a reversal was occasioned and allowed—in other words, the master used his prerogative and power to play a different game, one in which he suffers because suffering fulfills his fantasy and because, unlike the Slave, his fantasies have "objective value." Such role reversals do not imbue the encounter with reciprocity. The changes that begin to occur after the Civil War and up through the Civil Rights Movement, Black Power, and the American election of a Black president are merely changes in the weather. Despite the fact that the sadism is no longer played out in the open as it was in 1840, nothing essential has changed.

5

Josephine and Cody and another man I'd never seen before carried boxes and crates along the side of the house. We heard them go in the side door and up the stairs to Josephine's apartment. We heard them clinking away at whatever it was they had in those boxes. But it started even before that.

I once called Cody to fix the plumbing after our standoff in the courtyard. I was in the kitchen. Stella was in her bedroom at the front of the house. Malika was in the back in her room. Cody didn't knock. He didn't ring the bell. He was suddenly behind me in the kitchen. I told him he had to turn around, go back out to the porch, close the door behind him, ring the bell, and wait for me to come let him in. He must have stood there looking at me for no more than fifteen seconds but I knew I aged fifteen years. I don't know what made him do it, but he did. He didn't have the look of rage that Josephine had. He had the look of a man who strikes back in his own time. Cody's own time came slowly, in drips and drabs. He and Josephine spent more time together, not only upstairs in her apartment but in the basement, under our dwelling. We could hear them laughing sometimes. Shortly after that the radiators hissed incessantly—but only at night. When we complained to Cody, he went down to fix them and he'd pop up to Josephine's flat. In the night, the radiator made popping noises— not hisses anymore. The pipes would sometimes clink and clang for a minute or two, then stop, only to start again an hour, two hours, three hours later.

Sometime after that was when we saw Cody and Josephine and another man I'd never seen before scuffling down the walkway by the side of the house with the boxes and crates. We listened, our eyes now and then cast up to the ceiling, to the muffled tromp of far more feet than we were used to hearing up there. A day or two later came the muted clang of metal, sounds that were similar but distinct from the noises they had made in the basement when the radiators went berserk.

It wasn't long before we felt first heat, then stinging, then slight burning sensations on our skin.

We didn't call them burns. Beyond our complaints to one another we didn't pay attention or seek medical advice until the itching grew into a slightly singed sensation. It seemed most intense at night. A general practitioner told us we needed to see a specialist, and the best in the field, he said, were across the river at the University of Minnesota Medical Center. I called them. They said they were booked for some time. I said, "This is urgent. My name is Frank B. Wilderson III; my father is vice president for Student Affairs. My partner and I have been told by our GP we should be seen by someone in your department." We were seen within the week.

Dr. Vivian Zhou had a full, attractive face, but her smile gave off no more heat than the stars. She could have stamped passports at a border crossing. She examined us separately, then brought us to her office and closed the door. As I recall, she asked us what we did work-wise. She thought we worked with radiation and she insinuated that there were OSHA standards that had been breached.

"We don't work with radiation," Stella said.

Dr. Zhou implied that Stella was lying because she was afraid of on-the-job retaliation; or, worse, because of some misplaced loyalty to her employer. She suggested that Stella and I had a moral obligation to report the radioactive waste or the misuse of instruments, if not for our sake then for the sake of our coworkers and the general public.

"The woman upstairs did this to us," Stella said.

Dr. Zhou put her pen down. I could see the gears of other options whirring in her brain. I wanted to stop this before we both ended up in the psych ward.

"This has been an ordeal; you can see how we're out of sorts," I said, adding we needed time to go home and think about it.

"I don't understand," said Dr. Zhou. "It's a simple question. How were you exposed to radiation?"

"We're a bit confused about the details," I said.

"I'm not confused," said Stella.

"There's every indication that you both have been exposed to radioactive material. I'm at a loss as to why scar tissue is on your groin area and why it's on your lower side. We need answers."

"I told you why. He sleeps on his back. I sleep on my side. It's coming from Josephine's apartment upstairs. She works in a lab here at the U. She has access to—"

"Even if she does work in a lab, it's not legal for her to take this material—"

Stella cut her off. "You think we're lying?"

"We'll go home," I said, "and iron out the confusing details—"

"What's the matter, Frank?" Stella was livid. "Are you afraid we'll tarnish your father's reputation?"

"Why would your neighbor do such a thing?" asked Dr. Zhou.

"You haven't lived," said Stella. "The Japanese internment camps didn't teach you a thing." (Stella was aware that Zhou was Chinese and not Japanese, but as a child during World War II, Stella had seen how the word *menace* stuck like Velcro to a color, *yellow*, more frequently than it did to a specific ethnicity.) At the door, Stella said, "Frank drives a cab part-time for Blue & White. I work part-time as a teacher's aide at Marcy grammar school. He's on general assistance and I'm on welfare. Knock yourself out going after our bosses. You'll find radioactive isotopes in the seat of the cab he drives."

6

Our home is on the other side of campus from the hospital. We cut through campus, walking, for the most part, in silence, afraid that any word that we might say to one another will strike like flint on our raw nerves. I don't tell her how I fell for her right over there, on the steps of the armory, when she told a busload of inductees not to go to Vietnam. We pass Burton Hall, where she once worked with my father. She doesn't say how cute I was when my principal sent me to my father's office for skipping classes or smoking weed in the bathrooms. When we walk through the main gate and across the street to Dinkytown, I don't tell her the stories of days when Bob and I stole horses together up and down the street.

When in Dr. Zhou's office, Stella had said, "What's the matter, Frank? Are you afraid we'll tarnish your father's reputation?" she had put her finger on the pulse of a desire to be special that beat inside my heart. In my unconscious I wanted to latch on to an element of Whiteness, or Humanness (since Dr. Zhou wasn't White), that would set me apart from other Blacks. But this desire was deeper than Stella or I suspected at the time. An unconscious wish for my father's prestige (which was as faux as the prestige Solomon thought he had accrued from his skills as an engineer and his talents as a musician) to seep into my being by osmosis. I had dropped his name to get us the appointment. I would drop his name in the weeks and months to come to open other doors as well. This kind of reasoning is universal. But what is *not* universal, what belongs to Black people and Black people alone, is a deeper desire sparked by a deeper structure of oppression. When you intuit for the first time in your life that you live in a soup of violence that is prelogical, a kind of violence that is as legitimate if it's wielded by "ordinary" citizens, such as Josephine, as it is if wielded by sanctioned enforcers of the law, and that your father's position and prestige are no more the keys to a sanctuary than the position and prestige of someone who is Black and orphaned, you are faced with two choices: stare unflinchingly at the abyss as it stares unflinchingly at you, or take it out on the Black person near you who won't leave you to your fantasy of being truly alive. Anything to not have to face the fact that your sense of presence is no more than "borrowed institutionality."*

This dynamic, this intra-Black imbroglio, is harder to discern in the twentieth and twenty-first centuries, for the simple fact that the personas of the master class are no longer solidified in evil White men and evil White women who wield real whips on a real plantation. The

---

* Jared Sexton, private conversation, November 22, 2007.

master has been dispersed across the entire racial spectrum of people who are not Black. Dr. Zhou is as much a master as Edwin and Mary Epps, the antagonists in *12 Years a Slave*. In fact, the twentieth century shot the Eppses through a prism—they are not just people, they are ideas. They are ideas and personas that a young middle-class Black man like me had consciously fought against to the point of being kicked out of college, while deep in my unconscious I was a loyal supplicant who cared more about not simply the master's feelings, but the stability of the master's world, than I did about my own suffering and the suffering of Stella. It is hard to be a slave and feel that you are worthy, truly worthy, of your suffering as a slave.

One hundred twenty-seven years before Josephine, before Cody, before Urban Risers, and before Dr. Zhou, the rift between Stella and me would have been clearer to see. We wouldn't have walked home in symptomatic silence; our discord would have been played out in the open. At times, Stella would throw her sense of herself as a being from a special, quasi-Black dimension at me the way I threw my father's status and my Dartmouth pedigree at her. She would let me know of the competence exhibited by the White men she had been with and the Jew she had married; she held them up as object lessons that I could never be or learn. That's how most Black couples fight and argue, by firing White and non-Black people at each other. No, it's more subtle than that. The bullets aren't the White or non-Black people themselves but the ambience of recognition and incorporation in a world beyond the plantation. We load our guns with deadly intangibles and shoot straight for the heart. Anyone who thinks nineteenth century slave narratives are reports on the past isn't paying attention. Such a person will experience the analysis of Afropessimism as though they are being mugged, rather than enlightened; that is because they can't imagine a plantation in the here and now.

But Afropessimism is premised on a comprehensive and icono-clastic claim: that Blackness is coterminous with Slaveness: Blackness *is* social death: which is to say that there was never a prior meta-moment of plenitude, never equilibrium: never a moment of social life. Blackness, as a paradigmatic position (rather than as a set of cultural practices, anthropological accoutrements) is elaborated through slavery. The narrative arc of the slave who is *Black* (unlike Orlando Patterson's generic Slave, who may be of any race) is *not an arc at all*, but a flat line, what Hortense Spillers calls "historical stillness": a flat line that moves from disequilibrium, to a moment in the narrative of faux-equilibrium, to disequilibrium restored and/or rearticulated.

This kind of change, the transformative promise of a narrative arc, belongs to White men and their junior partners in civil soci-ety (non-Black immigrants, White and non-Black people who are queer, and non-Black women) *but only in relation to each other*. By transformative capacity I mean that, through struggle, non-citizens (in the legal and libidinal sense of the word—legal being Latinx undocumented immigrants, for example, and libidinal being any-one from a *documented* immigrant of color to a gay person to a non-Black woman) can become citizens, because they are still Human; they are simply oppressed and therefore not so fully vested. But their transformative capacity stems *not* from their positive attri-butes but from the fact that they are not Black, they are not slaves.

These fully vested citizens and not-so-fully vested citizens live through *intra-communal* narrative arcs of transformation; but where the Black is concerned, their collective unconscious calls upon Blacks as props, which they harness as necessary implements to help bring about their psychic and social transformation, and to vouchsafe the coherence of their own Human subjectivity.

Nevertheless, the slave is a sentient being. Therefore, an existence void of transformative promise, which narrative holds out to human subjects, is a painful lesson for the slave to learn, much less accept. I am not suggesting that Black people should resign themselves to the inevitability of social death—it *is* inevitable, in the sense that one is born into social death just as one is born into a gender or a class; but it is also constructed by the violence and imagination of other sentient beings. Thus, like class and gender, which are also *constructs*, not divine designations, social death can be destroyed. But the first step toward the destruction is to assume one's position (*assume, not celebrate or disavow*), and then burn the ship or the plantation, in its past and present incarnations, from the inside out. However, as Black people we are often psychically unable and unwilling to assume this position. This is as understandable as it is impossible.

I was a lot like that when I met Stella. Stella was skeptical about the willingness of the FBI to help us unravel the skeins of aggression that were coming our way (from Josephine and Cody's violence to the violence of whoever did not want Stella to bring her evidence against Urban Risers to court). Looking back, I realize that I believed that my father had standing in the community, that his position on multiple boards and his vice presidency at the university had somehow imbued us both with Human capacity, the capacity to be recognized and incorporated as something other than Black. I had no idea that the FBI had tracked me for four years, that there was a file on me; nor did it dawn on me that Stella's social-change activism, especially her civil disobedience against the war and her plethora of counter-culture and revolutionary friends, would militate against our being helped. But those aren't even the fundamental reasons why I should have been skeptical: If the FBI has been tracking Black creative writers since 1919, if the FBI has been constantly updating and revising its list of Black writers earmarked for preventative detention (concentration camps?),* if the FBI, like every law enforcement agency in the United States, is organically anti-Black, then where is the line between prison and home?

7

Now Stella and I have walked the width of campus, from Dr. Zhou's office to Dinkytown, without breaking our silence, afraid that any word we might say to one another would strike like flint on our raw nerves. I wanted to show her the steps of the armory, where she told a busload of inductees not to go to Vietnam, the exact spot where I as a fifteen-year-old boy fell in love with her. If she wanted to point to Burton Hall, where she worked in the dean's office with my dad, and say how cute I was back then when my principal sent me to my father's office for skipping classes or smoking weed, she too walked in silence and let the moment pass. We cross the street to Dinkytown; I don't say a word about my best friend Bob and the horses we stole up and down these streets.

Our home is in sight when Stella finally speaks. Beside us at a stoplight a couple expresses their relief that Teddy Kennedy has beaten Jimmy Carter in the Massachusetts Democratic Primary. We need a Kennedy, the woman says, as the WALK sign flashes, to beat Ronald Reagan. We let them walk ahead of us. *Then* Stella speaks.

"We'll send Malika somewhere safe," she says.

---

* William J. Maxwell, *F.B. Eyes: How J. Edgar Hoover's Ghostreaders Framed African American Literature* (Princeton, NJ: Princeton University Press, 2015).

8

DAY ONE.

Two weeks after we sent Malika away.

The car that I have stolen from my parents' garage is a fern-green station wagon with faux-wood panels and thirteen stickers from the national parks we visited when I was a child. Stella and I have no more than one hundred dollars, and our food stamps, of course. We've been wearing the same clothes for the past two days, for we've had to sleep in them; and we've sent Malika away, hoping she'll be safe. We'll send for her when we feel safe ourselves. But "when" is looking more and more like "if." We left our home without thinking to bring Jamal's gun. Stupid. Stupid.

As Stella and I roam the streets of Minneapolis looking for a place to crash, I imagine Malika hearing how her mother and I were gunned down on Hennepin Avenue. Malika is at her father, Uri's, house in Idaho. There would be no one to explain our deaths to her. More than once I want to believe that I have Stella's back; that I would meet any violence that is headed our way bravely and forthrightly, without thought of personal loss or discredit.

9

DAY TWO.

It's our second night in the living room of Stella's friend, a White woman named Olivia. Stella met Olivia eleven years before, in 1969, at an anti-war demonstration, but she had only grown close to her later, when they were LPNs on the preemie ward at Hennepin County Medical Center. It's Olivia's apartment, but Chase is her man and he acts like it's his. Thank God it's not his. We would be gone if it was. He manages a restaurant and can't watch *Johnny Carson* when he gets home because we're camped out in his spot. His fingertips are yellowed from smoking cigarettes and his clothes carry hints of griddle grease.

I don't know if they think we're out here asleep or if they don't know the kitchen door is ajar. As a nurse, Olivia is trained to speak in soothing tones; she can wrap heartbreak in cotton. But Chase is another story. I think he wants us to hear.

"Olivia, don't give me that crap about repairs being done at Stella's flat. Stella's toy-boy's freaking shit-scared. You can see it in his face. He wants out."

My bedding is a shag rug, some blankets, and a pillow on the floor beside the sofa. Stella is billeted on the sofa itself. I don't look up at her when Chase says "he wants out"; and my jaw tightens when he calls me a "toy-boy." For two years I've wondered if Stella's friends think of me like that. A part of me wanted them to say it out loud, as Chase just did. Give it form. Make it who I am.

Olivia tells him she doesn't know the details, and that he wouldn't believe Stella if Stella told him the truth.

"You're right. I wouldn't believe her. She's had you and those Dinkytown freaks hoodwinked for years. You all thought she was Angela Davis. She's not Angela Davis. You're no longer Olivia from the suburbs looking for a thrill; and the war ended five years ago."

"The war didn't end for Black people," Olivia says.

"Black people? Like the man who beat you for seven years?"

"Give me a number, Chase."

"A number for what?"

"The number of years you're going to keep punishing me."

"*He* beat you, but *I'm* the one who's punishing you."

"You punish me for sleeping with Sonja's father; you punish Sonja for being mixed. Sue me, Chase, for not being a racist."

"Sue me for being an independent thinker. And I'll tell you this for the price of a doughnut-hole, before it's over her boyfriend's gonna bail."

After two nights we leave Olivia's apartment. We don't say why and they don't ask. We drive twenty miles south to the suburb of Edina.

10

DAY THREE.

8:30 a.m.

We sit low in the front seat of the station wagon. We're parked down the street but not so far that we can't see the front door. When the certified public accountant pulls out of his drive, we leave the car where it is, walk around to the back, where she lets us in, and slip down to the basement. It's cold down here in the cinder-block basement, where another White woman Stella knew from back in the day lives with her CPA husband. But we can only sleep here in the daytime. (As we roamed from house to house, never telling all—and sometimes none—of our story, I noticed that we never went to any of the homes of Black women or men Stella had known. Stella said that some of them had fallen on times harder than ours; and that they were also either under surveillance or might end up that way if we brought this to their door.) On beach chairs we crash by the washer and dryer without taking off our coats. At four in the afternoon, Stella's friend comes down to wake us. We must leave before the CPA gets home.

10:30 p.m.

We drive through the streets of the Twin Cities, waiting for morning when we can get some sleep. We've already learned where all the late-night diners are.

DAY FOUR.

9:00 a.m.

This morning we're stopped at the back door. Stella's friend says a neighbor has noticed. She'll die if that woman talks to her husband. She's sorry, but we can't come in.

11:59 p.m.

March at midnight can be colder here than much of Alaska in winter. We sleep in the station wagon on the windless side of the Golden Gophers football stadium. We sleep in shifts so that the person who's awake can regulate the heat and crack the window now and then. If we stay here too long we'll be hassled by the cops.

DAY FIVE.

3:00 a.m. Downtown Minneapolis.

At three in the morning we drive across the Mississippi River and make our way through downtown. The streets are empty. The traffic lights blink without purpose in the vacant night. Stella asks me if we're being followed. We smell like a week without soap.

11

Chase was right. She's not Angela Davis, though folks have thought otherwise when they see her at a distance. But Angela Davis would have more people to rely on if she were in Stella's shoes. In the dim light of my parents' car, I think how beautiful she is, despite the lines in her forehead that I hadn't seen before her lawyer Noam Davidov came to say her court date was less than a year away.

The lawsuit Stella had filed against Urban Risers, a government anti-poverty program born in the era of LBJ, is going to trial in November. Since Noam Davidov came to Stella's place to tell us the date of her court hearing against Urban Risers and, by extension, "perhaps" individuals in the federal government, individuals whose identities might become known when he took depositions from members of the Urban Risers board, our lives had been turned inside out. Last week we went to see Imani Price, a woman who once was a major player in the Black community in the Near North side. Maybe she would tell us who's gunning for us.

When I first met Imani I was seven or eight years old. She was one of roughly thirty people, university students, Black community organizers from the Near North side, and university professors, gathered for a meeting in my parents' living room. My parents had given me Negro history picture books and I recognized Imani immediately. "Are you Harriet Tubman?" I asked her. Everyone in the living room laughed. I felt small and embarrassed. She touched my cheek and said, "Baby, that's the finest thing a man's ever said to me."

She and Darnell Price, her husband, had been on the board of Urban Risers with Stella. If I remember correctly, Stella said that Imani was innocent, though who knew what evidence the trial would reveal about her husband's involvement? The main defendant was a man named Kapalei Kenyatta, a dashiki-wearing hustler who, so went the scuttlebutt, had worked with Darnell (and, presumably, Imani) on other poverty programs besides Urban Risers, where money was skimmed off the top and where the resources were used for everything from the lining of their pockets to financing drug deals and prostitution to the purchase of real estate—such as one of the two largest homes in Kenwood, a baronial building that resembled a small Scottish château with a massive tower made of large hand-laid stones. This Scottish château in the heart of Kenwood was where Imani was living. She and Darnell separated after the last time he beat her. Darnell agreed to give her this grand house if, I presumed, she agreed not to press charges against him for his last episode of domestic violence against her.

Shooting up the front façade of the mansion was a large stone tower with ramparts at the top. In sixteenth century Scotland there would have been grain for the winter, or possibly weapons to fend off an English invasion, stored in a tower such as this; but in the enclave of Kenwood, the ground floor of this tower was a lavish study where Stella and I met Imani. The house I grew up in was less than two blocks away. For many years the neighborhood had been cordoned off by Highway 394 from North Minneapolis where Urban Risers was, what people in town called the ghetto. How Imani Price was able to purchase a home in Kenwood—making her the fourth Black home owner in Kenwood since my parents broke the barrier in 1962—was lost on me when we first arrived. In my youth we had called this house a castle and believed it to be haunted. Imani said "the foundation" she and Darnell had set up bought the house. It was owned by their nonprofit organization. But that still didn't answer my question: How did two poor Black people who had always lived from opportunity to opportunity, and had no pedigree that the Kenwood Committee could accept, get the money, the means, and the opportunity to breach the Iron Curtain of Kenwood? The Kenwood Committee had rallied five hundred households to try to keep my parents out of the neighborhood. The committee had even balked eight years later when a prominent Black architect moved in with his family. They had tried to keep a wealthy Pro Bowl football player, Alan Page, from building a modern home there (even though Frank Lloyd Wright had built a modern home there to great acclaim).* They had turned a cold shoulder to a Black surgeon who bought a mansion almost as big as Imani and Gabe's Scottish château. Given all of this, how in the world did they let a woman whose husband was known to this city as a Black radical as well as a shady schemer buy the second-most-prized mansion in the wooded enclave on the western edge of Minneapolis?

Imani Price moved into Kenwood with a north side White cat who liked to hang, and was twenty years her junior, at least. His name was Gabe and he made me feel diminished; but not by anything he said or did, for he didn't really *say* nor *do* anything at all. He stood behind Imani like the Queen's Guard at Buckingham as Imani sat at her desk and listened to Stella tell our story. It wasn't words or deeds that made me feel small, it was his body. The taut, muscular body of a football tight end; a body that eats the way I used to eat at the football training tables at Dartmouth College, five years ago, what now felt like a lifetime ago, in 1975; a body that had the leisure time and the money to train at the gym, just as I once trained. Over the past

---

* In addition to having been a Minnesota Viking, Alan Page was also a lawyer, and would become an associate justice of the Minnesota Supreme Court.

two years, I had lost much of my musculature and I didn't have the same access to the kinds of food that I once had. It hurt my ego to covet a body that was no longer in the cards for me. It hurt my pride to be poor.

Stella told Imani about the gun a north side brother named Jamal, whom both of them knew, had given Stella for protection; about the clicking on the phone that started right after Stella's lawyer, Noam, left the house; about the tampering with our telephone, how we got calls in which no one spoke when we answered; about the Daniel Ellsberg–like break-in at my apartment; and how we feared we were being followed. That was all I had wanted Stella to say to Imani. I didn't trust Imani, not completely, though I knew she was a victim of domestic violence and therefore had no more allegiance to Darnell— who was tight with Kapalei Kenyatta; they had the same skeletons in their closet. Nor did I know this White dude who stood behind Imani as Imani sat in her high-backed office chair behind a mahogany desk that could double as a runway.

Stella didn't want to heed my warning. Before we went inside, and while we were still parked by the carriage house away from the main building, I had said that she shouldn't tell Imani everything. Imani and Darnell have dealt with state surveillance, she'd told me, their phones are always tapped, and they've come home to find their house turned upside down, just as you did, Frank, that night when you came home to find that your apartment had been locked from the inside, and two men climbed out your window and ran down the alley. But they've never been forced out of their home, I rejoined; Imani's going to ask why we had to leave our home. And even if she believes you, I said, why would she tell us the truth?

Why would she tell us the truth? Stella had told me that the last time Darnell beat Imani, he broke her arm.

"She's living with a White guy now," Stella had said, "a guy about your age. He coldcocked Darnell Price, a punch so hard he flipped backward over a chair."

"That's why you need a young man," Imani said later that day as we sat in the two plush chairs in front of her desk. She touched Gabe's hand. She winked at Stella like they'd won the same prize. "Young men know how to treat a woman."

Imani told us in detail, and without being prompted, about the last few times Darnell had beat her. Stella responded with a story of her own—how Uri Shapiro, her Jewish ex-husband, the father of her child, grabbed her by the armpits and hoisted her in the air. He ran her back against a plate-glass window. He didn't mean to hurt Stella. He had no idea the window would break, but it did. Shards of glass dropped like daggers in a cave of ice. A glass dagger pierced her deltoid. Unlike Darnell, Uri hadn't meant to hurt Stella. He was sick with sorrow.

One night, I had asked her about the scar on her upper arm. She called it an "industrial accident." After we made love, I stroked the scar and asked her the details. She nestled her head in my neck. She laughed without raising her head. She said, "Bow Wow the dog did it." Then her whole body rippled in laughter against mine. I didn't get the joke, nor did I think she would stop laughing. I placed my fingers beneath her chin, but she wouldn't raise her face to look at me. She barked, several small puppy barks. "Bow Wow the dog," she said and she was off to the races laughing again. Her laughter was not contagious. It wasn't a happy laugh.

At first I was annoyed that for the nineteen months we had been together she hadn't told me, but now she was telling Imani Price, who hadn't even asked. These days I'm embarrassed by the way that I felt then. They were two women bonding over what two men had done to them. The two men in the room were as relevant to this exchange as any two random items of décor. Or maybe they *were* speaking to Gabe and to me. Maybe they were signifying, telling us they knew that deep inside both of us lay a Uri or a Darnell, just waiting to beat them. Maybe they were saying, Don't think too highly of yourselves. If that's true, however, it's a secondary truth. What's of primary importance is the way Imani and Stella, by sharing their stories (as though Gabe and I weren't there), acknowledged each other as Black women whose flesh had been the sites of the most gratuitous acts of violence—interracial violence in the case of Stella's abuse by Uri, and intramural violence in the case of Imani and Darnell. It was as though they were saying, Since there's no auditor for our suffering as Black women, no paradigm of recognition and redress, we will be for each other the world's missing ears.

As Imani heard about what had happened between Stella and Uri, she seemed to want to go back in time and protect Stella from that wound her ex-husband had inflicted on her. I often have wondered, if this communion hadn't happened between these two women, whether Imani would have opened up and told Stella what she knew about the skullduggery at Urban Risers. As if to say, I can't save you from the scars of the past, but I can shed some light on the scars that are to come.

When Stella told Imani and Gabe our story, and stopped at the point where I asked her to stop, I was relieved. Gabe seemed satisfied, but Imani was not. She asked the question that Stella had told me she would ask.

"Why did you leave your duplex?" Imani said.

Stella inhaled and let the air out slowly. She looked at Gabe.

"He all right," Imani said. "He knows all about Urban Risers. I'd tell him anyway, after you two left. Besides, he saved my life."

"Imani," Stella said, "it's going to sound crazy."

"No, child, not to me."

"It sounds crazy to me when I play it in my mind."

"Then speak. Get it out of your mind."

"This beast has so many limbs."

"That's what makes it a beast, child."

As Stella spoke, I clasped my hands in my lap and squeezed until they almost pained me. This is what she said.

"The White woman who lives upstairs was poisoning us. We were able to prove it, but one by one the people who helped us gather the evidence, including a private detective that we hired with money Frank borrowed from his parents, backed down. In the end, they weren't willing to testify. They all flaked out in the end—and this all happened after Noam came with the news of the court date and after we went to the FBI to report what was happening to us—not just Josephine, the woman upstairs, but all of it, like the break-in at Frank's apartment. We don't know what it all means."

Imani laughed for the first time all afternoon.

"You're screwed," she said. "That's what it means, child."

Stella wasn't laughing, and neither was I, nor even Gabe, for that matter. Stella had one question for Imani. Stella said that our only hope was to find the two U.S. marshals to whom Stella had spoken almost eight years ago when she brought the issue of corruption to the fore. They had seemed like straight shooters, she said. She didn't want to go to the U.S. marshals office cold, the way we had gone downtown to the FBI. She wanted those two individuals *specifically*, since they had been so accommodating to Stella in the past.

"Imani," Stella, implored, "will you make contact with those two for us, and tell them we want to meet with them?"

Imani shook her head.

"Honey," she said, "leave it alone. Those two U.S. marshals were in Kapalei Kenyatta's pocket. He was in their pocket. They were stroking each other's dicks. The marshals led you on. Why do you think it's taken all this time for you to go to trial?"

12

DAY FIVE.

3:10 a.m. Downtown Minneapolis.

I could have made the light at Third and Hennepin, and I would have, if I didn't need to turn. Stella is asleep and a sharp left turn would jar her. The Minneapolis Central Library is here. In the daytime it's graphite, glitter, and glass. Tonight it's a fortress, like something from the previews of the second *Star Wars* film that they say will come out in May. It was a lifetime ago when Stella, Malika, and I made this library our home away from home. Stella taught Malika how to use the Dewey decimal system and took her to the puppet shows and children's reading hours. We read there. I wrote there. Stella studied languages and borrowed sheet music there. Three people without the money or the means for recreation can live well at the library. It seems like ages since we shed the skin of that life and sent Malika to safety. It seems like a life that belonged to someone else.

3:10:37 a.m.

There's a car growing large in my rearview mirror. It's bearing down on us. The light is still red. If it doesn't stop it will ram us from behind. Stella hasn't seen it because she's asleep.

3:10:38 a.m.

Why can't I take my foot off the brake and floor the gas pedal? I can't scream. I can see Stella in a neck brace. I can see myself folded into a wheelchair. I feel a clutch in my chest but I still don't move.

Just before it rams us from behind, the car swerves. It stops beside us. Two lean faces leer at us. The driver revs the engine. It's a souped-up Datsun 240Z. The motor growls again. They're teenagers in letter jackets, not men. They want to know if we want to drag-race down Hennepin.

The light changes twice before I can stop shaking and drive.

3:20 a.m.

I drive on Hennepin the length of downtown, and follow it even as it turns toward uptown at the Basilica of Saint Mary where my parents have a pew.

At Franklin and Hennepin, the Lowry Hill liquor store is dark and blinkered. I can almost smile at those nights, right at closing, when Dad would careen this fern-green and wood-paneled station wagon that we have now stolen into that parking lot. Under the liquor store's neon sign, he'd leave me in the car with the engine running. Hans Knudsen, the night cashier, had a soft spot for my father, which helped a lot at closing time. "Gophers were down by a field goal," Dad might say, by way of apology and explanation, and Hans, who might have just turned the inside lock, might smile and say he knows how it is, as he unlocks the door and lets Dad inside.

Stella awakes and turns the radio off.

"We aren't married," she says. "You don't have to put yourself through this."

She wants me to say I'll stay to the end, whatever the end might be. Perhaps she wants to tell me that she too is afraid but she wants to be brave for both of us.

3:26 *a.m*

It starts to drizzle as we pass the Lowry Hill liquor store. Raindrops pearl on the window and whisper in the tires. I turn the radio back on. The tenor saxophone of Gene Ammons lays some leather on a ballad I've heard Stella play on her flute. She taught me the lyrics. But it's not a night for singing. We drive on without the human voice. The saddest of instruments.

"Where should we go?" she asks me.

I say I don't know. We've run through all of her friends. Most of my friends are away at college. Some live at home with their parents. But we can hardly rock up to their houses with our story and all its moving parts. The one who isn't at college or at home is dead. While I was at Dartmouth, Bob Stone went to prison. We didn't write for the four years I was gone, not even during the year he spent behind bars. Rumor has it he was raped inside. All I know for sure is that when they released him he walked down to where the trains pass the river and lay down on the railroad tracks.

"They're going to hate me even more," she says (and I know by "they" she means my parents), "when they get back from Moscow and find out you took their car."

"They don't hate you and they won't find out."

"Your long-tall dad said he liked my corncob pipe when I worked in his office at the university. It was like the one his grandmother smoked."

"You told me."

"She was standing right there. She didn't say anything." I knew Stella meant my mother. "She must hate me now that we're together."

"Why would she hate you? Because my dad liked your pipe?"

"I'm sure she wonders what's wrong with you. I'm not the first old woman you've been with."

"Forty isn't old."

"I'm old enough to be your mother."

"You would have been sixteen." It's my way of saying, I'm sick and tired of your negativity. Sick and tired of hitting-set at strangers' houses with stories about being followed, about Kapalei Kenyatta and his henchmen, about Josephine poisoning our flat with radiation, about the FBI and U.S. marshals and whoever else doesn't want *you*, okay, *you*, Stella, not *me*, to blow the lid off corruption in some poverty pimp program no one gives a damn about. I want to go back to Dartmouth. And that's enough about my mother. But I say none of this. Stella goes on as if she hasn't heard a thing I've thought.

"If I were her, I'd feel threatened. All the older women you've been with."

I tighten my grip on the steering wheel. My gaze is fixed on the gloom.

A friend of my mother's, a woman she was in college with in New Orleans, sometimes left my parents' cocktail parties to come upstairs and tuck me in bed at night when I was nine years old. Her name was Leontyne Dupré. Her father was a "sporting man" down in New Orleans; and though I never knew exactly what that meant, from the way my parents laughed when they said it I knew that it was not an occupation to aspire to. Leontyne Dupré would sit on the edge of my bed as I lay there; she balanced my globe on her knee and marveled at the way I explained the topography and climate of far-off places on the globe that I would visit one day. When I was in my last year of high school, she and I went into business together, selling Amway. Once, we turned my parents' huge living room into a theater with folding chairs, where fifty people, from the president and vice president of the local bank to folks my parents called my "little hoodlum friends" from the Black part of town, all sat together in the same sweaty room listening to the pyramid pitch of a major dude from headquarters in

Michigan. My parents returned from one of their European sojourns a day early and walked in on the whole affair. I don't think my mother ever spoke to her friend after that.

Then there was the Rada priestess in Trinidad. It was just five years ago and I was a sophomore studying abroad. I thought my mother would be pleased, since she came from New Orleans where voodoo, though in a fragmentary way, was practiced by people in our family's past. But she could only see the woman's age. I could tell Stella that story. I could lighten the mood between us. But I don't have the will to meet her halfway.

3:29 a.m.

At Twenty-Fourth and Hennepin I can see up ahead the Uptown Diner. When I was a junior in high school it was called Embers and I worked there as a busboy, and flirted with grown-ass women. As I cleared the tables of dirty dishes I tried out tired lines ("You ladies need an escort to the after party?") like a forger passing bad bills. One night a Pan Am stewardess (they weren't called flight attendants at the time) called my bluff and took me home and fucked me blue.

"I've got a long layover in Malaysia," the stewardess said before sunrise. "Take my car." It was a turbocharged Trans Am. This happened more than once. Once I drove her car home at six a.m. I sat at my parents' kitchen table in the morning, still smelling of sex. My mother, who had seen this car once or twice before and knew no girl at my high school had given it to me, came down in her robe and looked at me sideways.

"Did she charge this time or was it for free?" I can tell Stella this story and give her a sense that, come what may, I am always on her side. But I drive in silence with a clenched jaw and my ass on my shoulders.

3:31 a.m.

It suddenly dawns on me that we have abandoned our apartment without taking Jamal's gun. A fine rain coats the windshield. The streets are deserted. And I feel no need to see clearly. Colored beams from streetlights splinter on the glass. Stella tells me to turn the wipers on.

More than anything, I want to go back to school. More than anything, I hate myself for this feeling. I keep thinking of the grown-ass men Stella has been with whom I can't hold a candle to. None of them would be driving aimlessly through the night, running from Josephine and the people who don't want an Urban Risers trial. Men like Carl Eller, a Pro Bowl defensive end, or her ex-husband Uri, a Jewish biker and drug dealer who left her and the daughter they had together. Men Stella had shaped her life with when I was just a kid.

"What are you doing to protect my daughter?" Uri said to me when we called him after seeing Dr. Zhou. He knew the answer to that. He had just spoken to Stella. I didn't need a dressing-down from him. I should have shaken my head when she handed me the phone.

I felt like a runaway slave who crossed the river and left his family on the other side to meet the bloodhounds alone. "What are you doing to protect my daughter?" That's what Uri said from his cabin somewhere in mountain time. *Fuck you, Uri, and the horse you rode in on.*

I said, "What do you expect—for me to get a gun and go upstairs and bust Josephine's door down?"

Uri didn't say anything. I thought, at that moment, that I had won. *Cat got your tongue, White boy?*

But then Uri said, "You don't have a *gun?*" In my mind's eye, Uri was shaking his head. "Jesus. Put Stella back on."

Over the next two-week period we asked some of our friends to spend a night at our flat. We wanted to see if they experienced the same sense of heat on their skin that we thought was the source of our burns, but we didn't tell them what Dr. Zhou said. We couched it in terms of the noise and the racket that Josephine and Cody had somehow created in the radiators at night. They slept on the sofa outside of our bedroom. In the morning they told us that they felt strange sensations in their skin. One of them was a concert pianist whose sense of touch and hearing were as wired as the sense of smell in bears that can smell anxiety on a human body from five miles away. He said he had dreamed that he was on fire. He went to the bathroom and washed his face in cold water. At breakfast we would tell our friends what Dr. Zhou had said.

They all said they would give their testimonies in sworn affidavits when the time came. Olivia, whose partner, Chase, would soon want nothing to do with us, was so concerned for our safety that she brought rolls of aluminum foil and a bucket of thin nails to the house. On a ladder she nailed huge swaths of foil to the ceiling. She was satisfied with herself when she came down from the ladder. "You're not the only one," she said to me, "who's going to have their gonads burned. This'll give 'em a taste of their own poison."

But all of this wasn't good enough for me. So I went to my parents with an honest lie. I told them I needed money to get myself together—stopping short of saying that I planned to return to Dartmouth. The money in hand, Stella and I took the bus to the suburb of St. Louis Park. The private detective that we hired came to the house the next day. I can still hear the rapid-fire frequency of audible clicks, and the way Stella gasped—part in horror, part in vindication—as we watched him wave the wand of his Geiger counter around our bedroom and the living room. Today, as I write, I still feel the horror that we felt at that time, but the feeling of vindication that Stella and

I had shared has gone. Today, as I write, I wish his machine had made no sound at all. He promised us he'd write a report we could take to the police.

We thought we had what we needed to go to the authorities: A White detective was going to give us his report from the Geiger counter; our friends would tell the court about the sensation of singe they felt in their skin. And then there was Dr. Zhou. So we went downtown to the FBI, as well as to Tony Bouza, the brand-new chief of police, who was known as a Democratic Farmer Labor Party reformer and not a friend of the cops beneath him.

There were three agents in the conference room of the regional headquarters of the FBI. The agent who asked all the questions was a White woman. It would be wrong to say we were on cloud nine as we walked the streets of downtown from the FBI to Tony Bouza's office, but it is right to say we were proud of ourselves and—the suit against Urban Risers aside—we both had hope in the system.

Stella had calmly and meticulously told the female agent why this was a federal matter. Josephine must have violated some federal laws by bringing hazardous material home from her place of employment. That was the first reason. In order to explicate the second reason Stella told the agents the story of her suit against Urban Risers—and all of the strange forms of low-intensity harassment we had been receiving since Noam Davidov came to the flat last fall. If Josephine had been recruited by shadowy figures who did not want Stella's secret recordings of Urban Risers board meetings and the furtive copies of invoices and other documents that could prove embezzlement and collusion on the part of people in the government to be made public, then this was more than a police matter, it was something the FBI should look into in an effort to guarantee our safety from March to November.

If this were a novel, I would write it in such a way as to give Frank and Stella a bit more common sense. They wouldn't act so rashly.

They would know not to be so naïve as to think that one federal agency would help them investigate a can of worms that could lead to the indictments of an unknown number of people in another federal agency, in order to keep two Black people alive long enough to win a large settlement and send their colleagues to jail. That wouldn't make narrative sense. But it wasn't a novel and we were tired and hurt and bursting with hope.

A week went by and no one called, not even the private detective. We went back to the FBI. This time they were hostile. The White woman even yelled at me when I asked her to tell me what steps she had taken to investigate our claims. She told us we had to leave. There was archness in her voice when she said, "The only reason we listened to you at all was because of your father and his position"—she flung her arm toward the Mississippi River—"at the university!"

The second time we went to see him, Tony Bouza told his secretary to tell us he was gone. We thanked her and said we'd try to get him next week. Instead, we sat for at least an hour on a smooth wooden bench down the hall from his office. We saw him come out of a door a ways down the hall from the door to the reception area. He had taken two or three steps in our direction before he saw us. He turned and walked briskly in the other direction. We ran down the hall as fast as we could. The reformer's face was wild with rage as he told us to leave him alone.

One by one our friends told us they were sorry. Sorry, but they couldn't go through with it. They all felt bad about backing out, and (consciously) we did not hold it against them. I think that Olivia might have felt the worst about it. If we needed anything, she said, *anything* besides her testimony, she would be there for us. The concert pianist had just been accepted to medical school. He told me his dad told him to have nothing to do with me or with Stella and her case. I asked him when, precisely, his father had warned him off.

He gave me a look that said he didn't know what I meant. Did your father raise this out of the blue, I clarified, *before* you told him about the night you spent on our sofa, or did he give you this advice *after* you told him about spending the night? He didn't answer me. He didn't have to. I asked him, I begged him to let me speak with his father. Someone got to him, I explained. Someone's getting to everyone. But he just held both his palms in the air and shook his head and walked away.

It took me an hour to go by bus to St. Louis Park where the private detective's office was. Like Bouza's secretary, the detective's secretary lied to my face. He's been on a case in North Dakota; he'll call you first thing when he gets back. We were on the second floor of a modest office building. To her back was a large bay window. He scuttled through the parking lot. I told her to turn around. I called her a liar and I ran. I took the stairs two, sometimes three at a time. I know he heard me as I ran through the parking lot and told him to stop. Five, maybe ten yards away, we made eye contact in his side-view mirror. He drove away.

For several nights the noise in the radiators and the burning sensation in our skin continued. Stella called the management for the third or fourth time since this had begun. Stella's name was on the lease. She told me they told her that Cody had told them that we were lying, that Stella had physically assaulted Josephine, that *we* were disruptive elements living in the Courts; and that a person was living there (me) who shouldn't be there—translation: *We might have to raise your rent.* The hydraulics of forces known and unknown had become too much to bear.

I stole my parents' fern-green station wagon with faux-wood panels and thirteen stickers from the national parks. Stella and I made sure that Cody saw us vacating the flat. And Josephine surely saw us from her upstairs window.

It's a haze, the faces of all the people who put us up. I marveled at the way Stella could hold her head high when she asked people if we could stay with them. She was calling in her chips for gifts of her time and guidance that she had given to them over the years. A young White woman said, ten years ago, as a student at the U, she'd learned more from Stella than she had from any of her professors. Stella seemed to be whatever these White people wanted her to be—a source of psychic sustenance, Hattie McDaniel to Vivien Leigh. I grew hot with shame whenever we rocked up to the house of someone from her past and she fed them what they needed in order to let us stay; but she spoke to them as if access to their homes were her birthright, and in some true way it was. But something always happened—a parent of the young radical that Stella had groomed might not want us there anymore, or our presence threw the calculus of someone else's life into disarray—and we had to leave.

A few nights before we ended up at Olivia and Chase's place, we both had a eureka revelation. Josephine and Cody thought we'd left for good, we surmised. If we parked my parents' station wagon by the university and walked six blocks, late at night, we might be able to sneak back in the flat and sleep in our own bed. We thought if we were careful not to flush the toilet until we were sure Josephine had gone to work and that Cody wasn't around, if we used flashlights at night, and if we let the blinds stay closed, we might be able to stay for a couple of nights without notice and without being burned (assuming they thought we were gone and had dismantled whatever they'd used on us before we sent Malika away and vacated the premises the first time).

Forty years later my chest still tightens and I feel a phantom wound on my skin near my groin when I think of the morning we woke up in our own bed to the sound of tires crushing the gravel in the courtyard. We peeked through the blinds. We didn't recognize the car. It was more pristine than any car that usually came to the Courts. The woman from the FBI got out. I was stunned by a rush of joy. *Justice*, I thought, *at last we'll get justice*. As she walked toward the house she veered to the side. We heard the muffled spike of her heels on Josephine's steps. They were up there for thirty minutes or more. Then the same muffled sound of shoes descending, but this time it was doubled. They stood outside next to her car talking amicably. As they shook hands like old friends we knew we had to leave again.

13

3:37 a.m. Uptown Minneapolis.

Stella says she knows an ex-Weatherman. "We can crash at his crib." Not only had the Weathermen (and -women) found safe houses for the Black Liberation Army, but they had made false driver's licenses and purchased guns in shops where Black buyers couldn't without being put on a list marked "in need of surveillance."

When the war ended they grew tired of the rank isolation of being on the run. They missed their moms and pops and their friends, but most of all they came to the realization that they were not Black: they were not genealogical isolates, slaves whose relational status had been denied them from the day they were born. They had chosen this life of armed response against the state. They woke up one morning and realized that the color of their skin meant this isolation wasn't a fait accompli. In September 1979, Jalil Muntaqim, a Black Panther turned Black Liberation Army soldier, sent a communiqué from prison that expressed his sense of betrayal on the part of the kind of White revolutionary Stella and I were on our way to see:

By 1973–75 . . . Euro-American revolutionary armed forces refused to give meaningful material and political support to the Black Liberation Movement, more specifically, to the Black Liberation Army. Thereby, in 1974, the Black Liberation Army was without an above-ground political support apparatus; logistically and structurally scattered across the country without the means to unite its combat units; abandoned by Euro-American revolutionary armed forces; and being relentlessly pursued by the State reactionary forces—COINTELPRO (FBI, CIA and local police departments).

At Twenty-Sixth and Hennepin, I park near a phone booth. Moonlight glistens in the rain-slick street. I ask her why she didn't mention her Weatherman before. She tells me he could still be under surveillance. No cars are behind us and, as far as I can see, from here to Twenty-Eighth Street where Hennepin humps in a small bridge over the railroad tracks there is no one ahead of us either.

"How will we know if he's not still under surveillance?"

"We won't know," she says, "unless they want us to. And that could be worse than not knowing."

On the southwest corner of Twenty-Sixth and Hennepin I am eight years old again with two wrinkled dollars for a bucket of Kentucky Fried Chicken. My mother is waiting in the car. This is the only KFC with elegance, my mother tells me, the only one wedged in the protruding corner of a stylish Victorian complex of flats, reminiscent of the triangular Flatiron Building in New York. The door is built into the base angle of the building and above the threshold twirls a giant red-and-white-striped bucket with the Colonel's face emblazoned on it.

This is the memory that floats back to me as I watch Stella put coins into the telephone. How I loved buying food for my mother.

I loved skipping into KFC beneath that giant candy-cane-striped bucket of chicken that rotated on a rod above the door. But at night, however, I dreamed the striped bucket fell on my head and cracked my skull. I would wet the bed and wake up hungry.

It's raining harder now. Stella cradles the phone. She slides the door and sprints to the car. I lean over and open her door.

"How much did you tell him?" I ask her.

"I said I'd explain when we got there."

I plead with her not to tell him about Josephine. "And don't tell him that we saw the FBI agent who was supposed to be helping us go into her flat."

"He can handle it," she says. She tells me he's seen and heard of worse.

I gird myself. I follow my breath, in and out of my nostrils. Count to ten and hope to die, the saying goes, and don't say anything else. But she can read my mind.

"There's more than a hundred thousand dollars at stake, in this case that'll take Urban Risers down for corruption" she says. "We could be in Spain or Morocco right now. I wouldn't be on welfare. Malika would be here, if all I wanted was the money."

3:51 a.m.

A dark form draws nearer in the rearview mirror. But we are still arguing and it doesn't take shape as a word in my mind.

Now cats of light claw in the mirror.

I floor the accelerator.

"Don't speed!" Stella warns.

"He's in my ass!"

"Slow down, the streets are wet."

I slow down, as she says, but he draws up to our bumper and

blinds us even more with his high beams. I speed up and she says, "You're going to get us killed."

3:51:30 a.m.

I switch lanes from right to left and, for a few seconds, the car behind us comes into focus as something more than a hulking shape in a shroud of light. I knew it wasn't a patrol car; no rotating beacons of blue running the width of its hood, no PROTECT AND SERVE painted on its sides. Nor does it seem like a watch commander's unmarked sedan. Mosaics of soot and salt are splashed on its flank, suggesting an absence of institutional care: no indoor garage, no slew of men pressed into service for cleaning and upkeep as the case would be if the car belonged to the cops. This car is driven by someone who doesn't keep a record of his kills. I press down on the gas, though I know I don't have the nerve to drive at the speed it will take for us to get away.

He swoops in behind us.

3:51:45 a.m.

I'm not hallucinating. He's so close he'll ram us from behind if I stop or slow down. I suddenly know why Stella won't settle out of court. She wants to see the face or faces of the force behind the torment she suffered during and after (and, in some strange way, even *before*) her ordeal with Urban Risers. She wants to flush them out into the open. Tonight, I want the same thing: to *know*; to see the face behind us. I grip the steering wheel as I would his throat.

"Fuck the dumb shit." I jerk the steering wheel to the right.

"No, Frank." But all I hear are my needs.

We lurch into the right-hand lane. Then I slam the brakes. Stella's body snaps forward and back like a punching bag; and the car that was behind us lurches forward in the left-hand lane. Now *he* starts to run. *No, you don't,* I think. *I must see your face.* Down this wet city street we race at fifty miles per hour.

Suddenly he slows; as though he wants to be caught. Holy shit—we don't have Jamal's gun.

3:51:47 a.m.

I turn to my left and see that he is alone. Rage roils in my brain because he will not look at me. From what I can see, he doesn't look as I thought he would look. I have thought about him many times since the day Noam Davidov came to the house with the news of Stella's trial date, and his somber admission that though he was her lawyer he couldn't protect her in the months between his visit and her court date. J. Edgar Hoover has been dead for eight years;* still, I thought when he caught us he'd be a plainclothes man dressed in gray flannel drab, a face that was pink and whisker-free; a spit-and-polished pig. He doesn't look like that at all now. I can see hair like his flouncing up and down on that night when two men rolled out of my studio window and hightailed it down the alley. Is it the same man? I wonder. I want to see his face.

Three times I look at him and then quickly back at the road so as not to run a light or anyone down, though no one seems to be out at this hour. His hair drapes down to his shoulders. His profile reminds me of Uriah Heep, that angular rogue from *David Copperfield* whose veneer of humility proves as empty as his morals; a man whose hands are always moist. And like Uriah Heep, he is pretending that Stella

---

* He was the first director of the FBI, and died on May 2, 1972. In Dinkytown, one could buy tie-dyed T-shirts that read J. EDGAR HOOVER IS ALIVE AND WELL IN HELL, the day after he died.

and I are not even here. He drives down this street with the two of us speeding next to him and he won't look my way; just as I am not looking at Stella, though she is yelling, telling me to leave it alone. I yell at him, as though I think he can hear me through my glass and his. I spin the steering wheel to the left, forcing him to veer into the oncoming lane. *Yeah, that got your fucking attention.* He swoops back into his lane. We're jostled like rag dolls in the inside of the car as I veer away from him and the right front tire bounces up and then off the curb. This time, when I look at him, he's holding a gun.

3:56 a.m.

A moon swims out of a cloud. It pours crushed glass on the face of the lake. The engine hums as the station wagon idles on Lake of the Isles Parkway. Stella is saying, "What *possessed* you to run down a White boy with a gun?" She rotates her head to ease the pain in her neck. My temples are buzzing. I feel light-headed and sick. I know I can't vomit, in this car of all cars, but my hands won't let go of the wheel. The spacious home where I grew up lies three blocks north on this lakeside parkway and six blocks up the hill. Across the lake there's a hole in the night where a stone church stands, vacant as any tooth; and a hole where my grammar school has carved itself into the gloom.

It's strange, the things that pierce your mind in the moments after you think how you could have died. Seven years have passed since the last walk my father and I took around this lake. It was summer. A hint of algae blossomed in the breeze. I was seventeen and the world was new because I was new in it. I was being courted by the Dartmouth football coaches even though I was still a junior in high school. Dad and I were just a few paces from where Stella and I are parked. We were standing by a willow at the water's edge. I told him I was going to Berkeley, I said I needed to be nearer to the revolution. Not on my dime, he said. That's when we saw Walter "Fritz" Mondale being pulled toward us by Lonnie, his Rough Collie.

Lonnie strained at his leash as we talked in the thin shade of the willow.* Senator Mondale wore penny loafers and the arms of his sweater were crisscrossed over his shoulders and neck. He had lazy eyes that gave his face a quiet kindness, which belied his record on the Vietnam War. Mondale asked my father if he would stand for the House of Representatives. It probably wasn't the first time Dad had been asked to run for public office by a highly placed notable; nor was it the first time he said how honored he was by an offer he would have to decline. He didn't want to leave his job as a professor and a dean. Besides, he wasn't sure that Kenwood's Republican incumbent could be beaten. At the curb of the parkway, Mondale turned and said, What are your plans after Dartmouth, son? (*First off, Mr. War Criminal, I'm not going to Dartmouth.*) I shrugged. I smiled. I told Mondale that four years was a long time, that I didn't even know what I wanted to major in. Thank you, said my dad when the senator was out of range.

"Answer me," Stella says for the second time. She rubs her neck, and she might have whiplash. "Don't sit there like you don't hear me, Frank!"

The smell of puke is rising in my esophagus, churning with the rank smell of my body. An odor that I had only ever smelled on a subway in New York, when the doors opened and a man who lived rough got on. His pants looked like they had been soaked in oil and stiffened by the sun. *What*, I wondered, as he held the hand grip and looked right through us, *is the story behind that kind of smell?* The bile clogs my throat. I open the door. I slump out and retch over Senator Mondale's shoes, a yellow spume that smells to me like lunch meat and the fecaloid rot of a swamp.

---

* The dog wanted a walk, not a chinwag.

4:00 a.m.

"Chase saw right through me," I say. "After Josephine ran us out, I began thinking about leaving. We don't even know what or who we're up against. My brain and my stomach want to explode."

Stella holds me as I cry. I feel like I'm crawling out of my skin, because I'm the man and I think that it's she who should be crying; that I should be comforting her. I would look up and kiss her, but I have mustang breath.

"When you have a child, you learn to hide your fear." She may have felt me flinch in her embrace, for she's quick to add, "I'm not saying you're a child. You didn't leave." She kisses my forehead. I tell her that I'm sorry that my having lost it caused her pain in her neck and shoulders. Sitting up, I start to massage her, but she says we should be going.

4:45 a.m. The Seward neighborhood.

Lace doilies drape like toupees on the mantel where framed family photos are displayed: toboggan sledding in Theodore Worth Park; a summer picnic by the band shell at Lake Harriet. But no black-and-white scenes from the Days of Rage,* no portrait of Ho Chi Minh; no echoes of my expectations. Stella had said he'd been a Weatherman, but it hardly seemed like the home of anyone who had fought the cops in the streets of Chicago or bombed the U.S. Capitol; and the man

---

* Outraged by the Vietnam War and racism in America, in what was called the Days of Rage, hundreds of Weathermen wielding lead pipes and clad in football helmets marched through an upscale Chicago shopping district. They pummeled parked cars, smashed shop windows, and engaged the police in hand-to-hand combat from October 8 through 11, 1969.

himself had the ambience more of a therapist than of someone who'd thrown his body on the wheels and gears of the machine when the machine became odious and made him sick at heart.

"I see you're not flying your freak flag," she says. By which she means, You've shaved your beard and cut your hair. Stella and I are slow to sit down.

"I needed a job," he says, without arch or irony in his voice, and ignoring the disappointment in hers. "So I joined the Human race."

He asks us what brings us to his house at four in the morning. I wish he would offer us some food. But he serves only tea and honey.

Tell him about your suit against Urban Risers. Tell him about the clicking on our telephone. Tell him why Jamal gave you a gun. Tell him about the break-in at my flat, how my books were lined in neat garden rows on the floor, my typewritten pages scattered with care, and not a cent was stolen. Tell him that Imani Price alleged Kapalei Kenyatta and the U.S. marshals were in each other's pockets. Tell him you strained your neck as I swerved down Hennepin's wet streets, playing prey and hunter with a man who enraged me because he wouldn't look at me; how a mongrel once looked at me with more connection when it raised its head from its scraps; how we made a U-turn in the middle of the street, and for some unknown reason he let us get away. But, please, Stella, don't tell him about Josephine.

Stella isn't listening to my thoughts. She tells him the story from the beginning to this moment.

5:30 a.m.

He asks her if there's more, and she shakes her head. He takes the teacups to the kitchen. When he returns he asks her what she wants from him. Salmon-colored light bleeds through creases in his venetian blinds. We hear the hum and whir of thick-whiskered brushes cleaning the streets. The world is waking up. He then tells us that he's sorry but we can't stay here. I am livid. I tell Stella that I told her he wouldn't believe us. Stella asks him if that's true. There are three possibilities, he is trying to say as I get up to leave. But do I think the Feds recruited Josephine to poison you? That's one possibility out of maybe three. But it's not one that I believe. Come on, I say to Stella, I've heard enough.

14

My father and I have hardly spoken since I got kicked out of Dartmouth College two years ago and I told him I wasn't going to return. So much for a seat in the House of Representatives. Mom and Dad are Democratic Party stalwarts whose oldest son is a communist. Life isn't easy for them.

It's April now, and we've almost forgotten those March sheets of rain. I've just turned twenty-four. Last month I stole my parents' car while they were in Moscow, or Peking, or was it Bremen or Belize? A two-month tour studying the pitfalls of Soviet mental health clinics, three weeks of consulting to Chinese special education administrators, a Ford Foundation study of German urban renewal, or a rescue mission of American students who smoked too much dope and were bounced into jail in Belize—I don't know because I don't live with them anymore.

Dad contacted me and asked if we could meet on Hennepin Avenue at the Uptown Diner. His full-length black leather coat made him look like Shaft, with a pipe instead of a gun.* I wore an Army-Navy surplus coat and my hair was cornrowed under a skullcap. He dis-

---

* John Shaft was a Black PI, played by Richard Roundtree, in the original 1971 film *Shaft*, directed by Gordon Parks.

missed the dinner menu and ordered a beer. He did not come to the point. But he knew Stella and I had taken his car, he might have even sensed our smell in it and known that we slept there. When I neither confirmed nor denied what he said, he changed the subject.

He told me that the Iran hostage crisis had now gone on for more than one hundred fifty days. He said it was bad for Jimmy Carter's (1980) reelection. He reminded me of the importance of going to vote; by which he meant, the importance of voting for Jimmy Carter and Walter Mondale so that Reagan/Bush wouldn't win. I almost told him that I was going to vote for the Ayatollah Khomeini, since he and the Iranian students had released all the Black embassy staff, as well as the women, the previous fall during the first days of the occupation. But my father and I had been estranged for almost two years, and sarcasm is the last refuge of the weak; and even though the burns on my inner thighs had stopped stinging, and were now just a low, hot itch, I wanted him to hold me. I wanted him to let me cry.

I was tense. I thought we were meeting so he could tell me, face-to-face, to leave Stella. She was, as he knew, sixteen years older than me and had a child half my age. I thought Dad came to speechify on the pitfalls of entering a "ready-made family" with a woman on welfare and her biracial kid. But he never showed dissatisfaction with anyone I'd ever dated and, besides, he liked Stella, for they had been colleagues in the College of Education at the university. I didn't balk as he went on about voting; but when he asked when I planned to go back to Dartmouth and finish my degree, I pushed back from the table. He held up his hand. Forget Dartmouth, he conceded, I need to tell you something.

He said he shared a pew at the Basilica of Saint Mary with the regional director of the FBI, Special Agent Lindberg. As he spoke, his face was creased with concern. When Dad and Mom left Mass last Sunday, Special Agent Lindberg "pulled me by the button after church." This is where my memory plays tricks on me. Sometimes I remember my father saying that Lindberg told him to tell me and Stella to "leave it alone." Sometimes I see us sitting in the booth at the diner and he tells me this: "Special Agent Lindberg shares a pew with me. He told me that you went to his office and spoke with his agents." When I remember it like that, the words "leave it alone" are not on Dad's lips, they are uttered through his eyes.

Dad didn't ask me what the "it" was that I and Stella must leave alone; nor did I ask how Lindberg explained "it" or if he even did. Looking back on it now, I'm reminded of a scene from a time before diners and station wagons, a time when we were still chattel slaves. It's a scene from the film *12 Years a Slave*. Solomon Northup, the slave who, in 1853, penned his life story from which the film was adapted, hangs by his neck from a tree. The tips of his toes touch the ground. It's the only thing that keeps him alive. From the balcony of the big house the overseer wields a shotgun and looks down on him. Slave cabin doors start to open as the slaves begin to go about their day. No one looks at Solomon. No one asks what the "it" was that got him strung up in that tree. They just tend their meager gardens and fix their meager meals. They know the folly of calling up to the overseer for an explanation. They know it would be suicide to cut Solomon down. They know how to go unnoticed. If I'd been asked, at twenty-four, if it was me or Dad hanging from that tree, I would have said me. But now I know it's all of us: Solomon, Stella, me, Malika, my mother and father, and all the people who came out that sultry bayou day and didn't see a thing; and Special Agent Lindberg was in the balcony looking down on us all.

We left the Uptown Diner together. As I opened the door of a Blue & White cab I drove part-time he hugged me until I felt his life begin to wake in mine. In the crush of his arms I almost cried. "You're our eldest child," he said, in a voice I hardly recognized. "Please call your mother. We love you."

I should have driven straight north on Hennepin, through downtown, and crossed the Mississippi to Southeast Minneapolis where I had lived with Stella and Malika, until we sent her away. Instead, I drove west three blocks and parked by the shore of Lake of the Isles. It was the shank of the evening. A man and a woman in a canoe picked their way through the lily pads to the shore where a willow I had known since the age of six dipped its beard in the water. Now the sun was setting behind stone mansions that slumbered along Lake of the Isles Parkway. They looked like bunkers abandoned in war. A loon cooed. In grade school I had played Bantam hockey when the lake froze out to the island, where a loon now hid among the reeds. I was six blocks from my childhood home but it felt like a foreign land.

I'm sure Special Agent Lindberg was a pious man; most people were who sat in my parents' pew. But the quality of his character is not what's at issue, nor should it be if we want to understand Lindberg's paradigmatic position compared to that of Black people. Less than nine years had passed since a group of anti-war activists broke into an FBI office in Media, Pennsylvania, on March 8, 1971, grabbing whatever documents they could find, and in that way exposed the labyrinth of violence that J. Edgar Hoover had created.

Thanks to the investigative research of William Maxwell, we know a good deal about this violent labyrinth that "protects our freedom." Maxwell's *F. B. Eyes: How J. Edgar Hoover's Ghostreaders Framed African American Literature* broke the story, which revealed that the largest African American literature department does not exist on a university campus but is a part of the Federal Bureau of Investigation. In fact, the year 2019 marked the one hundredth anniversary of this department within the FBI whose special agents read and analyze the nation's Black poetry, fiction, and creative nonfiction. But this literary/investigative department is not just an FBI think tank. For one hundred years it dug its secret talons into the lives of Black writers by harassing them at home and overseas, by adding or subtracting their names to a running list the FBI keeps of the most "dangerous," by which they mean *influential*, Black writers who should be rounded up and incarcerated in an internment camp in the event of widespread unrest in the Black community. This FBI department has even launched literary journals to help special agents "capture" new Black writing from emerging Black writers—the FBI keeps lots of unpublished manuscripts of Black writers on file and it keeps tabs on their authors, as much as it does on established writers.*

So, we have the impact of libidinal economy (the phobic notion that Blacks are and always have been a threat to stability) coupled with the structural violence of state capacity, the Federal Bureau of Investigation's African American literature department, which was started in 1919, when J. Edgar Hoover read a poem by Harlem Renaissance poet Claude McKay, "If We Must Die"—a poem that was a response to the anti-Black race riots of the 1910s. Hoover would have been more strategic as a crime fighter if, instead of demonizing McKay for writing a poem about self-defense, he had set up a *White* American literature department, so that he and his agents could take the violent pulse of White civil society; since the riots McKay referenced in his poem were the violence of lynch mobs that invaded the Black community. The FBI example of literary lockdown can help us reimagine Black incarceration, not as a place in space and time (that's only one iteration of incarceration), but to think of incarceration as a paradigm of *permanent and ongoing* containment that non-Blacks (what Afropessimism calls Human beings) pass in and out of, but one in which Black people greet them upon arrival, bid them farewell when history liberates

---

* Per Maxwell's book *F. B. Eyes.*

them, and remain, awaiting the next provisional round of unfortunate souls. "There is no golden age for blacks before the criminal law. Structural vulnerability to appropriation, perpetual and involuntary openness . . . should be understood as the paradigmatic conditions of black existence in the Americas, the defining characteristics of New World antiblackness . . . Policing blacks in the colonial and antebellum periods was . . . the prerogative of every white (they could assume the role or not) and was only later professionalized as the modern prison system emerged out of the ashes of Reconstruction." This raises the next conundrum, one in which for Black people it is impossible to discern where the violence of the state ends and the violence of one's White neighbors begins.

It was this conundrum that forced me and Stella from our home.

15

HANOVER, NEW HAMPSHIRE. MAY 1980.

The students, the professors, and even the deans on the College Committee on Standing and Conduct are not the same as the ones who kicked me out two years ago and told me to get a job in a corporation or enlist in the Army before I petitioned to return. I pruned my Afro and shaved my beard, and I wore a blue necktie in lieu of an elegant noose.

A dean asks me what I have been doing for the past two years. Like windows to compartments in a train passing swiftly on the track next to mine, I see the answers flicker by.

(I hitchhiked in a blizzard from Minneapolis to Columbus, Ohio. I smoked hash with a wounded Green Beret who picked me up at the St. Croix River; he was tattooed with bullet wounds on both arms from his wrists to his shoulders, where the flak jacket caught the spray as it crossed his chest during the Tet Offensive. I slept in a homeless shelter and worked day labor. I hauled garbage in Columbus. I tripped on LSD for the eleventh time; a squirrel in a park dropped an acorn from its mouth just to tell me, Jesus saves. I know Jesus saves, I said with impatience, but where the hell does he shop? The squirrel jumped out of a bag; it got all siddity and told me it could not divulge such details. I came down off my high and went back to Minneapolis three months after you kicked me out. A four-night stint as a stand-up comic in a country and western bar; they wanted Redd Foxx, who, as it turned out, got his start with Malcolm X before he went mainstream, but I gave them Lenny Bruce. I didn't last the week. For a month or two I worked for Prince, as a bouncer at his nightclub in a hollowed-out Greyhound station in downtown Minneapolis, just a block off Hennepin Avenue. I got a beat-down from two drunk-ass White dudes and a woman in the middle of the club. But the College Committee on Standing and Conduct should take into consideration that I stayed on my feet for a minute, at least; then, my hands and knees did their best. Was it strobe lights or the stars that exploded in my eyes when the woman hit the back of my head with a mug or a bottle of beer? She rode my back like a steer and all kinds of "niggers" rained down on my neck from her sweet blond mouth, while the men kicked me in the ribs. I earned good money waiting tables. But that didn't last and I don't know why. Or, I do know why, but if I told you you'd have to hear the rest: how I fell in love with Stella; how we were stalked by ghosts.) The train passes, with its windows of unspeakable scenes.

I give the dean the other truth.

"Freelance journalism for Twin Cities' newspapers; I worked as a researcher for the Urban League; a PR person for the Legal Aid Society of Minneapolis; and I studied Dickens and Hardy for two quarters at the University of Minnesota."

The dean, as I speak, is reading my updated file. As he reads he says, "There are gaps between jobs that are unaccounted for—and almost nothing here on the last three months."

16

Across the Green are Reed, Wentworth, and Fayerweather Halls, the long white colonial buildings, with their latticed windows, winged with shutters painted Brunswick-green. I smile to myself remembering my first night in my Fayerweather dorm room six years ago in 1974 and wonder who that newly minted man was, staring up at the ceiling as he lay in bed and wanted to leave. Now students and alums decked in green sweaters with white D's emblazoned walk up and down a sunny Main Street as though they have nothing to fear. There's a scent of pine needles in the air and conifers smother the mountains that surround the town of Hanover. People here say it hasn't been this warm in weeks. The grass on the college Green is dry.

In an oak-paneled phone booth in the Hopkins Center I feed the coin slot with quarters. Two years have gone by. Long enough for me to have forgotten why I stopped calling home from this booth that's third in the line of booths. There's graffiti here that reads, *The nigger is living proof that the Indian fucked the buffalo.* But the quarters have dropped and her phone is ringing and today I'm too happy to be hurt.

"Stella, they let me back in!"

"Oh . . . That's great. How?"

"They were confused about the charges. In the end the dean looked at the last lines of my sentence, from 1978 and said, 'It says to get back in you have to show that you've inculcated the esprit de corps of an Ivy League institution. So, we put it to you, in the past two years have you inculcated the esprit de corps of an Ivy League institution?' Like there was more than one answer. Everyone on the committee nodded when I answered; and that was that. I'm going to start house-hunting. Be back by, say, Saturday, and we'll come out together and then send for Malika. I'll be an Ivy League graduate soon. I'll get a fancy job and pay for you to finish your B.A."

"After the trial I'll have my own money for school. We're coming back in November for the trial, right?"

"Well, yes."

"Promise?"

"We'll go with Noam to and from the courthouse. We'll just be in Minneapolis for a few days."

"It could take longer."

"Okay, Stella, as long it takes."

17

There's a photograph of Stella that I took with my Miranda camera in Morocco. We were on a quay in Tangier about to board the hydrofoil to Gibraltar. It was taken four years after that night on Hennepin Avenue. The Rock of Gibraltar, Spain, and a blue, misty sea lace the background behind her. At home, in the darkroom, I felt a tremor of grief when I saw how worn thin was her smile in that photo. It made me think of the way she looked when we left the house of her Weatherman friend and sat in the Uptown Diner, planning our next move in a room drizzled with insomniacs and a rendezvous of strangers at the counter by the coffee urn. Vacation photos shouldn't remind you of

that kind of past. I stayed in the darkroom and superimposed a photograph of colored lanterns I took on the outdoor patio of a Chinese
restaurant in Torremolinos, that the eye might be distracted from that
night on Hennepin Avenue.

18

Before we left the ex-Weatherman's apartment he had tried to explain
as best he could why we couldn't stay.

"I don't want to think that my tribe is hardwired for evil," he had
told us.

Then he said when the Vietnam War ended and the Weather
Underground started to disband, some people who wanted to go on
fighting went south and infiltrated the Ku Klux Klan. For a long time
he had tried to forget the stories one of them told when he returned.
He said there were no limits to the imagination down there when it
came to the violent acts committed against Black people. They get
migraines, his friend said, communal pressure on the brain, if they go
too long without killing someone or burning someone.

"Stella, I can fight the war machine but I can't fight that," he
said. "The U.S. marshals won't let you bring those tapes and invoices
to court."

The ex-Weatherman said even if the U.S. marshals weren't running interference for Kapalei Kenyatta, some agency was.

"The FBI scares me, but it's only fear," he admitted. "Everyday people like Josephine *terrify* me. It's like looking at the face of my mother
or of me. I'm terrified by the intimacy. That female agent from the FBI
might have just made a routine visit to Josephine; the facts of the matter
aren't the point. The point is, it's the North but it's just like the South."
By which he meant, you can't tell where the people end and the pigs

begin in the hall of mirrors through which Stella and I were running. Then he laughed for the first time that morning, but it wasn't a laugh that gave him relief.

"The pigs and my mother, or the pigs and me, for that matter—" He stopped. Then he said, "You know me, Stella, I was in the trenches when I thought it made sense, but I can't fight an army of ghosts. It's because I believe you that I'm asking you to leave."

CHAPTER FOUR

Punishment Park

1

Copenhagen is a city without scent. Unlike Berlin with its fragrances of bratwurst and beer, shawarma spits and strong coffee, in Copenhagen one is never sure if one is breathing clean air or gusts of organic hand sanitizer. To be fair, Copenhagen's lack of urban grit, even in the center of town, wasn't the only reason I thought my talks on Peter Watkins's iconoclastic 1971 film *Punishment Park* would be much better received in Berlin than in Denmark, "The Happiest Place on Earth."

I'd been invited to give a presentation at a conference in Berlin. Since the ticket to Berlin required a change of planes in Copenhagen, I made plans to spend two days there, and then go by road, rail, and ferry across the Baltic Sea from Copenhagen to Berlin, to the conference on the fiftieth anniversary of May 1968. For me, 1968 had been a watershed year (I turned twelve and left the Roman Catholic Church that year), so I was thrilled when fifty years later I got an invitation to speak at a symposium on art and revolution in 1968, at the Berlin center of a well-endowed American university.

I planned to screen two clips from *Punishment Park* in the Afropessimist workshop set up for Danish activists—the same two clips that I planned to screen and critique at the conference in Berlin. Most people under the age of sixty have never heard of Peter Watkins. (And that may well be true for most people sixty and above who were not, so to speak, "in the Movement" back in the day.)

Punishment Park offers a disturbing look at the backlash against leftist activism that emerged in the wake of such events as the 1968 Democratic Convention in Chicago and the shootings at Kent State University. The plot goes like this: It's the story of Nixon's Silent Majority seated in judgment over young people who are fighting (some peacefully, some violently) for the end of the war in Vietnam and social justice at home. The story oscillates between the mise-en-scène of the tribunal (which is deciding the fate of activists from Group #638) and the desert where the convicted members of Group #637 are given the "opportunity" to travel fifty-three miles on foot in three days, with only minimal provisions of water or food under 110-degree heat. They're told if they reach the American flag in the allotted time, they'll be allowed to go free.

In a "normal" courtroom setting, nothing more than the hum of an air conditioner, the shuffling of feet as people make their way to their seats, and, perhaps, a cough here and there would complete the soundscape. But in the *Punishment Park* tribunal hearing, the canvas walls of the desert tent in which the hearing takes place offer the defendants no sanctuary from the invasion of ambient sounds. They can hear the sonic boom of fighter jets breaking the sound barrier over the desert, reminding them of the napalm raids and bombing missions that these planes will make over Vietnam and Cambodia. The tribunal's defendants, such as Charles Robbins (Stan Armsted) and Nancy Jane Smith (Katherine Quittner), can also hear occasional gunshots, reminding us that the National Guard, the LAPD, and the

L.A. County sheriffs are out there in the desert hunting down the members of Group #637, and that the members of Group #638, who are, one by one, being interrogated, will be joining them in short order.

2

Midway through the movie, Nancy Jane Smith enters through a flap in the tent where the tribunal waits. She is handcuffed and flanked on both sides by a sheriff. She is only as tall as their shoulders. Peter Watkins's British voice-over introduces her to the viewing spectator as "Nancy Jane Smith. Popular singer and composer." The handcuffs are left on her wrists and, as we hear the chairman of the tribunal confirm with the defense attorney that Nancy Jane Smith wishes to defend herself, the sheriffs settle her into a metal office chair facing the tribunal and shackle her ankles to the legs of the chair. Once Nancy Jane Smith is chained to the chair and the proceedings are about to begin, we cut away to Group #637 in the desert. The youths in the desert are suffering from severe thirst, dehydration, and various physical ailments from being exposed to triple-digit temperatures in the daytime and extreme cold at night.

As the proceeding intensifies, so does Nancy Jane Smith's confrontational response to her interrogators. The scene ends with Nancy Jane Smith screaming at the tribunal—"How many children have you killed?"—as members of the tribunal scream back at her, accusing her of composing songs that sent the youth into the streets to fight (and ultimately sent them to be convicted by this tribunal)—as the sheriffs lift the chair she is sitting in into the air and carry her out of the tent.

Charles Robbins's interrogation opens with him seated in the same chair where Nancy Jane Smith had been seated. He is also handcuffed and his legs are also shackled to the legs of the chair. But unlike

Nancy Jane Smith's hearing, Robbins's interrogation does not begin
with members of the tribunal asking him questions about his politics
(much less his family background or his moral code). The interrogation begins with the chairperson of the tribunal minimizing the size
and the political relevancy of the Black People's Army.

The scene of Robbins's interrogation cuts back and forth to the
members of Group #637 in the desert. At one point in the crosscut-
ting, we come to a scene where a Black woman and a White man are
holding a West German soundman hostage. Police on the ridge above
them have them pinned down on the rocks. The lead officer takes
aim with a high-powered rifle (with the aid of a scope) and shoots the
White radical, thus freeing the West German soundman. All of the
police chase the lone Black woman for several yards; they shoot her in
the back several times, and then shoot her six more times as she lies
facedown on the ground. Meanwhile, miles away, inside the desert
tent of the tribunal, the interrogation of a Black revolutionary named
Charles Robbins continues. The film contains extended footage of his
and others' interrogation at a secret location somewhere in the desert
due east of Los Angeles: a courtroom inside a tent, a situation that the
McCarran Internal Security Act of 1950 has made perfectly legal. The
McCarran Act authorized the president (then Truman), in an emergency (defined as invasion, declaration of war, or insurrection in aid
of a foreign enemy), to arrest and detain persons he believed might
engage in espionage or sabotage.

From the summer of '68, when I was twelve, until 1974, when I
went to away to college, my teachers were the young, heroic women
and men who could have played the women and men who were handcuffed, shot, and killed in *Punishment Park*. After having spent the
first six years of school at Kenwood Elementary School, named for the
all-White enclave where it was located on the western edge of Minneapolis, I was unexpectedly thrust into a parallel universe, in Seattle,

the summer after sixth grade. I met many doppelgängers of Robbins, Smith, and the unnamed Black woman in the desert who held a German sound technician hostage, all of whom were murdered in *Punishment Park*. Nancy Jane Smith was twenty-one. The unnamed Black woman could not have been older. Charles Robbins was twenty-five years old and already a member of the Black People's Army (an underground organization whose name and guerrilla philosophy was close, if not identical, to Assata Shakur's Black Liberation Army).

When the summer of '68 ended, my family left Seattle, returning to Minneapolis, to Kenwood, where I started and completed seventh grade. We went away again, in eighth grade, this time for an entire school year—a yearlong sabbatical for my father, and a chance for my mother to study for her French exam and finish writing her dissertation. We lived in Detroit's St. Antoine projects, not two years after the riots and the Algiers Motel incident; we were in Chicago when Fred Hampton was gunned down in his bed; and we lived near campus, in Berkeley, California, when Nixon bombed Cambodia, and Kent State and Jackson State went down.

On this trip across the country, I met a doppelgänger of the unnamed Black woman whom Peter Watkins had interviewed in *Punishment Park* while she was on the run. Hidden from the L.A. County Sheriff's Department, the National Guard, and the police in the split of a rocky crag, she cradles a rifle she had taken from a cop she and her comrade had killed. She's short of breath from running. She knows the posse is closing in.

She tells Peter Watkins and his crew, "It's a game, man. A fucking game. This whole establishment. You either win or you die."

Then there is footage of her sprinting over the flat, hot terrain below where the interview was recorded. The LAPD, the sheriff's department, and the Guardsmen are chasing her. Off-camera, one of them says, "Get the bitch." Then, from a ridge above her, one of them shoots her in the back. She is facedown in the dust, but they keep shooting and shooting.

I met her doppelgänger in Chicago the month Fred Hampton was murdered. She was one of the Black Panthers who opened to the public the bullet-riddled flat where he was murdered. Four months later my family and I left Chicago and went to Berkeley, where I saw her again. In Berkeley, I never knew what her political affiliations were, but I knew that revolution was her dream. I was thirteen and fourteen when we were friends, and she was at least twenty. She worked at a fish-and-chips takeout on Telegraph Avenue, halfway between my school and the university. I wanted her to marry me before my parents hauled me back to Deadsville (Minneapolis) when the school year ended. The fact that to take the vows and kiss her I would've needed a stepladder didn't dampen my desire. Her skin glowed like marble. We laughed and talked on slow spring afternoons. Sometimes I brought the latest edition of *Ramparts* to the fast-food restaurant and she'd take her break with me. We talked about the stories in the magazine. I'd try to impress her by reading what I thought were notable passages from articles on the Chicago Eight trial, demonstrations in Latin America during Nelson Rockefeller's fact-finding mission for Nixon, or the musical demise of Jefferson Airplane.

It never once occurred to me that a woman in the struggle who was six years my senior might not *need* a little thirteen-year-old boy as an interlocutor or a would-be lover; that perhaps she was perfectly capable of finding the relevant paragraphs in *Ramparts* herself; and that, furthermore, perhaps she might have actually read the magazine before I bounced and grinned my way in. When, on the rare occasion, these thoughts violated my space, I'd look in the mirror, holding my chin in my hand, and nod: "Age ain't nuthin' but a number, you dig?" That's what I would say to her one day, I thought, just not tomorrow.

Instead of actually telling her how enchanted I was with her, I fantasized about my future with her while standing in front of my bedroom mirror. Her name was Bernadette. When I fantasized about her, I gave her connections to the underground she never claimed in that fish-and-chips shop on Telegraph Avenue. On the masthead of the Black Panther newspaper, there was always someone on the editorial board who wasn't named. One day, at after-school school in the Panther office, a brother told me that that unnamed person on the masthead was underground; she or he was their link to the secret cells that operated in what he called an "offensive-defensive" manner. I gave that person the name Shirley, and I imagined that she was Bernadette's cousin; and that, on the journey that Bernadette and I would take after we were married, Bernadette and I would raise money and support for Shirley and the "offensive-defensive" operations of Shirley's Black Liberation Army underground cell. In my reverie, Bernadette and I hit all the places my father and mother had brought me to—the University of Washington, the University of Chicago, UC Berkeley, Wayne State University, and the University of Minnesota—bringing the message of Nation Time!

I am wearing shades and a black leather jacket, a cross between a young Bobby Seale and "Linc" Hayes of *The Mod Squad*. Bernadette is decked out in a black miniskirt, hoop earrings, and her Afro's blown out wide and full. Six microphones are bunched together like steel tulips on the podium in the student union. When I make a point and pound my fist on the podium the steel tulips shudder and the feedback pierces the auditorium. No one has been seated since I raised my fist and warned, "If you don't want no trouble, keep your filthy white hands off our beautiful Black women!" A beautiful sea of black faces roars; and ofay newsmen in faded raincoats look up in awe at the stage. Conga players at the far end of the stage beat rhythms with callused palms.

Now Bernadette comes up beside me. I edge to the right, and she leans in to the microphone. She tells them that she brings them greetings from her cousin in the revolutionary underground.

"Her name is Shirley Jones! *My* name is Bernadette Jones. That's right, Shirley Jones's my cousin. Now, run 'n' tell *that*!" she says to the press below. "The pigs say my cousin's on the run. But y'all ready for this?"

Sparrow voices lace the air with, *We ready! We ready!*

"All right, then, here it is. Here it is. Shirley Jones ain't on the run; she's puttin' *Oinky-Oinky* on the run! That's who's on the run. Now, rescue me if I'm wrong."

I'm standing beside her, applauding, saying, *Rescue me if I'm wrong*, into the din. Bernadette holds up her hand. The auditorium begins to quiet.

"Open your windows," Bernadette tells them. "That's right, open your windows and hear Oinky-Oinky squealing! Shirley Jones ain't going nowhere; and she sent me and my man, Frank, to tell you that she is *right here*, you dig, right here in Babylon. Shirley Jones is in *me*. Shirley Jones is in my man here. Shirley Jones . . . okay, okay, hold up, now, I only got a little bit a time."

Bernadette wipes sweat from her forehead with the handkerchief I hand her.

"Shirley Jones is in *each and every one of you beautiful Black sisters and brothers*."

She waits again for them to get as quiet as they can get. She leans in so close the feedback makes her words nearly unintelligible.

"Y'all run 'n' tell *Oinky-Oinky* he best eat his Wheaties, now." She peers down at the press. "You got to eat so you can protect yourselves." The reporters aren't sure if she's joking, even though the room is in stitches. Then, to the crowd, she says. "Go back home. Grease some pieces. Sight some scopes. *And blow that pig away when he jumps out of a bag!*"

The room rocks like a minor quake.

"One more thang, y'all, one more thang. Hold up. Hold up. One more thang. My man Frank, right here, my husband. This man right here beside me." A young woman from the front row yells, He sure is fine! Bernadette stops, she's still smiling but she stops. "Okay, okay, okay, my sister, hear me, okay? I'll off a cleanup woman quick as a pig." The whole room breaks out laughing. "My husband's gonna rap on about the Spring Offensive; and what we need to do to get ready for the get-down."

Now I ease back to the podium and start to speak again. But it never failed, my daydream always disintegrated when my "wife," Bernadette, called me back to the mike.

It was during this time, the spring of 1970, that I met Nancy Jane Smith, as well. But unlike Bernadette, there is no footage of her murder in *Punishment Park*. But we can assume that the police or the Guardsmen offed her. In the film, Nancy Jane Smith knows she's going to die; she says as much to the tribunal as she gives testimony while she's handcuffed. Nancy Jane Smith may have been in Students for a Democratic Society, but the records of the tribunal don't reflect this.

When I met a double of Nancy Jane Smith she taught social studies at Willard Junior High School in Berkeley, on Telegraph Avenue half a mile from UC Berkeley and the fish-and-chips shop where Bernadette Jones worked. She had brunette hair that hung down her back, and her earrings were two blue feathers attached to the piercings. One day Nancy stood in front of the class, in her customary miniskirt and peasant blouse. She asked if we understood the symbiosis between the "White woman" and "American imperialism." First she explained *symbiosis*: a mutually beneficial relationship between different people or groups. Then she put a 45 on the Dansette portable record player on her desk. Hard-rock licks from a lone guitar introduced a song we'd all heard—it had just been released in March. Then Burton Cummings, lead vocalist for the Guess Who, started singing "American Woman." When the song ended, she lifted and cradled the tone arm. For the rest of the period she broke it down, the symbiosis between the White woman and American imperialism, through the lyrics of the song.

3

When Nancy Jane Smith enters the tent of the tribunal, the ensemble of questions is ratcheted downward from ethical dilemmas elaborated by affilial conflict (such as class warfare) to moral dilemmas elaborated by filial anxieties (such as the proper conduct of young women, the future of White reproduction, and a general anxiety about the status of the nuclear family).

Smith's interrogation is under a constant hydraulics that, through the selection of topics, the distribution of concerns, the emotional weighting and emphasis afforded to questions of sexual conduct instead of questions of institutional power, and the tribunal's preoccupation with mental hygiene, child-rearing, and decent vs. indecent speech, pressures the interrogation's scale of abstraction downward, from the political to the personal.

An ethical assessment of Richard Nixon's war machine, capitalism's economic disparity, the prison-industrial complex, and sexism and patriarchy as manifestations of institutional power (and not mere interpersonal practices) is shunned in favor of the tribunal members' fixation on the moral hygiene of a young White woman. Ethical assessment is crowded out by the hydraulics of moral judgment. *Unfortunately, this penchant for the personal over the political, and for morality over ethics, is as much the preoccupation of Nancy Jane Smith as it is of the tribunal.*

The proceedings begin with the labor union official (and draft board member), a conservative Chicano, asking Nancy Jane Smith to tell them a little bit about herself. But the "herself" that they want to hear about is not grounded in her *affilial* choices (her political affinities) but in the *filial* world into which she was born and had no say in, that of a well-to-do White family.

He says, "You came from a wealthy family and had the best of everything, so how did you end up like this?"

This filial pressure on the ensuing interrogation and the complementary discourse about the state of her mental health—in other words, this constant pressure to steer the conversation from position and power, to identity and personal choices—is something that Nancy Jane Smith *consents to* rather than rails against. Her consent, of course, is spontaneous, meaning not something she thinks out—which makes her complicity in the interrogation's scale of abstraction *more* constitutive of her desire, not less. The unconscious is a faith-based initiative. In other words, even though Nancy Jane Smith is a revolutionary insurgent, hell-bent on the overthrow of the U.S. government, and the tribunal members are exemplary of Richard Nixon's "Silent Majority," at a deep unconscious level they are equally *invested* in the status and integrity of the White family.

The tribunal members *and* the person they are about to put to death care about the same thing: the status of the White family. And this shared, unconscious investment drives the interrogation in ways that are more essential than their political and ideological disagreements over revolution and the Vietnam War.

Then the FBI agent reads a report into the record that concludes with a psychiatric evaluation that declares Nancy Jane Smith to be a schizophrenic. The implication is that she is a female hysteric and not a "real" revolutionary.

"I'll bet your mother and father are really proud of you," says the housewife who chairs an organization called the "Silent Majority for a Unified America."

But this diminishment of Nancy Jane Smith's politics also works to fortify and extend her relational status. Put differently, her Human subjectivity is *secured*, not diminished, by these attacks as well as by her responses. As counterintuitive as this might seem, the *structure* of the exchange—and not the *content* of the exchange—is what affords Nancy Jane Smith the kind of essential relationality that Charles Robbins and the Black woman in the desert are barred from ab initio.

Right off the bat, the tribunal makes it clear that Smith has a mind, a mind about which they are all concerned. (We need to bracket the fact that their concern mimics Victorian views of female hysteria— that's not essential here, because it cannot extend to Black women, so its oppressive dynamic remains important, but takes a backseat to the more essential dynamic, which is how it fortifies and extends the paradigm of Human relations between the tribunal and Smith.) Unlike the Black, the Slave, Nancy Jane Smith has what Frantz Fanon calls "ontological resistance in the eyes" of her interrogators by which he meant the spatio-temporal labors of one subject have transformational potential on the spatio-temporal labors of another subject. This shared capacity for transformation, and for recognition and incorporation, does not extend to the Slave.

It is important to reiterate that Nancy Jane Smith does not attempt to change the *perimeters*, or the structure, of the exchange in any meaningful way. When she is confronted with her psychiatric review, she shouts, "Is that your opinion, dummy?" She is then given an opportunity to sing one of her songs. After reciting the lyrics, laden with sexual expressions that the tribunal, no doubt, consider seditious and pornographic, Smith makes a sarcastic remark to the housewife who chairs an organization called the Silent Majority for a Unified America.

"Do you know what 'snatch' is, lady?" The remark is meant to have shock value and to establish Nancy Jane Smith's credentials as a liberated White woman at the expense of her older, and repressed, White female interrogator.

This pageantry of strike/counterstrike that ensues throughout Nancy Jane Smith's interrogation betrays a proclivity to imagine political conflict, which is to say "affilial" (meaning, political and institutional) struggles, through filial (meaning, family) frames. Questions of citizenship and state power that would ordinarily be categorized as affilial dilemmas, questions of institutional power, are displaced onto questions that would ordinarily be categorized as filial, questions of family loyalty. The interrogation weaves a tapestry of articulations, "connections, transfers and displacements," between affilial frames of reference and filial frames of reference in which the stability of the White family becomes hegemonic throughout the interrogation, while questions of political power (Nixon's war machine and the scourge of capitalism) become secondary, at best.

What this framing mobilizes is a deep unconscious saturation and naturalization of White family authority as state authority, wherein "characteristics of the family are projected onto the social environment" in such a way as to allow for "no disproportion between the life of the [White] family and the life of the [state]."

In stark contrast, Charles Robbins's interrogation begins with an assault, in the guise of an assertion.

"We know from our records that there are only a handful of Black militants that are running the so-called People's army"—so begins a member of the tribunal. "It does not represent the community. You are trying to overthrow the government—and you're only a handful."

The camera then provides a close-up of one of the other men on the tribunal. Unlike the men and women during Nancy Jane Smith's interrogation, this man is not looking at Charles Robbins, the person being interrogated. He is doodling.

Another interrogator snarls, "Martin Luther King was opposed to your violence!"

The opening of this scene is exemplary of the ways in which the master's prerogative, beyond deciding that Charles Robbins and the Black People's Army have not secured a Black mandate, goes so far as to designate what kind of politics will be allowed to secure a mandate and what the nature of that mandate will be. All of this transpires prior to Charles Robbins having said one word! In fact, the interrogation closes as it opens, though more emphatically: Robbins is bound and gagged, as a tribunal member keeps shouting.

"Shut him up . . . Shut. Him. Up!"

And a white defense lawyer rises to articulate the ethical dilemmas that Robbins has been barred from speaking since the beginning.

On some level, this is the same discursive violence meted out to Nancy Jane Smith, in that the members of the tribunal quash any hope of the interrogation flowering on a rich semantic field of affiliation—an ethical assessment of institutional power predicated on competing political and philosophical orientations. In other words, on face value, the kind of argument that Marxists like Negri and Hardt make—that, in this post-industrial dystopia in which we have been living since the end of the 1960s, that is, since the end of the Golden Age of Capital, the temporality of incarceration, or "prison time," has usurped the time of civil society, for *everyone* regardless of race or gender.

But unlike Nancy Jane Smith, Charles Robbins is not even given the opportunity to participate in a ratcheting downward of the scale of abstraction, that is, from affiliation to filiation. He is not someone's wayward son, in the way that Nancy Jane Smith is someone's wayward daughter. Charles Robbins is not even a Human subject; which is to say that he experiences civil society *not* as a system of laws, codes, and mores that dispense violence against those who transgress its laws and codes of behavior. For him, civil society is a juggernaut of murderous vengeance void of contingency, trial, or debate. For Charles Robbins and the Black woman in the desert, civil society has *always* been a juggernaut of violence. Civil society has never been a terrain characterized by consent as opposed to coercion. For the two of them, the usurpation of civil society by violence is not a new phenomenon, predicated on changes in political economy (such as the end of the gold standard). *On the contrary, violence without sanctuary is the sine qua non of Blackness.*

Like Nancy Jane Smith, he is a stimulus to anxiety; but not anxiety of an ideational nature. It is not as though Robbins's ideas are a threat to deep-seated ideas held by the conservative tribunal. Their interrogation of him is symptomatic of the fact that the only ideas he has are the ones he embodies, that is to say, the ideas *they* have of him. Like my interrogation at the hands of Elgar's mother, Celina Davenport, when I was a child, a woman whose unconscious prompted a complaint about her husband's lack of home team spirit when my answers ran afoul of her frame of reference, the tribunal has no need for Robbins's actual testimony.

His "*flesh*" (his color, size, genitals—the *bio-facticity* of Blackness), not his philosophical or sexual orientation, is the stimulus to anxiety. There is no need for the tribunal to parse out his rhetoric as they did when, in their filial fixation, they asked Nancy Jane Smith to sing one of her songs for them; or when, in a rare moment in which they granted her the noblesse oblige of official engagement, they asked her what her philosophy of government was. The inability of the tribunal to imagine Charles Robbins as a relational being, their unconscious inability to see him as a Human being, as someone imbued with the spatio-temporal capacity to possess relational status—the absence of resistance in the eyes of the other—extends to Black people writ large, and, I might add, is also the essential limitation of the filmmaker, Peter Watkins, and of the film itself.

Black people form a mass of indistinguishable flesh in the collective unconscious, not a social formation of interests, agendas, or ideas.

At the beginning of the interrogation, Robbins is *told* he has absolutely no political mandate, no political effectiveness.

Later, he is asked, by the same tribunal member, "Why are you leading your people into the mass hysteria?"

Which is he, void of agency or in possession of superhuman powers? He is both. He is neither. The truth and where it lies is immaterial. What *is* substantiated is that the species that sits before them threatens their collective unconscious beyond their powers of speech. Charles Robbins is a phobogenic* object; an embodied stimulus to anxiety.

The breadth of his agency is so totalizing as to make agency warped, unrecognizable, and without borders. This is the same orientation White people and their non-Black junior partners have toward Black sexuality; a sexual ubiquity and power that is so comprehensive as to make it impossible to speak of it in sexual terms. Something to be abandoned to, given over to, as though jouissance had no beginning and no end; something to be terrified of, as though boundless pleasure can lead only to death. The Black is held captive in the joy and terror of the master as it whiplashes between Negrophilia (as, for example, in the vapid consumption of hard-core rap by White youth in the suburbs) and Negrophobia (as in the interrogation, void of meaningful dialogue, of Robbins by the tribunal).

It is important to remember that this is not a reciprocal dynamic. Whereas the committee was indeed concerned as to where Nancy Jane Smith would seek her pleasure and how, and was concerned with what ideas motivated her hatred for America (her "paranoia" after the Kent

---

* Something that is induced or caused by fear.

State massacre), there is *no* concern regarding the motivations that underwrite Charles Robbins's pursuit of personal pleasure or political retribution. As a slave, his jouissance, like his political intent, is always already usurped, given over, to the power and desire of those who are not slaves.

Franz Fanon reminds us that the Jew, like the White woman, is a phobic object at the level of the *ideas* others have of their *ideas*, and as I have argued in *Red, White & Black*, American Indians are phobic objects due to their embodied demand (again, ideation) for territorial redress. But the Black is not a phobic object who stimulates anxiety around their articulations (real or imagined) regarding time (the anti-Semitic fear of Jewish "financial domination") or space (a conflict over indigenous claims to land). The Black is a threat, to paraphrase Fanon, at a genital level. "He's a beast!" is the most commonly uttered phrase of appreciation for a Black athlete. In other words, anti-Black violence murders, *destroys*, subjectivity (eviscerates the capacity for relationality), whereas misogynistic and anti-Semitic violence, along with the genocide of indigenous people, exploits and alienates subjectivity *without* obliterating relational capacity. In other words, the violence that will ultimately kill Nancy Jane Smith cannot be analogized with the violence that will kill Charles Robbins and the Black woman in the desert—even if the same gun is used on both *species*. Though they all will stop breathing, death for Nancy Jane Smith in no way resembles death for Robbins and the Black woman in the desert. The difference between some*one* dying and some*thing* dying cannot be analogized.

This is what makes *murder*, rather than exploitation and alienation, the generative mechanism of the "relationship" between Charles Robbins and the tribunal; that is, the Slave/Human "relation." A paradox is embedded in this murder, in that it can never be anything but murder; but it must be a kind of murder that is comprehensive enough to obliterate the Slave's, the Black's, yearning for, and attempts at attaining, recognition and incorporation for their spatio-temporal labors, even though the comprehensive nature of the homicide would not wipe Black people out altogether. Without Black people, Human existence would be unintelligible, in the same way that "cat" has no meaning without "dog." This is very different from Native American genocide. For Indians are, in fact, Humans. Wiping them out, empirically, does not threaten the stability of Humanity. Any more than the anti-Semitic violence of the Holocaust would have made "Humanity" unintelligible should the Holocaust have wiped out the Jews.

But if Blacks were completely genocided, Humanity would find itself in the same quandary that would occur if Black people were recognized and incorporated as Human beings. Humanity would cease to exist; because it would lose its conceptual coherence, having lost its baseline other. Humanity would find itself standing in the abyss of an epistemological void. The Black is needed to mark the border of Human subjectivity. Without the pageantry of violence meted out to Charles Robbins and the Black woman in the desert (a pageantry of violence that is not contingent upon their giving the "wrong" answers to the tribunal, a violence that considers them a mass of flesh, not members of a social formation), there would be no way for Human Beings to know that they are Human. By way of contrast, Nancy Jane Smith will die, that much is clear, but her death is contingent upon her "misbehaving" sexually and politically. This contingency imbues her death with meaning and thereby rejuvenates her species (the Human race and its most hallowed institution, the White family) even as she lies cold and inert in the desert soil. As Jonathan Lee writes, in his paraphrasing of Lacan, "Death is such an essential and revelatory future moment. One's death is unavoidably one's own." In other words, even when she dies, Nancy Jane Smith's songs and countercultural ideas will live on (albeit as thorns) in the psyches of her interrogators and in the psyches of Humans yet to be born; hence the efforts of the tribunal to discipline her into a properly Oedipalized young woman.

But we must turn to Patterson to understand the meaning of murder when it comes to Charles Robbins and the Black woman in the desert: "The slave dies, it is true, but he [sic] dies in the master." This passing does not mark the death of a relational subject, but the expiration of an implement; a speaking implement with no auditor for the sound it makes.

What is remarkable about Charles Robbins's interrogation is that, unlike Nancy Jane Smith, Robbins is given no opportunity to have his ideas recognized and incorporated by his interlocutors—not at the level of filiation or at the level of affiliation. In the libidinal economy of the Human vs. Slave antagonism, he cannot be imagined as someone's son or father or brother, and nor can he be imagined as someone who speaks a philosophical language, the politics of which would either concur or conflict with members of the tribunal. He has "no ontological resistance in the eyes of the white man." Like objects in a grammatical structure, Charles Robbins and the Black woman murdered in the desert are objects upon which the subject of a sentence acts, and the stability of the Human race depends on these roles never being altered or reversed.

4

In Copenhagen, the publisher of a small left-wing press had asked me to give a public lecture at his press's launch of an anthology featuring the work of Jared Sexton, Saidiya Hartman, Frantz Fanon, and me. I said yes, but I had one request: I wanted to meet with a group of Black organizers with no one else in the room in order to facilitate a three-hour workshop on Afropessimism that would be similar to workshops I had facilitated in North America, South Africa, and other parts of Europe.

"Denmark is a very white place," he said, in a Skype conversation. Though he knew of multiracial organizations doing political work in Denmark, finding one that was exclusively Black would be a challenge. A week later, he came back with the name, a relatively new group called Marronage; a "people of color" organization. The kind of group I had asked for didn't exist. But since Marronage came into existence to counter Denmark's self-aggrandizing celebrations commemorating the one hundredth anniversary of its abolishment of colonialism, when, in 1917, it sold the Virgin Islands to the U.S. (which also allowed it to shed the taint of its past as a slave-dependent economy), it made sense for me to conduct a workshop for people who were interested in the political ramifications of the long durée of slavery.

5
—

I arrived in Copenhagen steadfast in my conviction that even the most persecuted White women are a priori positioned as masters, in relation to Black people, *even* to Black men. This assertion gains greater clarity when we consider that at the level of consciousness, what psychoanalysis calls preconscious interests, the realm of the psyche that can be brought to consciousness—and spoken—it would *appear* as though Nancy Jane Smith, Charles Robbins, and the unnamed Black woman in the desert are all of the same species. They are all Marxist revolutionaries who would argue that they are of the same species: the working class. But what becomes clear as one compares their interrogations is that though they share the same consciousness, and though they would *say* they are of the same species (working-class Humans), in point of fact the unconscious realm of the psyche has no capacity to recognize Charles Robbins and the unnamed Black woman in the desert as Human beings. They cannot be incorporated into filial or affilial imaginaries of family or political relations, *regardless of the preconscious/conscious mind's protestations to the contrary*. In short, the conscious mind of a radical says, "I don't see color," whereas the unconscious mind is "saying" (in ways that are rarely legible) "I live in fear of a Black planet." This duality is sustained by the fact that the violence that positions Nancy Jane Smith as a White woman and as a Human being is structurally different than the violence that positions Charles Robbins and the unnamed Black woman in the desert as Blacks and Slaves.

This flies in the face of theoretical and political assumptions that non-Black intellectuals and activists hold dear about violence and gender. The challenge this argument presents is not intellectual, but rather it is emotional; especially when it comes from a cisgender Black man who critiques the paradigm of White femininity in less than dulcet tones.

But White women, as Human beings, *are* structurally more powerful than Black people, because they, White women, are members of the Human species, whereas Blacks are the sentient beings *against which Humanity is defined*. Even in the horrible act of rape (of White woman by a Black man, for example) the *structure* of the relation does not change. This is an incendiary assertion. But no theory worth its salt should shy away from pyrotechnics. To begin with, Afropessimism in no way condones or seeks to explain away sexual violence. On the contrary, violence, as structure or paradigm, and sexual violence, as an ensemble of practices within that paradigm, is at the heart of Afropessimist meditations, albeit in ways that run counter to received wisdom.

In the centuries when slavery was still on the books, and not strangely sublimated by euphemisms like "citizen" and "universal suffrage," a male slave forcing a female slave owner into sex against her will was as *morally* wrong as a male slave master forcing a female slave into sex against her will. Sex as a weapon is revolting and cannot be condoned. Despite all the *moral* injunctions against such acts, to suggest that the male slave's rape of his female master is also a problem of *ethics* is to mistake *force*, the musculature of the Black male rapist, for *power*, the web of institutional capacities that make him an extension of her prerogative and power, even in the act of rape. At the level of performance, she is his victim. At the level of paradigm, he is still her tool. What does one do with that? One does not look for answers that "solve" the problem of performance while ignoring the problem of paradigm. One sits with it.

No Marxist revolutionary would say that shorter working hours and higher wages for workers redress the unethical paradigm of capitalism. But when many people encounter the Black, a sentient being who, unlike the worker, does not *have* a problem but, rather, as Du Bois has written, *is* a problem, the image burns too intensely for the eyes.

But, even at the risk of searing our retinas, we will gaze unflinchingly at this flame.

Even though women in the room where the Copenhagen workshop took place were not, for the most part, White women, many of them were not Black women either; and they knew enough from my introduction that the White woman in Peter Watkins's *Punishment Park* (a radical, left-wing prisoner named Nancy Jane Smith) was a stand-in for any non-Black woman. I planned to return to this thorny proposition—that the status of non-Black women vis-à-vis Black men hasn't changed over time—with a quote from an article by Jared Sexton, where he writes:

[It] seems counterintuitive . . . [but] because of her historical implication in the structures of white supremacy (marked
by her limited capacity to marshal state violence or state sanctioned paramilitary violence), the white woman can have the
black man (or black woman) brutalized for transgressions real
or imagined. However, and because of this relation of power, *she
can also rape him*, thereby reversing the polarity of a rape fantasy pervasive in the anti-black world; regardless of his size and
strength, his prowess and his pride, he is *structurally vulnerable*
to her. (Contrary to many standard legal definitions, she is able
to rape him without his necessarily being physically penetrated
against his will. In this sense, the fear of rape and the fear of
penetration must be *carefully distinguished*.) Perhaps rape is better understood not as an isolated act, but as part of *a spectrum
of sexual coercion generated within a broader set of social, political,
and economic relations* regulated (but not simply controlled) by
the racial state and enabling permutations of enactment.

During my evening lecture to one hundred forty audience
members—which followed the three-hour workshop with thirty Danish radical activists—I distributed handouts with Sexton's quote on it
to the people who came after the workshop, so that they could read it
when I came to it in my speech; and so that they would have it in front
of them if they wanted to discuss it during the Q&A. The reception
of these ideas was thoughtful and engaged, in both the workshop and
the talk that followed; which meant my guard was down when I got
to Berlin to discuss these ideas with left-wing academics who, presumably, had more theoretical chops than the activists in Copenhagen.

Most of the people who attended the Marronage workshop had read
very little about Afropessimism. They were hardscrabble organizers,
many of whom had seen Denmark's state violence up close. This made

them open to a deeper theorization of that violence, even if what they learned might shatter their previously held ideas about the structure—not simply the performance—of that violence. I was impressed by their willingness to sit, for three hours, in discussions and exercises that challenged so much of their received wisdom and, more to the point, *so much of the foundation upon which their organizing was based.*

The workshop and the speech I gave that followed took place in Folkets Hus. These were two really special events for the thirty people in the workshop and the people who came to my public lecture, because the building, Folkets Hus (the Peoples' House) had been the hub of radical activism and community struggles for decades. Arts and crafts, as well as rebellion and resistance to the Copenhagen police, had emanated from Folkets Hus in the past. The police had closed it down for about two years. My workshop and speech were the first events of its reopening. People were excited and also a bit on edge, wondering if the cops would raid it, as they had in the past, and haul all one-hundred-plus people to jail.

An Asian-Danish woman asked me, "If the violence of White supremacy and capitalist, patriarchal violence is what I, as an Asian woman, suffer, and if you're suggesting White supremacy and anti-Blackness are not the same—in fact, I hear you saying that the people who suffer White supremacy are also the people who, along with Whites, perpetrate anti-Blackness—then my question is what does that mean . . . what does that do . . . maybe what I want to say is, how do we forge solidarity in multiracial coalitions such as Marronage?"

(I'd be asked the same question in two days' time, in Berlin; but the tone and intent would be hostile, and I would say, "I don't give a rat's ass about solidarity." Which wasn't true; but the *way* I cared about solidarity wasn't the way the mob that had packed its bags to meet me in Berlin cared about it.)

"What we're doing in this workshop is a form of solidarity," I replied.

"The important things we need to understand are the ways non-Black people of color can crowd out discussions of a Black grammar of suffering by insisting that the coalition needs to focus on what we all have in common. It is true that we all suffer from police aggression; that we all suffer from capitalist domination. But we should use *the space opened up by political organizing which is geared toward reformist objectives— like stopping police brutality and ending racist immigration policies—as an opportunity to explore problems for which there are no coherent solutions. Anti-Black violence is a paradigm of oppression for which there is no coherent form of redress, other than Frantz Fanon's 'the end of the world.'* Solidarity means not crowding out discussions of Black social death just because there is no coherent form of redress on the horizon. I think that's what we've done today. Your participation in this workshop with the Black people in Marronage is an act of solidarity."

There is no point-for-point pilgrim's progress that can explain how the clips from *Punishment Park* made the Copenhagen workshop a success; or why the same analysis went south when I got to Berlin.

6
___

Berlin was as hot as it had been two days earlier in Copenhagen. But the greater density of buildings there, the teeming throngs of tourists, and the fact that, unlike Copenhagen, Berlin is not bordered on three sides by the sea made it bake even more. The room used for the conference on May 1968 didn't smell like the Folkets Hus room in Nørrebrogade.* That was the first thing that I noticed: there was no smell. It was a clean room of sharp angles and floor-to-ceiling windows

---

* The Arab, African, and White working-class neighborhood of Copenhagen where Folkets Hus is located.

that trapped cold, odorless air inside. The pentagon of white Formica tables on wall-to-wall carpet was a far cry from the unvarnished tables at Folkets Hus in Copenhagen, most of which had to be hauled from a storage room and were clearly donated over the years, because they didn't fit together the way the tables fit together in Berlin. In Nørrebrogade we had all chipped in, hauling tables, unstacking chairs, working with the whiteboard that had been donated for the workshop by Kapelvej 44, another Nørrebrogade community center run by a cheerful and direct woman named Lisbeth Bryhl; a whiteboard we propped on a chair, and which had to be held up with one hand to keep it from sliding down as I wrote on it. Ladders and empty coatracks dotted the room at Folkets Hus; and the floor was a palimpsest of scuff marks from metal chairs or the rubber soles of SWAT teams. Folkets Hus smelled lived-in, contested, a room which weed and teargas had each called home; it smelled of dry sweat and laughter and *fuck the police*; and the windows had broad sills where comrades who came late sat.

In contrast to the People's House in Copenhagen, the conference room in Berlin was on the fourth floor of an office building with cameras embedded in keypads at the entrance of each of the floors. You had to wait for someone inside the panopticon to recognize your face in the lens by the door and buzz you in. The well-pressed staff replenished white bone chinaware and coffee, tea, and cakes twice a day.

Compared to the Danish activists in Copenhagen, who I thought would be most dismissive of Afropessimism, the gathering of academics in Berlin was a sad, milquetoast menagerie.

For the most part, dustups between academics seem to matter not one bit to people on the ground. All too often academics ascribe more gravitas to the stakes of their debates than is warranted. The dustup over and around Afropessimism is different, however. It is different not because of its importance to people within the academy. On the contrary, it is different because of the way it has captured the imaginations of Black people around the world. In Afropessimism, the imaginations of Black people on the ground, and the intellectual labors of Black people in revolt, have, finally, found an unflinching resonance in an ensemble of interventions being produced by Black intellectuals. One would think that the left-leaning intellectuals would find reason to rejoice in this. Afropessimism is not an ensemble of theoretical interventions that *leads* the struggle for Black liberation. One should think of it as a theory that is legitimate because it has secured a mandate from *Black people at their best*; which is to say, a mandate to speak the analysis and rage that most Black people are free only to whisper.

For some bonehead reason I thought these White academics in Berlin, and their Asian junior partner, would coalesce as a safe gathering to share what, under normal circumstances, should not be shared. The hint of sanctuary was in the invitation that Professors Ian Bryce and Helmut Jahn sent me. "At every turn, we will resist circumscribing the conference's subject in terms of date and place (i.e. May 1968, Paris 1968)," read the letter of invitation. It went on to suggest that the purpose of the conference was to challenge encrusted narratives by reflecting on how the fifty-year gestation of 1968 has allowed us to consider the period's new racial, sexual, and practical coalitions, both aesthetic and political, with new eyes.

"At every turn"? Maybe I turned too hard. But I believed that if any group of people were trained in the theory needed to discuss and debate Afropessimism's first principles, as a means of assessing 1968 with fresh eyes, that group was more likely to be the pedigreed Marxist scholars at the conference in Berlin than activists much younger and less pedigreed in Copenhagen.

Professor Ian Bryce was strong and stocky and not too tall. During the conference breaks, he picked his way between the conference table and the chairs, heading for the tea and coffee trolley like a pulling guard on an end-around play. I played outside linebacker in college and was flattened more than once by a pulling guard on an end-around sweep. But I didn't think Ian would lead the charge in Berlin. Indeed, I thought just the opposite, given the fact that in one of his emails to me, and then again in person, he said how much my critique of Antonio Gramsci's assumptive logic had aided him in writing his monograph on Pasolini. After the conference, I realized that he was no different from most White academics who dabble in Afropessimism for their own ends without regard for the fact that they are holding a grenade that has no pin. Afropessimism is a looter's creed: critique without redemption or a vision of redress except "the end of the world." In the hands of a Marxist academic it tends to be corrupted and contorted into something with no purchase for Black revolt. In hands such as these, hands that craft visions of antagonisms as dustups between the worker and the capitalist, and have no clear understanding that the *essential* antagonism is the antagonism between Blacks and the world, two birds are killed with one stone: the centrality of Black people's social death, the grammar of suffering of the Slave, is dispensed with or given short shrift; and, secondly, the imagination of the Slave (which often dreams of the world's undoing without being burdened by a vision of a new world, such as socialism or a liberated nation-state) is made to fit within the limits of what non-Black people have the stomach for. James Baldwin said it best, in his essay "The Black Boy Looks at the White Boy Norman Mailer," where he wrote about "the terrible gap between [Norman Mailer's] life and my own." It is a painful essay in which he explains how he experienced, through the beginning and ending of his "friendship" with Mailer, those moments when Blackness inspires White dreams of liberation, and how it felt when he suddenly realized the impossibility of the inverse: "[T]he really ghastly thing about trying to convey to a white man the reality of the Negro experience has nothing whatever to do with the fact of color, but has to do with this man's relationship to his own life. He will face in your life only what he is willing to face in his." His long Paris nights with Mailer bore fruit only to the extent that Mailer was able to say, "Me too." Beyond that was the void that Baldwin carried with him into and, subsequently, out of the "friendship." "I am afraid that most of the white people I have ever known impressed me as being in the grip of a weird nostalgia, dreaming of a vanished state of security and order, against which dream, unfailingly and unconsciously, they tested and very often lost their lives." He is writing about the encounters between Blacks and Whites in Paris and New York in the 1950s, but he may as well be writing about Ian and the posse that came for me at the Berlin conference on May 1968. In short, there was blood on the floor, and most of it was mine. But I could not imagine this when Ian Bryce called my name. Happily, I screened the two clips from *Punishment Park*. The lights came on and, in my lecture, I proffered the critique of the film that had been well received in the Copenhagen workshop: how and why the putative political solidarity between Nancy Jane Smith and Charles Robbins did not mitigate the structural antagonism that they embodied; how the film's unconscious dramatized this antagonism while disavowing it at the level of its conscious, narrative intent.

I concluded by saying that, rather than advance the project of revolution (both politically and aesthetically), the White radical revolts of the late 1960s and early 1970s, as well as well-intended films such as *Punishment Park*, when perceived through the Slave's eyes (Charles Robbins and the Black woman in the desert), did more to fortify and extend the interlocutory life of Western civil society than to hasten its overthrow.

I was stunned by the magnitude of the applause. More than once I was told how "elegant" and "sophisticated" my talk had been. Sandra Dove, a British art historian, even used the word *beautiful* in reflecting upon the élan of the prose. But the emotional resonance of those words was familiar. It's what Black women, and some men, experience when our hair is touched by a White person who doesn't ask permission but assumes that because this violation came with a compliment ("It's so soft"), you should, like a Lhasa Apso being petted, be grateful for their attention; it's what it means to be told, "You're so well spoken." You can make them swoon but it doesn't mean they're hearing what you say, it means they experience something close to orgasm in the way you say what you say. *Soul music!* Blowback occurs, however, as the lyrics to the song start to sink in. You can set your watch to the next three moments: *Guilt. Resentment. Aggression.* In Berlin, the clock struck resentment and aggression. The assembled professors skipped the hour of guilt.

It was then that Negrophobia kicked in, in a manner that was, to say the least, uncanny; uncanny in the sense that, for the next twenty minutes, we reenacted the same dynamics that characterized the interrogation of Charles Robbins by the *Punishment Park* tribunal. To be sure, the content of the "questions" the room fired at me were more diverse than a bowl of Fruit Loops, but they shared a common *affect* of hostility and patronizing condescension. On one level the scene was more, for lack of a better word, *civilized* than the tribunal. I was not handcuffed and chained to a chair and the ten members of the conference had no prosecutorial powers over me. But one could argue that the professorial code of civility made the interrogation more bizarre than what Charles Robbins endured.

In short order, the group's capacity for logic and debate disintegrated into righteous indignation at the way, as they saw it, I played "fast and loose with the film"; at my lack of appreciation for "the bonds of love that had been forged" in the 1960s between people like Charles Robbins and Nancy Jane Smith; and, finally, indignation at my claim that non-Black people of color (White civil society's junior partners) have something to salvage, whereas Blacks have nothing to lose—that

Asians and Blacks are structural antagonists *even when they are joined together in coalition fighting for civil and human rights.*

7

Professor Li-ling Chen took issue with Asians being cast as the junior partners of White civil society. She did not take issue, however, in the form of an engagement with and/or critique of my analysis. She simply said how "mad" it all made her; as though the most important thing to consider was how non-Blacks *felt* when critiqued rather than the material impact on Black lives that *necessitated* the critique to begin with. (Mobs might ask you if you really raped that woman or robbed that man as they string you up but rarely do they quiet down and wait for an answer.) I felt like I'd been cast as the facilitator of a group therapy session and I had asked the wrong question (or the right question), which sparked a chain reaction. I had, however, both unleashed this chain reaction and become the repository of its smoldering transference.

Ian Bryce led the charge. The way his chin thrust out when he spoke, and the small, involuntary cannonballs of breath that burst between his words bore a resemblance to Reg in Seattle as he steered young Luke to the parking lot; a man I had seldom conjured in more than fifty years.

Bryce began with an obliquely motivated form of chastisement. He complained that throughout my entire presentation he had heard the name "Peter Watkins" only once. He accused me of mounting an unsophisticated reading of the film—of not respecting the film as a cultural object. He accused me of casting the film itself as a transparent reflection of what happened in the segment of scenes during which Charles Robbins was interrogated. He wanted more "thick description" of the film, more exegesis on it as a work of art (in keeping, no doubt, with the other presentations at the conference).

I told him that my points of attention lay elsewhere. I could have added, Had you been paying attention, you would have heard how I touched upon the cinematic strategies of the film *which make the very case you say is too reductive*, that the film does in fact labor in ways that accompany—rather than critique—the anti-Black racism Robbins endures in the tribunal. *And, furthermore, it doesn't matter that the director thinks he's doing something different. What matters is how the film labors.*

But I didn't say this because I (naïvely) expected Bryce to respond by saying to me, Okay, so tell me about your points of attention. Sorry to harp on about what you did not do, let's use the little time we have productively, by discussing your presentation on its own terms.

That would have made too much sense. He had built up a head of steam or, more accurately, short little choo-choo train puffs of exasperation. He was the Little Engine That Could, huffing and puffing up the hill, pulling the others up the track behind him.

As Ian Bryce cloaked his exasperation about my lack of devotion to the film as a cultural object, another professor, Arthur Winter, cloaked his exasperation in a similar, Jesuit-like devotion to the history of the film as a cultural object: the context, in 1971, of *Punishment Park*'s production and distribution.

"Don't you realize," a prosaic translation of his remarks would read, "Peter Watkins was a White man who was in solidarity with people like Charles Robbins? Don't you realize that in the making and exhibition of this film he suffered for Black people?" In other words, Winter took it upon himself to school me, to tell me what I already knew and knew well. With the kind of restrained incredulity one employs when Little Johnny spills his milk on the floor for the *third time* (*damn it!*), Arthur Winter took pains to explain to me that *Punishment Park* and

Peter Watkins were viciously attacked in the press and on college campuses (when the film was screened there) for dramatizing a paranoid vision of America, and for being a foreigner who hates America.

The tribunal was enraged with Robbins because America had proffered a helping hand to Blacks (albeit discreetly) and his violent insurgency smacked of ingratitude. Professor Winter was saying the same to me—with Watkins as stand-in for the state. "One cannot be Black," Frantz Fanon once warned, "with impunity."

"No theaters would show the film," Winter protested. "And it was pulled in less than a week from the one obscure theater where it was screened." His eyes sent out distress signals. A flurry of hands waved to be recognized by Ian Bryce. Winter's voice seemed to crack; as though I had besmirched, not a filmmaker whom he had never met, but a close and revered relation. *This is family*, his tone betrayed. He ignored people whose hands were raised. He rushed on before Ian Bryce gave someone else the floor.

"When Watkins brought it to college campuses he was *attacked* by professors in the audience."

Winter gave a pitch for the angels. My eyes began to mist. I was sure he would end with a motion to put Watkins's name forward for sainthood or Friend of the Negro. Winter's commentary sputtered to an end as he reminded me that the end of the scene with Charles Robbins (Robbins being bound and gagged in the tent of the tribunal) was a cinematic quotation of the Chicago 8 trial, in which Bobby Seale was bound and gagged. His point being, in case I didn't get it, that this cinematic quotation, coupled with the hell Peter Watkins caught when he went on tour with the film and with the way the film was panned by the critics, is exemplary of how the film was in solidarity with my project and with the plight of Charles Robbins and the unnamed Black woman who was riddled with bullets in *Punishment Park*.

I laughed, for I had no wish to insult Winter by taking him seriously. But he wasn't joking. He was as pumped up and as serious as Ian Bryce had been when he chastised me for doing an end run around the aesthetic integrity of *Punishment Park*.

From the far side of the room, Bryce and Winter's professorial twaddle was modestly baptized by Professor Helmut Jahn, who nodded and grumbled into his neck, "I too worried about the place of history in your presentation."

The floodgates widened. More voices poured in. Sometimes people spoke over each other, as though they had arrived so late to the lynching they needed to push against the spines of others to get a closer look, or a better stab, at that not-quite-Human hanging in the tree.

It was what my students would call a "total mind fuck," in the sense that this scenario of charged affect in service to the most hysterical display of Negrophobogenisis was, *first*, projected onto the screen in the conference room, in the form of Charles Robbins's clip from *Punishment Park*, and then reenacted in the room by the people at the conference. In other words, the tribunal interrogation of Charles Robbins involved nothing on the order of a dispute between communist and capitalist *ideas*, nor was it, as in the interrogation of Nancy Jane Smith, a dispute between two divergent views about moral hygiene. Charles Robbins had been structurally barred from the dynamic of reciprocity. This structural injunction was what characterized the conference—and this characterization is exemplary of what happens to Black voices when those voices make arguments that are predicated on a theory of violence that (a) does not apply to all suffering people and (b) suggests that even people who suffer from the scourge of White supremacy, capitalism, and gender oppression are, *simultaneously*, agents and beneficiaries of anti-Black violence. Such arguments blow the lid off the unconscious as evinced by the fact that they stir a

communal wrath of half sentences, strong moods, and wagons beginning to circle. This is what Sebastiaan, a Canadian graduate student
who had introduced himself to me outside an *imbiss** the night before,
meant when he described the room's meltdown and its aggressivity
as "what Fanon might have called a tear in the psychic infrastructure of the conference on 1968; which is to also say that the work of
Afropessimism was accomplished, if only for a moment" in that Berlin
conference room.

The uncanny kicked in again. I experienced the same sensation
that I experienced the first time I saw the scene of the unnamed Black
woman, facedown in the desert of *Punishment Park*, when several L.A.
County sheriffs riddled her back with bullets. The conference room's
cacophony of raw exasperation mimicked the dry pop of gunshots
(and the voice snarling, "Get the bitch") as the hot and thirsty cops
stood on a ridge above her and spent all their ammo.

To my dismay, this affect was just as intense when two of the
women—a White woman, Professor Sandra Dove, and the Asian
woman, Professor Li-ling Chen—spoke. In some respects there was
an odd honesty to how those two women spoke. My presentation was
underwritten by the claim that everyone in the room was a structural
antagonist to me, to Charles Robbins, and to the unnamed Black
woman who was killed in *Punishment Park*. Everyone else had given
a presentation that was underwritten by the assumptive logic that the
structural antagonism was between workers (of whatever race, gender,
or nationality) and the capitalists of the world. Confrontation with a
lecture, mine, that argued that exploitation and alienation (the generative mechanism of the antagonism between the proletariat and the
capitalist) was *a mere conflict*, a struggle occasioned and allowed by the
essential antagonism between Blacks (Slaves) and Humans (masters),

---

* A German word that means a small food stand or street food shop.

made the professors in Berlin suffer from what Jared Sexton has called "the anxiety of antagonism."

The White men (Ian Bryce, Arthur Winter, and Helmut Jahn) had responded symptomatically, speaking away from the source of their trauma, knitting their brows as they conjured red herrings about my ahistoricism and my display of bad faith with respect to yeoman efforts on the part of Peter Watkins and the bleeding heart of his film.

The honesty of Sandra Dove and Li-ling Chen manifested itself in the fact that *they* actually had something to say about my presentation, unlike the White men who had something to say about what I didn't say. This is not to cathedralize the wisdom of Dove and Chen. Sandra Dove and Li-ling Chen were "saddened" and "angered," respectively, by my presentation. The honesty of their interventions (meaning, their scattered sound bites) manifested itself in the fact that they responded to what I had said. The *perverted* nature of their honesty was due to the fact that their responses did *not* manifest in an actual engagement of my argument but, instead, foregrounded the way my lecture made them *feel*: Sandra Dove felt hurt and disappointed—perhaps betrayed; Li-ling Chen was angry and at her wits' end.

Li-ling and I had met at academic gatherings several times in the past. So, on day one in Berlin, we had embraced and sat beside each other at the table. I had offered her cough drops and nodded in that amen-corner sort of way whenever she skewered a Deleuzian intervention by two prior speakers, whose arguments were theoretical accompaniments to neoliberal individualism rather than a blast of social iconoclasm that Deleuze and his spiritual progenitors anoint themselves as having. We were soul mates on the rampage; and might still have remained so had I not taken the critique of neoliberalism over a line she was not prepared to cross.

And, on day one as well, Sandra Dove had winked at me from where she sat at the other end of the table; that universal wink of friendship between the races.* And I, never chary with my charms, flashed my fifty-two teeth. I returned from a bathroom break to find her in the seat next to mine. She introduced herself and asked if it was all right to sit beside me. The sun was beating on her back where she had been sitting, she explained. I was sandwiched, snuggly, between Dove and Chen; and this had given me comfort. For, surely, Dove and Chen would be alive to what I had to say! I thought Sandra Dove and I were in a groove. There's nothing more deadly than Negro self-delusion that makes one forget that there can be no love without hatred. Guilt. Resentment. Aggressivity. The clock ticked on.

The force of their honesty was of a piece with the angry avoidance of the White men. In other words, Dove and Chen spoke to the presentation itself (foregrounding how hurt and angry they were by it), while simultaneously fortifying and extending the lynching *affect* that preceded them when the White men spoke. Their words were different than the words of the White men but the affect was of a piece; and, in this way, they mapped a cultural formation across gender and race, sutured by a shared anti-Blackness and, most importantly, subtended by their communal capacity for violence. *The community had been wronged; now it was time to get some justice.*

Instead of working through and *then* against my argument and the archive of critical literature that scaffolded it—something she was quite capable of and had done so well in her skewering of the faux-politics of Deleuze and in her own presentation and critique of Winnicott's theory by way of Lacan—Li-ling Chen sidestepped the archive of Afropessimism as well as my lecture's thesis. In other words, rather than debate the thesis she found to be so objectionable, she simply pronounced her objection ("Afropessimism is absolute and totalizing"!) and she then proceeded to foreground the way it made her feel.

---

* Or perhaps I'm mistaken and there was simply a mote in her eye.

"I am so angry!" "It makes me so angry!" "I don't want to say anything, because I'll get angry at Frank if I have to speak, and we're friends." She must have seen my eyebrow arch when she said *friends* because she blurted the same sentence out again, "I don't want to say anything, because I'll get angry at Frank if I have to speak," and modified the ending with "and we're *colleagues*"; before extolling for the third time, "And I'm *tired* and I'm *hungry* and I want to go to *lunch*!"

Not everyone in the room was stricken with multiple anxiety disorders, however. But of the six out of ten people who spoke, Professor Tilsen McMann was the only one who wasn't.

Tilsen McMann actually tried to reason with Chen. Indeed, he tried to reason with the entire room. He said that my critique mattered because my argument was cogent and had to be attended to. McMann noted the resonances between my presentation and Li-ling Chen's presentation, in which she, Chen, demonstrated how "Left cultural politics of 1968 created an opportunity for the Right to emerge as both a defender of tradition and as a pseudo-populist force."

It was clear that McMann was *not* saying that Li-ling Chen and Frank Wilderson were on the same page politically; or that our archives had anything in common. What he was saying was that if Chen and the rest of the room could tamp down the rage, we could have a decent conversation and debate about the two presentations that were similar to each other (and unlike most of what had preceded); how Chen's and Wilderson's talks were similar by virtue of the fact that they opened up a way for us to discuss overarching political and paradigmatic forces that affected the activism and aesthetics of 1968, and which continues today.

McMann was saying, Isn't it wonderful that you both share this penchant for analysis of larger political forces?

Li-ling Chen retaliated, "My work is *nothing* like Frank's! I don't go around the world saying Chinese women are the most oppressed people on the planet." (Presumably, the way Wilderson goes around the world saying Black people are the most oppressed people on the planet.)

Professor McMann was astonished and dismayed. He tried to reason with her again. But she repeated how angry it was going to make her if she had to talk about this and how much she wanted to go to lunch. McMann, no doubt, had not counted on the force of her unconscious manifesting itself with such tenacious fixation in her conscious speech. But the unconscious is a faith-based initiative where reason has no purchase.

Had there been ten Tilsen McManns in the room instead of the ten who were there, we might have had robust engagement—which is not to say he is an Afropessimist; nor is it to say that I would require that. Of the one hundred forty people in Folkets Hus in Copenhagen, and the thirty people in the workshop that preceded my speech, I would not presume that more than a handful actually *agreed* with me or with Afropessimism. But it didn't matter. Agreement was not my prerequisite. Honest engagement was. But the resonance between the FBI's document on Black identity extremism and the psychic infrastructure of Chen's objections to what she views as my brand of oppression Olympics is stronger than the resonance between her political analysis and mine.

Finally, Sandra Dove spoke. She was unwavering in her belief that Black men are *not* structurally vulnerable to White women. She believed that *all* women are structurally vulnerable to *all* men; as though female slave masters were disempowered in the face of their male slaves; or as though the paradigm of slavery is a thing of the past unreplicated in the present. Sandra Dove had been betrayed; and for several minutes she oscillated between lashing the whip and displaying her stigmata.

Earlier, during the screening of the Nancy Jane Smith segment, I sensed from the way Sandra Dove's laughter championed the feminist salvos Nancy Jane Smith hurled back at her sexually uptight interrogators that Dove might have difficulty with the way *I* critiqued both Nancy Jane Smith and the tribunal; with the way I characterized their display of hatred for one another as little family feuds that would end by strengthening the bonds between them *even if they killed* Nancy Jane Smith. Perhaps this is why my analysis seems to have hurt Sandra Dove so deeply. By way of Nancy Jane Smith, Sandra Dove was not only being critiqued but, in some respects, ridiculed for the puniness of the demand that emanates from White female suffering in the face of White male patriarchy.

The force of Sandra Dove's objections was as palpable as those of Li-ling Chen and the White men, and it came with the same sensation of victimization at the hands of a Black man. Perhaps she saw herself in coalition with the Black Panthers and she felt my presentation made a mockery of such desire. She was right, of course, but what gave her permission to not think twice before acting so pained in public, as though the legitimacy of my argument lay in how it made her feel? This is akin to the logic of several million football fans whose beef with the NFL protests is the fact that these protests interrupt their enjoyment (but the fact that we're being gunned down in the streets be damned).

Supplemental to the quality of her hurt was her expression of a deep sadness, for *me*. I had turned my back on the opportunity for a rich cultural connection that her plaintive voice told me she longed for. My thesis had snubbed her wink.

"What about coalitions?" she cried. "What about solidarity between the races?" Now Sandra Dove sat up straight, her cobalt eyes ablaze. She thrust her arm in the air and with her index finger pointed at the wall where a blank projection screen hung and said, "What about the picture we saw projected on the screen [one or two sessions before mine]—the photo of that beautiful interracial couple [a Black man, his White wife, their mixed-race child] from 1967, in Haight-Ashbury during the Summer of Love? Your presentation leaves no room for that photograph."

"My presentation shits on the inspiration of solidarity," I told her. "I don't give a rat's ass about solidarity."

Dove was an Oxbridge-educated don, who held her head so high as she scolded me she could drown in the rain. Her eyes widened at the sheer derision of my words. What, she must have wondered, happened to the friendly black face and those snowy teeth that had flashed when she winked the day before?

" That is *so* terrible," she groaned. "That is such a *shame*."

She went on to tell me that she had recently heard Angela Davis say that she had transcended the slave stature. She said this two or three times and I was about to ask her if she had heard of any other Black people when Ian Bryce ended the session and said it was time for lunch.

Sandra Dove stood up and blocked my way as I tried to leave. She said, once again, how sad I had made her. She then told me that, in the future, I needed to consider my audience when I give presentations. (!)

"Listen," I told her, "I'm not even talking to anyone in this room. Ever. When I talk, I'm talking to Black people. I'm just a parasite on the resources that I need to do work on behalf of Black liberation." Just as the world has always been a parasite on me in pursuit of its legibility and sense of presence. But I didn't need to say this, for she had moved to one side.

They went to lunch as a group. I did not join them. Instead, I went to lunch with Sebastiaan, the Canadian graduate student I'd met by chance the night before on a crowded Berlin street. Together, we debriefed. He was almost as shell-shocked as I was by what had just gone down. After lunch, I walked back to the building, collected my things, went back to the hotel, and packed. During the afternoon session, Ian Bryce emailed me:

Hi Frank, Are you OK? We're having our final roundtable here. Would love for you to be here. Ian.

One never really knows which is more severe, the blithe disregard one suffers at the hands of White people or the pious remorse with which they purify themselves.

8

You think you've seen it all, and you have. You met Sandra Dove when she sipped gin and lemonade and flicked her cigarette out the kitchen window. She called herself Celina Davenport. Celina Davenport was the *present* that packed her bags to meet you in the future, in Berlin, just to say she still didn't like your answers to her questions; that when you speak she hears only the noise of death drawing water. She winked, mistaking you for Eros, and you betrayed her in the worst way possible, when you could have thrived as a scalped-down duplicate of her desire.

Once, once, and once, in the same tree you were born. Sandra and Celina, Ian and Reg, Li-ling and all the Indians who chafe at the sound of a "nigger's" voice, gaze up at the branches and say, "Look what you made us do to you." You twitch apologetically. The last seeds of light are dying in your eyes.

You look down, and feel their pain.

II

The slave is the object or the ground that makes possible the existence of the bourgeois subject and, by negation or contra-distinction, defines liberty, citizenship, and the enclosures of the social body.

SAIDIYA V. HARTMAN

CHAPTER FIVE

The Trouble with Humans

1

In her meditation on slave women who had been raped, Saidiya Hartman impugned a thesis of the Marxist I held most dear, Antonio Gramsci, the father of cultural studies. She interrogated his theory of consent and, by extension, hegemony.* She argued, by way of case studies on the rape of Black women who had tried to prosecute their rapists (their masters) in a court of law, that the collective unconscious, *as well as the conscious discourse of nineteenth century legal statutes*, did not recognize consent as a possession of the slave. *Rape*, as a mode of injury, simply had no way of being translated when sexual violence against Black women was being adjudicated: there was no crime because there was no violation of consent. There was no violation of consent because consent was not a possession of a slave but an "extension of the master's prerogative." To be absurdist but no less correct, one would never say to an individual seen crushing an empty water

---

* *Scenes of Subjection: Terror, Slavery, and Self-Making in Nineteenth-Century America.*

bottle, "Did that water bottle consent to the way you are treating it?" What happens to the bottle of water is an extension of the prerogative of its owner. I read that book in the way that Hartman wanted it to be read: not as an account of history but as an allegory of the present. "I came into the world imbued with the will to find a meaning in things, my spirit filled with the desire to attain to the source of the world," Fanon writes, "and then I found that I was an object in the midst of other objects." In other words, Fanon tries to see himself as a subject, one imbued with the capacities of other subjects (consent being a key endowment). But Fanon is slapped upside the head with Hartman's lesson: he is not imbued with Human capacities. He would not be quite as shocked to learn that, as a worker, he lacked the capacity of a capitalist. All he need do is look at his bank account and his lack of ownership vis-à-vis the means of economic production. In other words, to face the realization that one is a worker and not a capitalist is far less traumatic than the realization that one is Black, a Slave, and not a Human. The former revelation is not nearly as traumatic as one in which the sentient being wakes up to find that she has no capacities for Human production; and, furthermore, comes to understand that just as economic production is parasitic on the labor power of the working class, the production of Human capacity is parasitic on the flesh of the Slave, the Black. As one must have capital (or natural resources) to be a capitalist, one must have a variety of *capacities* to be a Human being: consent is one of them. And this is vouchsafed by one's relationship to violence. The point that must be constantly repeated is that the Slave's/Black's relationship to violence bears no *essential* analogy to the Human's relationship to violence, even when those Human subjects represent extremely abused and degraded members of the Human family.

There's a television series that (unwittingly) drives this point home. It's called *Homeland*, and it's about the trials and tribulations of a mentally ill, bipolar CIA officer named Carrie Mathison. In one episode her cover is that of an investigative journalist who convinces the nephew of an Afghan Taliban leader that she can get him out of Islamabad and help him find safe haven in England. She convinces him that the two of them must stay holed up in a secret apartment for three days as transport is being arranged for his safe passage. It's all a lie. She's really using him as bait to lure his uncle into a trap, that she might assassinate his uncle. In point of fact, the apartment is a CIA safe house in which Carrie holds this young man captive. She then proceeds to seduce him; he thinks they are in the throes of some sort of love affair that is overdetermined by mutual consent.

In other words, he doesn't know that he is being raped . . . repeatedly raped . . . that his consent to this sex has been abrogated by the very structure of the conditions in which the sex takes place. It is a rape scenario because the sex that he mistakes for mutual attraction is really a series of multiple acts of aggression in which his consent has been eviscerated completely. The gun the White woman holds to his head needn't be in her hand. In fact, the gun she holds to his head is not one weapon but the weapons of three million soldiers in uniform and their arsenal of drones and technologies of death. She forces sex upon him through her capacity; the capacity that her white skin embodies. Another way of saying this is to say that White desire is always already weaponized. She forces sex on him through the capacity that White bodies have to weaponize White desire. The young Afghan man is fucked! He is fucked at every level of abstraction. The guns are in the bedroom (Carrie Mathison's hidden pistol). The guns are also pointed at his head from outside in the street: the CIA operatives who watch the house. And the guns are held to his head from high above, in the nine thousand drones that saturate the sky and track him as he makes his way back to Carrie's genuine objective—his uncle, whom she hopes to murder at long range with a drone strike.

Here we have a pristine example of the ways in which White femininity *and* White masculinity occupy the same *structural* position vis-à-vis a man or a woman of color. To paraphrase Frantz Fanon: the White family is a cutout of the state. Jared Sexton puts a finer point on this dynamic. We encountered his assessment in our discussion of *Punishment Park*, the Peter Watkins film in which Richard Nixon has declared martial law and sent young dissidents to the desert tribunal. In that film, we observed that though Nancy Jane Smith, on the one hand, and Charles Robbins and the unnamed Black woman in the desert, on the other hand, are all ideologically committed to the overthrow of the United States, to the end of the war in Vietnam, and to the establishment of a socialist or communist state, Nancy Jane Smith is their antagonist at the level of species, structure, and capacity. They are her slaves regardless of the fact that her conscious mind would recoil at the thought that she exists as a member of the same species as the people on the Punishment Park tribunal who are about to execute her. Let's hit the high points of Sexton's assessment of White femininity vis-à-vis the Black man (and, by extension the Black woman and/or Black transgender person).

- *She has a limited capacity to marshal state violence or state-sanctioned paramilitary violence against Black people of all genders and ages.*
- *She can have Black people of all genders and ages brutalized for transgressions real or imagined.*
- *She can also rape a Black man (as the CIA agent raped the Afghan boy), thereby reversing the polarity of a rape fantasy pervasive in the anti-Black world; regardless of his size and strength, his prowess and his pride, he is structurally vulnerable to her.*

In other words, the capacity for anti-Black violence is embedded in the ontology of the White woman's being; it is part and parcel of her Human inheritance. Sexton is careful *not* to include the young Afghan man being raped by a White woman, as I have (and which I will correct momentarily). Instead, he homes in on the specificity of the Black male in relation to the woman who is White.

Saidiya Hartman's historical explanation of the paradigm of anti-Black sexual violation concurs with Sexton's synchronic explanation of the paradigm: "[E]nslaved men were no less vulnerable to the wanton abuses of their owners, although the extent of their sexual exploitation will probably never be known, and because of the elusiveness or instability of gender in relation to the slave as property and the erotics of terror in the racist imaginary."

Geopolitical agendas of the White nation cannot be disentangled from the sex life of White femininity (and White masculinity). In other words, White sexuality is always weaponized. To put it differently, but no less to the point, the United States of America is a big, bad rapist; a big, bad rapist that *projects* the fantasy of *its* vulnerability onto Muslims, Mexicans, Native Americans, and Blacks. Fanon discusses the rape fantasy of the White woman in great detail in *Black Skin, White Masks*. I won't rehearse it here. For our purposes we should note that the rapist projects the fantasy of vulnerability by suggesting that she or he is the victim of Islamic jihadism or the victim of Black agitation and civil disobedience against killings by cops.

The big, bad rapist would have us believe that *America* is the victim; and underneath that phantasmagoric projection, underneath the fantasy of vulnerability, is a set of assumptions that America is indeed an ethical social and political formation; that the problems that America has are *not* structural, but rather that they are performative (that is, to be found in acts of discrimination or in the use of excessive levels of force). None of this would be a problem if not for the structure of violence that subtends this fantasy, the institutional violence that gives these fantasies what David Marriott calls "objective value."

Jared Sexton gives a concrete explanation of David Marriott's phrase "objective value" when he says, "You better understand White people's fantasies because tomorrow they'll be legislation." That's what the law is: White fantasies as objective value.

The White family and the White state have the firepower and the institutional infrastructure to enforce their projections. What people of color get to do when they go to the polls is decide what flavor of this rape fantasy they are going to support. In the words of George Jackson, "An electoral choice of ten different fascists is like choosing which way one wishes to die."

Voting is an important *performance* of dispossession for people of color who are *not* Black. But for Black people, voting is not just a performance of dispossession. We have to dig deeper and see how the very bedrock, the structure, the very paradigm of electoral politics is predicated on sexualized violence against Black people. Sexualized violence against Black people is electoral politics' *condition of possibility*!

From Willie Horton to gerrymandering to the auction block, anti-Blackness is the genome of electoral politics. In short, anti-Blackness is the genetic material of this organism called the United States of America. The fantasy projections that had been weaponized to rape the young Afghan man would not be possible if the paradigm of the weaponization were not already in place prior to the conflict between Muslims and the U.S.; and that weaponized paradigm is overdetermined by anti-Blackness. The U.S. government *could* become a democracy for people of color who are not Black (it's not likely, but it is entirely possible); but if it ever rid itself of the central ingredient that overdetermines its condition of possibility—that is to say, if the United States of America were to somehow not be anti-Black—then we would no longer have a country; the United States of America would cease to exist. Just as tomatoes overdetermine gazpacho soup! No tomatoes, no gazpacho. No anti-Blackness, no nation.

I've explained how the U.S. is an anti-Black polity by using a synchronic analysis of domesticity. Let me now point to how it is also *historically* unethical: how the U.S. is diachronically anti-Black. A recent history book does this job of diachronic explanation brilliantly. It's called *The American Slave Coast: A History of the Slave-Breeding Industry*, by Ned and Constance Sublette. A small portion of the book focuses on the Electoral College.

The Electoral College is a prime example of a so-called "democratic" institution that owes its *condition of possibility* to the sexualized violence against, and captivity of, Black people. Without the sexualized violence against and mass incarceration of hundreds of thousands of Black captives, Americans would not be able to elect a U.S. president. Thomas Jefferson would never have become president. In the late eighteenth and early nineteenth centuries, "389,000 [that's less than a half million] . . . African slaves, bred like horses or sheep, became four-million enslaved African-Americans . . . [T]he forced mating of slaves . . . gave slave states more voting power based on the number of slaves they held captive." Virginia was the largest slave-breeding state. As a result it gained twenty-five percent of the forty-six Electoral College votes, more than enough to send Jefferson to the White House.

Think about that. The kind of captivity needed to breed slaves dwarfs the kind of captivity Muslims are subjected to in Guantánamo or in the "love nest" where the female CIA agent raped the young Afghan. How else can 389,000 people be made to procreate, under pain of torture or death, into 4 million people if they are not incarcerated and forced into sex? Slave-breeding is a kind of forced sex that makes words like *rape* and *incarceration* puny and inadequate. The young Afghan man had a prior moment of freedom, and a prior space of consent, before the White woman held him captive and raped him. For Blacks there is no prior space and time of freedom and consent: the freedom of all others—in the form of electoral politics—owes its condition of possibility to the unfreedom (lack of consent) of and sexualized violence against Black people. People of color *experience this madness from time to time*; but the forced procreation of Blackness is the bedrock of this madness.

The young Afghan's rights were violated by the White woman; but the *concept* of rights that can be violated, or respected, rises up out of the breeding of Blacks like cattle. You can speak of prisoners' rights, but the term *slave rights* is an oxymoron.

A historical analysis of the Electoral College illustrates how Black people are political *currency*, not political *subjects*. And that is the paradigm of Black people's existence today. Black people are political currency or objects, not political actors or subjects. Subjects have homes, or at least the capacity for some sort of sanctuary. Objects exist as implements, tools, in the psychic life of Human subjects.

Hartman's analysis of the paradox that the idea of rape presents for the woman who is Black, who is a slave, alerted me to the fact that this universal possession of the oppressed and the oppressor—*consent*—wasn't universal at all. Consent was *not* an inherent, organic capacity, an element of political ontology that belonged to everyone, high and low. My mind abstracted in ever-widening concentric circles: if the Black woman cannot be raped because she had no consent to give or withhold, and if this absence of consent is both particular and general—in other words, if it applies broadly to the status of Blackness, and not only to the status of Black women who come before the court as plaintiffs in nineteenth century courts, and if, qua Sexton, the Black man can by raped by the White woman, and if (the culminating and most devastating *if*) "rape" is too feeble a concept to explain the violation* of Black flesh—then all of us who are marked as Black are of a different species than all of those who are not. We

---

* Here, words fail us again! For how can an object be violated?

are a species of sentient beings that cannot be injured or murdered, for that matter, because we are dead to the world. No narrative arc of dispossession can accrue to us. What do I mean by that? Just this: for there to be a narrative arc the persona in the narrative must move from possession to dispossession to (the denouement) the prospect of repossession. Another way of earmarking the points on the narrative arc would be: Equilibrium to disequilibrium to equilibrium (restored, renewed, and/or reimagined). Rape can be seen on this arc: consent as an ontological and social possession: followed by rape, which would be dispossession of consent: followed by consent restored via the trial of the perp, or his/her murder, or the narrative could explain how the victim regained their self-esteem and self-worth even if justice was not done. But even here, when the denouement does not include justice, there is an *assumption* that the victim had a "self" to be violated. In other words, no matter how you slice it, no matter the details of the arc, the narrative arc *itself* is possible because there exists within the ontology of the subject the Human capacity of consent that could be restored just as it was taken away.

This kind of logic makes no sense when thinking of the slave. Nor is the argument that all of this changed in 1865 in the slightest way convincing—it is not an argument, it is a sentimental assertion, mobilized by the interlocutor's fear of thinking slavery as a relational dynamic; the interlocutor insists that slavery is a historical event, a thing of the past. Such assertions are exemplary of the anxiety of antagonism. My breakdown in graduate school was of a piece with this anxiety. As a creative writer and as a critical theorist I could not fathom thoughts of myself as a sentient being exiled from the arc of narrative. And, to further complicate matters, I was in love with a White woman; and this meant that though we were partners in important ways, I was her slave at the level of what was essential about our relationship. I had fled the hell of the war in South Africa, and landed in the war in my mind. I was left with nothing—no enemies and no allies. Enemies and allies, war and solidarity, require Human capacity; a possession that had never been mine. Uppers and downers were my two best friends.

My mental breakdown didn't break me, not on the outside anyway. Perhaps, if I had really barked like a puppy at the nurse at the UC Berkeley psych clinic who looked at me as though I were a puppy, they would have held me for "observation." And who knows when or if I would have been released back into the graduate school population? But I did not bark, nor ask for a doggy biscuit. I went on with my Ph.D. studies in critical theory in the Rhetoric Department at the University of California, Berkeley, writing papers, attending classes and conferences, getting straight A's along the way. No one but my partner (and later my wife) Alice knew that I was on two highly dissonant forms of medication. And she did not understand the bomb that splayed so much shrapnel in my brain. We were lovers and antagonists; and the antagonism was constantly erupting to sabotage our naïve and quintessentially American view that "love conquers all." I knew, if only intuitively, that love had already been conquered by violence. But I refused to believe that anti-Black violence was a healing balm for the Human mind.

The realization that Black suffering is of a different order than the suffering of other oppressed people, and that Black suffering is the life force of the world, was waiting for the two of us eighty miles down the road.

Six months before the Twin Towers fell, I drove with Alice, a White woman I first dated, upon my return from living in South Africa for five years, then lived with, and finally married, down the rugged coast to a conference in Santa Cruz called the Race Rave.

Alice and I met in South Africa, when I was still married to a South African woman named Khanya. One of my assignments as an underground insurgent was to spy on Americans who came to South Africa; to sidle up to them and find out why they were there; to then write dossiers for my handlers. This included attending American expatriate functions to suss out who might be tied to the U.S. military or intelligence communities. I developed a knack for making people I met *want* to tell me about themselves and why they were there.

When someone found out that I was an American who was also an elected official in Mandela's party, they would sometimes reveal their agendas to me *not* by directly divulging their agenda, but indirectly, by the *questions they asked me (which suggested how much they already knew) about the inner workings of the ANC*. Afterward, I went home and stayed up until the wee hours of the morning typing out my reports. This was low-grade intelligence, more dust and gossip than gold, that I passed up the food chain. I only knew what was made of it on rare occasions, as when I found out an American "businessman" posing as an affirmative action consultant had, at one time, been an agent for the Department of the Treasury, and had worked in the Congo for the U.S. puppet Mobutu Sese Seko. Alice Wilson was the subject of one of my reports. She arrived, on sabbatical, at the end of 1992 to do research for world literature courses she taught at a college in Northern California. Nadine Gordimer and I had been friends and literary events collaborators for a year when Alice arrived. I introduced her to Nadine Gordimer, right after Gordimer won the Nobel Prize in Literature.

In February 2001, Alice and I attended the Race Rave conference at the University of Santa Cruz. Between two hundred and three hundred activists, scholars, students, and people who were non-academic workers or precariously employed met "to explore racism and the intersections of oppression, to promote reparations and healing, and to develop the framework for a truth and reconciliation process in the

United States." It was billed as the first of a series of such gatherings on college campuses across the country.

At the end of the day, we gathered in a large room. The two organizers told us to break into groups that reflected how we were seen by the police. This meant that there would be a White group, a Black group, a Brown group, a Red or Native American group, and a Yellow group.

I remember thinking, *At last, now we'll move from a politics of culture to a culture of politics.* The whispers sent out by a few of the Black people seated near me confirmed my feeling. A sister near me sighed as though she had been holding her breath for the past day and a half and said, "Now *we* get to talk." A brother seated in front of her chuckled. "Didn't know *Black* was in their vocabulary."

The resistance started before the exercise started; and it didn't come from the Whites. It came from the non-Black people of color— the Yellows, the Browns, and the Reds who didn't want to be known by their color, not even for two hours. They insisted that they were not simply colors but cultural identities.

In contrast, the Blacks, spurred by our joy at the opportunity to speak about the way state violence functions in our lives, were already at the door. But the commotion in the center of the room made us turn and look back. It felt as though a seismic tremor had cracked the parquet floor, split the room in half, leaving a small group of slaves adrift by the door, while the Humans argued about their cultural identities in the middle of the room.

The non-Black people of color were angry, in a scene not unlike my presentation in Berlin. They demanded a say in how they were categorized. The organizers did their best to speak over those in the crowd who wouldn't listen. They said that being pigeonholed was the whole point; that the police *treated* you as a color and ignored your cultural and ethnic singularities; and the point of the exercise was to assume that formation and see what came of the discussion. That's the exercise! Let's get to it! Right on! roared up from the Blacks waiting in the wings.

And it might have gone down like that. But something unexpected happened. One group of people who had formed part of this scrum of discontent became more vocal than the rest. But they didn't voice their objections on the basis of cultural integrity. In fact, they mobilized the same term as the organizers, *race*; but they mobilized race in service to the aims and objectives of the non-Black people of color who insisted on a *politics of culture* (versus the *culture of politics* that had animated the Black folks). It was weird, but it "worked." They were biracial (one Black parent and one White parent) and they didn't want to be "pigeonholed" as Black (though they didn't say that they would be just as irate to be "pigeonholed" as White).

As I watched the so-called biracial, half-Black/half-White people make their case for why they did not want to be grouped as Black, I was struck by how their argument in no way resembled the logic of the people of color; and by how little that mattered—meaning *no one checked them on this contradiction*. Rather than assert the specificity of their cultural heritage and ethnic origins—and why the catchall colors assigned to them would be an erasure of those cultural markers— the biracial people argued that the four colors (Red, White, Brown, and Black) did not account for them. They were neither Black nor White. They were both; and as amalgamations, they deserved their own room.

The two organizers were stunned. Stymied. But not by the argument—a child could have countered by simply saying, None of y'all look like zebras; and no pig would put you in a lineup of White perps, or blast you in the shoulder instead of the heart because he could tell your momma was White. Y'all *read* as Black, so go to the Black room and stop wasting our time! Perhaps the child would have said it without the clarity and rancor I've imposed, but nonetheless, it's not a difficult objection to handle, especially given the fact that the biracial people did not interrogate the assumptive logic, as was the case with the others; they simply said, "You haven't given us the right color room."

Why did the organizers look like deer in headlights; and, more importantly, what made them cave in?

It was the affect, the verve, the energy, the bodily performance of the biracial contingent. They postured and gesticulated in a manner more stereotypically "Black" than biracial. In other words, their loud talk, their indignation, their runaway slave rage made the organizers quake.

It was a different affect than the affect of the people of color. The non-Blacks had pleaded, whined, cajoled. The biracial contingent, to quote Queen Latifah, *Got buck with the muthafuckas!* They pressed a hyperbolic, N.W.A. performance of Blackness into service of their desire to be as far away from Blackness as they could. It worked like a charm. The organizers, confronted with the sound and fury of Black rage (cynically divorced from Black desire), gave the biracial people a room of their own. And, by necessity, they caved in to the other people who wanted to be grouped by culture, *not* color. Black affect (or the Blaxploitation of Black affect) had been weaponized for the death of Black desire.

Each group was given the same sheet of paper with the same instructions and discussion topics. The sheet of paper also included a charge: we were to come up with ways to talk about what happened in our groups with our "allies," when we returned to plenary ninety minutes later.

The first thing the Blacks did when we were alone and the door was closed was to tear the sheet up and throw it away. We realized that the regime of violence through which we were subjugated could not be reconciled with the regime of violence that subjugated our so-called allies; and what had happened in the auditorium confirmed this. In other words, what the organizers had unleashed was a realization that oppression has two, not one, regimes of violence: the violence that subjugates the subaltern and the violence that subjugates the Slave, or the Black.

Once we had liberated ourselves from the constraints of having to make our suffering analogous to the suffering of the people of color, something truly profound occurred. For me, someone who was beginning to move from Marxism to what would a year later be called Afropessimism, the session was instructive because I was able to see and feel how comforting it was for a room full of Black people to move between the spectacle of police violence, to the banality of microaggressions at work and in the classroom, to the experiences of chattel slavery as if the time and intensity of all three were the same. No one, absolutely *no one*, said, "Hey hold on," for example, when a young woman said she was forced to breast-feed all the White people at her job like she'd done on the plantation. No one said, "You're speaking metaphorically, right?" The room simply said amen and right on. The time of chattel slavery was the time of our lives. And this was not a problem, as some psychoanalysts would have it, of neurotic conflation between the imaginary and the symbolic. In other words, this was not a failure of our collective psyches to restore state violence to relational logic, to separate, that is, the time of chattel slavery from the time of discrimination, or to separate the space of the whipping posts from the cartography of the office. It was a collective recognition that the time and space of chattel slavery shares essential aspects with the time and space, the violence, of our modern lives.

Folks cried and laughed and hugged each other and called out loud for the end of the world. No one poured cold water on this by asking, What does that mean—the end of the world? How can you say that? Where's that going to leave us? Or, How will we make sense of *the end of the world* when we go back to speak with our "allies"? The dangerous fuse of the Black imagination had been lit by nothing more than the magic of an intramural conversation. No one wanted it to end.

With thirty minutes left in the session a sense of dread set in: the organizers would soon be calling us back into *that* dreaded auditorium. Someone floated the idea of not returning; of just going home. But someone else came up with a better idea: we would go back in and refuse to speak with them. Not a protest, just a silent acknowledgment of the fact that we would not corrupt what we experienced with their demand for articulation between their grammar of suffering and ours.

Now there was movement outside our door. We looked up, thinking that the organizers had recalled us early. But when we opened the door we found that it wasn't the organizers but the entire group of biracial people, people whose hyperbolic "Blackness" had rescued them from our room. They were greeted with grunts and cold stares. One of them asked if they could come in. Silence.

I broke the silence by saying, "You never left." They entered and sat down, cautiously. We made room for them, just as cautiously. We asked them why they decided to join us.

Their discussion had centered on the presumptuous notion that they could access the social capital of civil society. Their talk had been vertically integrated from discussions about what a special place on the U.S. Census could mean for their mobility and their quest for recognition on what they had described as their "own terms," to the gut-wrenching conflicts they experienced in the tussle of allegiance in their individual family lives. In other words, how do we honor both parents, both of our White and Black cultural heritages? But this discussion didn't have the gravitas needed for ninety minutes; so, eventually, they turned to the topic they had been given—their relationship to and experience with police violence. It wasn't long before they realized that to meditate on this through their biracialism wasn't going to get them anywhere. No cop had ever said, Look here, I'm going to shoot you in the shoulder and not the heart because you're only half Black.

When we returned to plenary, the room took note of us—all of us.

Someone said, "I want some of what that group has!"

We hadn't spoken a word.

Another person said, "Look at all that love!"

We still had not spoken.

A third person said, "So, what's up with y'all, every one of you is glowing!"

The organizers asked us who had been designated as the spokesperson for our group. I raised my hand. They asked me for our report.

"We have decided to remain silent," I said. They wanted to know why.

"We have decided to remain silent," I repeated.

Can you say *anything*? they asked.

I said all that I had been mandated to say: "We had a good session."

Well, we can *see* that! they said. Then they asked the biracial group to speak. One of them simply said, "We ended up joining the Black group."

The room was even more puzzled. But no explanations were forthcoming.

It went south from there. The Whites reported on their bric-a-brac dialogue. Alice had had her head handed to her. No one in her room was willing to think of themselves as White *in relation to policing*. The White women said it was important to divide the room along gender lines and have a discussion about how women fare under patriarchy. Several people said they were Jewish and perhaps they should have pressed the organizers for their own room, as the biracial people had done. One White man actually said that it was important for them to do a round-robin in which each person should say what state they lived in before they came to California. To Alice's horror, damn near everyone in the room thought this was a good idea. One by one they began to shout the names of states where they were born and raised, and they would have descended into personal narratives about how and when they came to California, and what brought them there, had my wife, Alice, not exploded.

"This doesn't have a damn thing to do with our relationship to the institution of policing! Let's get back on track."

But no one was willing to get back on track. The interesting thing about the trajectory of the conversation in the White room was the way it uncannily mirrored the absolute refusal of the exercise that was going on in the Black room—albeit for different reasons. Alice was shut down because the exercise threatened the most constitutive element of Whiteness: White people *are* the police. This includes those White people who, like Alice, at the level of consciousness, do not want this birthright deputation. At a deep unconscious level they all intuited the fact that the police were not *out there* but *in here*, that policing was woven into the fabric of their subjectivity. No wonder the discussion veered in myriad directions away from a conscious encounter with this horrifying aspect of their structural position into a chorus of declarations about gendered identities and stories about their individual sojourns to California. And, conversely, the Black people, in their room at the other end of the hall, understood that no kind of psychic or material immigration would ever be expansive enough to open such doors to them—to Alice and her people. But for the non-Black people of color the question of access remained an open one.

The Asians and Latinos and Native Americans' discussions had begun with questions of violence and ended with questions of access: immigration policy, Spanish in the schools, the question of Indigenous gambling casinos, and the question of land and sovereignty. It was clear: the articulation was between the Whites, whose access to civil society was so unquestioned that they had no reason to complain about it or question the regime of violence that fortified and extended it; and their junior partners, who were anxious for expanded access. None of these groups embodied an antagonism to civil society itself. What they embodied were gradations of marginalization. The antagonism was not between them and the police, but between all of them and all of us, even the ones who wanted their own room.

Even the two organizers were wrong, which is to say the exercise was right, if only accidentally right. The organizers had divided people up based on their color; on how the gaze of the police perceives them. But only one group of people is *essentially* elaborated and subjugated by this kind of gratuitous violence. The Blacks. The Slaves. For all the other groups of people there is a certain contingency that interrupts, as well as makes legible, the violence of the state. These people must transgress, or be perceived to transgress the Law before the anvil of state violence falls on their heads. For the Blacks, the Slaves, no notion of transgression is necessary. The pleasure of maiming Black bodies is its own reward. It is this pleasure that divided the conference *not into five colors, but into two species: Blacks and Humans.*

But the cognitive maps of the people at the Race Rave conference could not comprehend or explain this a priori species division between the Human and the Slave. The Black people and, ultimately, the biracial (Black) people knew this, if only, for most part, intuitively. But the terrain wasn't fertile enough for that knowledge to flourish. The Black people were shackled to the cognitive maps of their well-meaning masters.

2

Two months after the attack on the World Trade Center, and nine months after the Race Rave, an airport shuttle picked me up at my apartment in Berkeley. It was winter, just shy of five in the morning. The air was clear and frosty, as Bay Area winter mornings often are. The sun had yet to rise. Winter doesn't deserve its name in Northern California when set against the blizzards of my Minnesota youth. Now, in the early gloaming, broken knees of lightning kindled the blood-orange sky above the San Francisco Bay. It was going to rain.

Standing beside his idling van, the South Asian driver asked me twice if I was the person going to the airport—as though the wrong person had somehow come out of the right complex; as though I'd called him under false pretenses, not to go to the airport at all but simply to come out at that ungodly hour of 4:55 a.m. to annoy him, if not to rob him. I felt a chill of chastisement in his gaze.

I tossed my bags in the back and walked around and slid the door open. In the nugget of light that shone from the ceiling I found myself face-to-face with a middle-aged White woman and a hesitant middle-aged and bearded White man who peered at me from her left side. Their excess luggage took up the seat behind them; and we looked at each with that momentary, familiar, but all-too-mutual dread as we realized that I was going to sit next to her. I took more than ample care not to touch her thigh as I fished for my seat belt in the dark.

The van nosed down the road through the last seeds of night. The only light on Martin Luther King Jr. Drive came from the intermittent streetlamps. We were as quiet as death itself: the driver, the woman, her husband, and me. I felt angry; I had the sense that before I arrived they had all been engaged in spirited conversation, and that it had stopped when I got in. Was I the reason they had stopped talking?

Could I be sure that they had *been* talking? Was this Black paranoia kicking in where a little common sense might be in order?

The face of the Pakistani driver when I came out of my apartment was still branded in my brain. Now this quiet discomfort; this silence on my behalf; this churning of my gray matter to make sense of it; this doubt that it was anything at all. *Not that I want to speak with these ofays and their junior partner*, I thought. But I wanted them to want to speak with me.

"George here works at Cal," she finally said, stammering. "Are you at Cal? I mean, are you a professor or a grad student?"

No, lady, I'm a crackhead, just out on the prowl this morning.

"That's wonderful!" she said, "Do you know Judith Butler?"

I told them a bit about my research, but rather than couch my research project in the language that animated me most (a synopsis of the structure of U.S. antagonisms between the triangulated positions of the Immigrant/Settler/Master, the Red/"Savage," and the Black/Slave) I couched the synopsis of my research project in the language that animated me the least—questions of film theory and film historiography. I kept it simple and free of politics. When I finished speaking, everyone seemed to be relieved. Even the driver smiled at me through his rearview mirror and seemed to be at ease. I had accomplished the main objective of international Negro diplomacy: make them feel safe.

Now the taciturn professor ventured forth.

"Before you got in," he said, "we were discussing this new law, the Patriot Act. Ghastly business. Is this still America? This man here"—he motioned to the driver, who smiled again and nodded at us in the rearview mirror—"shouldn't have to come to this country and encounter xenophobia and persecution—what are we coming to?"

The Pakistani driver then weighed in with anecdotes dramatizing the injustices he and members of his community had been subjected to since the passage of the law. The Patriot Act was 400 pages long and neither the professor nor his wife nor the driver had read a word of it. I had read 170-odd pages of it and had written a synopsis of what I'd read for some Black folks in a retirement home in Oakland. They too had thought the law to be draconian and unjust—but, unlike the people in the shuttle to the airport, they did not think there was anything particularly new or un-American about the "new" law. A woman at the home, who was eighty, had looked at me, shaking her head. "And they keep going to the polls, these Caucasians. They go back to the polls like it matters."

But the memory of these Black folks' response to my findings was lost on me as I traveled to the airport because the people in the van had taken a renewed interest in me. I had advanced from being feared to being tolerated to being valued. I was no longer a stimulus to anxiety. *Tonight*, I thought, *I will be someone of whom the Pakistani driver speaks highly of to his wife or compatriots, the professor and his wife will talk about me and what I've said, on the plane and perhaps at their conference when they reach* their *destination*. My desire was to be the object of their desire. There was no more Black or White or Brown in that shuttle. Through my words, a common sense of joy and a sense of a common purpose bloomed inside that small shuttle, where before there had been dread and division. We were all people. Just people. People who demanded the same basic form of fairness and accountability from our government. The thought of sneak-and-peak searches, the thought of unlawful wiretaps, the thought of expanded prohibitions on our freedom of assembly, the thought of the government sniffing around in our libraries and bookstores—well, that does it, we all agreed, that's taking things just a bit too far. And I was not only part of and party to this multiracial consensus, but it was the miracle of *my* efforts, *my* research, *my* erudition, *my* labor, and my fifty-two-teeth charm that had sutured this vigorous populism, this fire-and-brimstone accord in the wee hours of the morning. Not only were they taking me seriously—which is to say they truly thought that they thought that I could think—but I was now essential to them: I kindled the fire of their nostalgia for a democratic past; and they seemed to need, at the very same time, for me to somehow castigate them, beat them, as though only I could fulfill their masochistic urge to hear how bad their future would be. To this end, the woman turned to me and said something like, *Sambo, now, don't you spare me, Sambo, you hear, don't you hold back, Sambo. Tell me just how bad it's going to be.*

Miss Anne, dey dun taken aw ciba lubbaties and sen' 'um waaaay up yonda.

The professor sat there shaking his head. Way up yonder. He gazed at the ceiling. Way up yonder.

Now the terrain of conversation was cleared, once again, for the driver.

"Let me tell you about my community, let me tell the story of the wrongful arrests, the detentions without trial."

We listened to him from within the folds of our renewed faith in redemption. We were more than a mere collection of common interests; we were an intrepid coalition of affect. Our mood and our will meshed into a warm cloth of *amen* and *ain't it a shame.*

The driver said, "I don't know why I ever brought my family to this country."

And before I could disentangle the structure of my unassimilable Blackness from the mesh and mush of multiracial affect, I said, "Me neither."

But these words shredded our mood.

The earth flipped. We all fell off.

The driver had said, "I don't know why I ever brought my family here."

And I had responded, "Me neither."

The van was again uncommonly silent. It was as though a period had been placed in the middle of a sentence. The driver's eyes flashed at me in the rearview mirror. The White woman beside me shifted the way she had shifted when I first got in. My "Me neither" was not being addressed. My "Me neither" hung in the air like a faint but unquestionably foul odor—an unexpected but not unattributable fart. To be sure, my odor had been emitted, but it had not been emitted in bad faith. I thought we were one—surely they could live with my smell if I could live with theirs. So robustly had I been hailed by the South Asian's dilemmas of access *to* civil society and the good White folks' dilemmas of the relative elasticity or rigidity *within* civil society that I had forgotten the first rule of international Negro diplomacy: make them feel safe. My presumed embodiment of the tenet of immigration (the presumption that moving from the plantation to the city was a form of immigration)—the presumption that I possessed the constituent elements of filiation ("*my family*" moved from the plantation to the city) rather than the ruse of borrowed institutionality, and that I furthermore possessed the constituent elements of volition and agency ("I brought my family from the plantation to the city"), all this, spoken in my "Me neither," had somehow tampered with the safety upon which the triangulated goodwill and warm feelings between what Jared Sexton calls citizen, non-citizen, and anti-citizen depended: the White professor and his White wife being the citizens, the Pakistani a non-citizen, and me being the anti-citizen. I had sutured the equilibrium of the universe through my recitation of the dreaded Patriot Act and then, with the same ease and unthinking intuition, I had dared to threaten the equilibrium of that fragile universe by thinking a Black thought out loud. In their thirty seconds of silence, I felt my flesh peel away. With two words, *Me neither*, I had fallen from grace. I went from warm and fuzzy Sambo to W. E. B. Du *Blac*.

The professor and his wife were ready for this ride to the airport to end. But the Pakistani driver had the same kind of new-arrival fight in him that the couple had possessed two hundred years ago when their people were immigrants. He looked at me unsympathetically in his rearview mirror, as if to say, Did you make a mistake, an honest, innocent mistake, the kind of mistake anyone can make in the joy and euphoria of the moment; or were you fucking with us—being a smart-ass whose sole intent was to shit on the inspiration of the personal pronoun *we*?

His eyes flicked from the street ahead to my image in his mirror. Slowly and deliberately he said, "Sometimes I want to pack my bags and go back home."

No one spoke. No one even breathed. The engine groaned uneasily as we turned onto the exit ramp.

I threw down the gauntlet, sat up straight, and cleared my throat. "Yeah," I said, "me too." This time, the smell was unmistakable. It was the stench of something burning; a field of cotton up in flames.

Into this fire the professor's wife rushed with the only water she could find. "Being homesick," she said, "now, there's a universal phenomenon. We've been going to this conference for years and we still miss the kids when we're gone."

"Which is more than we can say for the kids," her husband chimed uneasily.

I felt something pressing itself into the palm of my hand as it lay at my side—insisting I take hold. To this day I don't know if it was the cold hard door handle or the handle of a blade.

The shuttle that I took to the airport in the wake of 9/11 was a microcosm of a captive scenario where Blackness exists inside and beneath the specter of policing, thinly disguised as the work of social movements dedicated to the expansion and democratization of civil society.

It shows how the libidinal economy of values (access to institutionality, universal suffrage, unfettered mobility, etc.), when set in motion by social justice initiatives, is predicated on the intensification of Black suffering and death. Four people rode in that van that morning. But one of those four was subjugated by a regime of violence that bore no resemblance to the regimes of violence that subjugated the others. The people in the van policed my pain, my bearing witness to the singular structure of anti-Black violence.

3

As with the Native Americans, the violence that subjugates the Pakistani driver has temporal limits (the time of, for example, the War on Terror), as well as spatial limits (the occupation of Iraq and the gulag at Guantánamo Bay). Not only is there no punctuation or time limit on the violence that subsumes Black people, but, furthermore, no cartography of violence can be mapped, for that would imply the prospect for a map of nonviolent space: the possibility of Black sanctuary, which is, by definition, an oxymoron. Instead, Black people exist in the throes of what historian David Eltis calls "violence beyond the limits," by which he means: (a) in the *libidinal* economy there are no forms of violence so excessive that they would be considered too cruel to inflict upon Blacks; and (b) in *political* economy there are no rational explanations for this limitless theater of cruelty, no explanations that would make *political or economic* sense of the violence that positions and punishes Blackness. Whereas the Human's relationship to violence is always contingent, triggered by her transgressions against the regulatory prohibitions of the symbolic order or by macro-economic shifts in her social context, the Slave's relationship to violence is open-ended, gratuitous, without reason or constraint, triggered by prelogical catalysts that are unmoored from her transgressions and unaccountable to historical shifts. In short, the violence inflicted upon Black people is not the effect of symbolic transgressions, nor is it the result (as Allen Feldman would have it) of a new, global shift in political economy—it is an "extension of the master's prerogative." Orlando Patterson clarifies this distinction between violence that positions and punishes the Human (worker, postcolonial subject, woman, or queer, for example) and violence that positions and punishes the Slave (the Black) by emphasizing the difference between the violence that constitutes capitalism and the violence that constitutes slavery.

> The worker who is fired remains a worker, to be hired elsewhere. The slave who was freed was no longer a slave. Thus, it was necessary continually to repeat the original, violent act of transforming free person into slave. This act of violence constitutes the prehistory of all stratified societies . . . but it determines both the prehistory and (concurrent) history of slavery.

To put it bluntly, Blackness cannot be separated from slavery. Blackness is often misconstrued as an identity (cultural, economic, gendered) of the Human community; however, there is no Black time that precedes the time of the Slave. Africa's spatial coherence is temporally coterminous with the Arab, and then European, slave trade. The time of Blackness is the time of the paradigm; it is not a temporality that can be grasped with the epistemological tools at our disposal. The time of Blackness is no time at all, because one cannot know a plenitude of Blackness distinct from Slaveness. The prior references of the worker, a time before the Enclosures, for example, or of the postcolonial subject, *a time before the settler*, are simply not available to Black people. From my book *Red, White & Black*:

Historical time is the time of the worker [the time of the Pakistani driver], the time of analysis. But whereas historical time marks stasis and change within a paradigm, it does not mark the time of the paradigm, the time of time itself, the time by which the Slave's dramatic clock is set. For the Slave, historical time is no more viable a temporality of emancipation than biographical time—the time of empathy. Thus, neither the analytic aesthetic [the demystifying cure of ethical assessment] nor the empathetic aesthetic [the mystifying "cure" of moral judgment] can accompany a theory of change that restores Black people to relationality. The social and political time of emancipation proclamations should not be confused with the [time of the paradigm itself, a temporality] in which Blackness and Slaveness are imbricated ab initio, which is to say, from the beginning.*

Blacks are constituted by a violence that separates the time of the paradigm (ontological time) from time *within* the paradigm (historical time).

At every scale of abstraction, violence saturates Black life. To put it differently, for Black people there is no time and space of consent, no relative respite from force and coercion: violence spreads its tendrils across the body, chokes the community, and expands, intensifies, and mutates into new and ever more grotesque forms in the collective unconscious through literature and film.

Working-class *ideas* are contaminants: threats to capitalist economy, to a capitalist conception of the world. Black *bodies* are a differ-

---

* Frank B. Wilderson III, *Red, White & Black: Cinema and the Structure of U.S. Antagonisms* (Durham, NC: Duke UP, 2010), 339–340.

ent kind of contaminant: they are threats to the Human body ideal, and to the psychic coherence of Human life.

This schema is even different from the one that attends Native American genocide. The Native American was and is genocided for her land. There are pre-logical or libidinal elements to the murder of eighteen million people—to be sure. But land acquisition and usurpation give the genocide a kind of coherence and reasonableness similar to a massacre of workers who have gone on strike—who have withdrawn their consent.

You can't make an analogy between the violence immigrants, Native Americans, and workers are subjected to and the violence that attends to Black people.

It is absolutely necessary for Blacks to be castrated, raped, genitally mutilated and violated, beaten, shot, and maimed. And it is necessary for this to take place in the streets as well as in popular culture—as on TV and in the cinema. Blacks can even be genocided, but only up to a point! Because, unlike Indians, Blacks are not in possession of something exterior to themselves that civil society wants. Civil society does not want Black land as it wants Indian land, that it might distinguish the Nation from Turtle Island; it does not want Black consent, as it wants working-class consent, that it might distinguish a capitalist economic system from a socialist one, that it might extract surplus value and turn that value into profit. What civil society wants/needs from Black people is far more essential, far more fundamental than land and profits. What civil society needs from Black people is confirmation of Human existence.

Of course, the Human being can say, I know I am alive at the level of identity because I speak Spanish, or French, or English, because I am straight or gay; or because I am rich or middle-class. This is a kind of life at the level of identity, or culture, or sexual orientation. But to be able say, I am alive at a paradigmatic level, that I am really and truly a Human being and not the other thing . . . this can only be guaranteed to the extent to which one can say, I am not Black.

It would be misguided, even mendacious, to have said to the people in the van that the Patriot Act did not affect Black people; or to champion an anti-immigration sentiment of any sort. But it would be just as misguided and mendacious to suggest that the Patriot Act's relative corruption of the integrity of the Bill of Rights, or the relative rigidity or elasticity of access to (and within) the institutionality of civil society, can help us think through Black folks's unique grammar of suffering. Put another way, Black thought (and therefore Black liberation) is threatened not only by the state, but by the interests and actions of the loyal opposition in the airport shuttle.

In fact, Black thought is threatened by a three-tiered ensemble of terror. Our intellectual capability to do the work is not what's at issue here. What's at stake is our capacity to work against the constraints of analogy, the terrorism of intra-Human exchange—the hydraulics of my ride to the airport.

First, there is the terrorism of what Gramsci referred to as "political society": the police, the army, the prison-industrial complex.

Second, there is the terror of civil society's hegemonic blocs and its clusters of affilial formations: like the mainstream media, the university, or the megachurch.

But there is also a third tier of terror with which Black thought must contend. *And that is the terror of counter-hegemonic and revolutionary thought: the logic of White feminism, the logic of working-class struggle, the logic of multicultural coalitions, and the logic of immigrant rights. The unrelenting terror elaborated whenever Black people's so-called allies think out loud.*

The stakes of this three-tiered terror are high because of their impact upon Black people's capacity to capture and be captured by our own imaginations. These three tiers scaffold *the death of Black desire.* And our capacity to imagine and to fantasize while assuming our position is imbricated in our capacity to think theoretically: to give our political desire "objective value."

This third tier of terror that threatens the imagination and the enunciation of Black thought—the terror of left-wing counter-hegemonic alliances—should not be dismissed as incidental or inessential, nor should it be trivialized as an ensemble of bad attitudes that can be overcome through dialogue, as the Race Rave conference in Santa Cruz had assumed. For it is an essential terror; it is as constitutive of an anti-Black world as the military and the megachurch. It doesn't simply kill or warehouse Black thought the way the first tier kills and warehouses the Black body. Nor does it simply crowd out a Black emancipatory ensemble of questions the way traditional organs of hegemony crowd out the performance of the common man or woman's ensemble of questions. This third tier terrorizes through an interdiction *against* Black performance, coupled with a demand *for* Black performance—dance, Johnny, dance. We might say that it demands the performance of Black thought, albeit under erasure. It wants us to sing the blues; but instead of those Ain't Got No Life Worth Living Blues (instead of the social death blues), it wants Black folks singing the:

> —Ain't Got No Green Card Blues
> —Ain't Got No Abortion Blues
> —Ain't Got No Right to Privacy Blues
> —Ain't Got No Border-Crossing Blues
> —Ain't Got No Same-Sex Weddin' Blues
> —Ain't Got No Ciba Lubbaties Blues

Civil society expands and contracts to accommodate or diminish (but never banish carte blanche) a multitude of positions and identities—Jews, Arabs, Asian Immigrants, Latinos, Italians, White women, and Native Americans. The annals of history show nineteenth century transitions from territories to states as being manifest with a great and conflicting diversity of views with respect to all of these groups. These fledgling fifty states even found themselves, on rare occasion (as in the case of California), debating the civic and social membership of Native Americans. But civil society would not know the boundary, the frontier, of such debates, which is to say it would lose all coherence and not be able to draw the line between social life and social death, if not for the presence of Black folks. Black people hold that line for White people and for everyone else. Blacks give even the most degraded position a sense of human possibility because we are the locus of human impossibility. Whatever grace others may fall from, they will never be Black. This is a comforting thought. The flame of human warmth.

There's something organic to Blackness that makes it essential to the construction of civil society. But there's also something organic to Blackness that portends the destruction of civil society. There's nothing willful or speculative in this statement, for one could just as well state the claim the other way around: there's something organic to civil society that makes *it* essential to the destruction of the Black body. Blackness is a positionality of "absolute dereliction," abandonment, in the face of civil society, and therefore cannot be liberated or be made legible through counter-hegemonic interventions. Black suffering is not a function of the performance(s) of civil society, but of the existence of civil society. For the Pakistani driver, the White professor, and his White wife, civil society is an ensemble of constraints and opportunities. But for the Black, civil society is a murderous projection.

In light of this, coalitions and social movements—even radical social movements like the Prison Abolition Movement—bound up in the solicitation of hegemony, so as to fortify and extend the inter-locutory life of civil society, ultimately accommodate only the *satiable demands and legible conflicts* of civil society's junior partners (such as immigrants, White women, the working class), but foreclose upon the *insatiable demands and illegible antagonisms* of Blacks. In short, whereas such coalitions and social movements cannot be called the outright handmaidens of anti-Blackness, their rhetorical structures, political desire, and their emancipatory horizon are bolstered by a *life-affirming anti-Blackness; the death of Black desire.

4

What sets the Black apart from the Human? It is the division between social death and social life; a divide between the structural violence of, for example, capitalism, postcolonialism, and patriarchy, and the structural violence of social death.*

The violence of capitalism or any Human paradigm of subjection, for that matter, has a prehistory. In other words, it takes an ocean of violence to transpose serfs into workers. It takes an ocean of violence over a couple of hundred years to discipline them into temporalities that are new and more constricting—and to have them imagine their lives within new constraints: urbanization, mechanization, and certain types of labor practices. Once the system is set up, then violence recedes and goes into remission. The violence comes back at times when capitalism needs to regenerate itself or when the workers transgress the rules and push back (when they withdraw their consent).

---

* It is worth reiterating that, through the lens of Afropessimism, slavery is, *essentially*, a relational dynamic, rather than a historical era or an ensemble of empirical practices (like whips and chains).

The violence of the slave estate cannot be thought of the way one thinks of the violence of capitalist oppression. It takes an ocean of violence to produce a slave, singular or plural, but that violence *never goes into remission*. Again, the prehistory of violence that establishes slavery is also the *concurrent history* of slavery. This is a difficult cognitive map for most activists to adjust to because it actually takes the problem outside of politics. Politics is a very rational endeavor, which allows activists to work out models that predict the structural violence of capitalism in its performative manifestation. But you can't create models that predict the structural violence of slavery in its performative manifestations. What the Marxists do with slavery is they try to show how violence is connected to production, and that means they are not really thinking about the violence of slavery comprehensively. The violence of social death (slavery) is actually subtended to the production of the psychic health of all those who are not slaves, something that cannot be literally commodified or weighted on an actual balance sheet. That's the more intangible, libidinal aspect to it.

In other words, activists want to make sense of the death of Sandra Bland, and the murders of Michael Brown, and Eric Garner; when what these spectacles require, in order to be adequately explained, is a theory of the *non*sense; their absence of a tangible or rational utility: Black people are not murdered for transgressions such as illegal immigration or workplace agitation. The essential *utility* of Black death is, paradoxically, the *absence* of utility.

Black death does have a certain utility, but it's not subtended by the extraction of surplus value; not in any fundamental way. And it is certainly not subtended by the usurpation of land. Black death is subtended by the psychic integration of everyone who is not Black. Black death functions as national therapy, even though the rhetoric that explains and laments these deaths expresses this psychic dependence not directly, but symptomatically. It is complex, but it is simple too.

Blacks are not going to be genocided like Native Americans. We *are* being genocided, but genocided *and* regenerated, because the *spectacle* of Black death is essential to the mental health of the world—we can't be wiped out completely, because our deaths must be repeated, *visually*.

The bodily mutilation of Blackness is necessary, so it must be repeated. What we are witnessing on YouTube, Instagram, and the nightly news as murders are rituals of healing for civil society. Rituals that stabilize and ease the anxiety that other people feel in their daily lives. It's the anxiety that people have walking around. It can be stabilized by a lot of different things—marijuana, cocaine, alcohol, affairs—but the ultimate stabilization is the spectacle of violence against Blacks. *I know I am a Human because I am not Black. I know I am not Black because when and if I experience the kind of violence Blacks experience there is a reason, some contingent transgression.*

This is why online video posts of police murdering Black people contribute more to the psychic well-being of non-Black people—to their communal pleasures and sense of ontological presence—than they contribute to deterrence, arrests, or even to a general sensitivity to Black pain and suffering.

Afropessimism helps us understand why the violence that saturates Black life isn't threatened with elimination just because it is exposed. For this to be the case, the spectator, interlocutor, auditor would have to come to images such as these with an unconscious that can perceive *injury* in such images. In other words, the mind would have to *see* a person with a heritage of rights and claims, whose rights and claims are being violated. This is not the way Slaves, Blacks, function in the collective unconscious. Slaves function as implements in the collective unconscious. Who ever heard of an injured plow?

Afropessimism is premised on an iconoclastic claim: that Blackness is coterminous with Slaveness. Blackness *is* social death, which is to say that there was never a prior moment of plenitude, never a moment of equilibrium, never a moment of social life. Blackness, as a paradigmatic position (rather than as an ensemble of identities, cultural practices, or anthropological accoutrements), cannot be disimbricated from slavery. The narrative arc of the slave who is *Black* (unlike the generic slave who may be of any race) is *not a narrative arc at all*, but a flat line of "historical stillness": a flat line that "moves" from disequilibrium to a moment in the narrative of faux-equilibrium, to disequilibrium restored and/or rearticulated.

To put it differently, the violence that both elaborates and saturates Black "life" is totalizing, so much so as to make narrative inaccessible to Blacks. This is not simply a problem for Black people. It is a problem for the organizational calculus of critical theory and radical politics writ large.

Foundational to the cognitive maps of radical politics is the belief that all sentient beings can be protagonists within a (political or personal) narrative; that every sentient being arrives with a history. This belief is underwritten by another idea that constitutes narrative: that all sentient beings can be redeemed. History and redemption are the weave of narrative. As provocative as it may sound, history and redemption (and therefore narrative itself) are inherently anti-Black. Without the presence of a being who is, ab initio, barred from redemption (a being that is generally dishonored, natally alienated, and open to naked violence), history and narrative would lack their touchstones of cohesion. Without the Black, one would not be able to know what a world devoid of redemption looks like—and if one could not conceive of the absence of redemption, then redemption would be inconceivable as well.

At the heart of my argument is the assertion that Black emplotment is a catastrophe for narrative at a metalevel rather than a crisis or aporia* within a particular narrative. To put it differently, social death is aporetic with respect to narrative writ large (and, by extension, to redemption writ large).

If social death is aporetic with respect to narrative, this is a function of both space and time, or, more precisely, their absence. Narrative time is always historical (imbued with historicity): "It marks stasis and change *within* a [human] paradigm, [but] it does not mark the time *of* the [human] paradigm, the time of time itself, the time by which the Slave's dramatic clock is set. For the Slave, historical 'time' is not possible." Social death bars the Slave from access to narrative at the level of temporality; but it also does so at the level of spatiality. The other element that constitutes narrative is setting, or mise-en-scène, or for a larger conceptualization, we might follow H. Porter Abbott and say "story world." But just as there is no time for the Slave, there is also no *place* of the Slave. The Slave's reference to his or her quarters as a "home" does not change the fact that it is a spatial extension of the master's dominion.

The three constituent elements of slavery—naked (or gratuitous) violence, general dishonor, and natal alienation—make the temporal and spatial logic of the entity (a character or persona in a narrative) and of setting untenable, impossible to conceive (as in birth) and/or conceive of (as in assume any coherence). The violence of slavery is not precipitated as a result of any transgression that can be turned into an event (which is why I have argued that this violence is *gratuitous*, not contingent); the dishonor embodied by the slave is not a function of an event either; his or her dishonor is general, it is best understood as abjection rather than as degradation (the latter implies a transition);

---

* Aporia: an irresolvable internal contradiction or logical disjunction in a text, argument, or theory.

and since a slave is natally alienated, she is never an entity in the metanarrative genealogy.

Afropessimism is a theoretical lens that clarifies the irreconcilable difference between, on the one hand, the violence of capitalism, gender oppression, and White supremacy (such as the *colonial utility* of the Palestinian Nakba or the Sand Creek massacre*) and, on the other hand, the violence of anti-Blackness (the Human *necessity* for violence against Black people).

The antagonism between the postcolonial subject and the settler cannot—and should not—be analogized with the violence of social death: that is the violence of slavery, which did not end in 1865 for the simple reason that slavery did not end in 1865. Slavery is a relational dynamic—not an event and certainly not a place in space like the South; just as colonialism is a relational dynamic—and that relational dynamic can continue to exist once the settler has left or ceded governmental power. And these two relations are secured by radically different structures of violence. Afropessimism offers an analytic lens that labors as a corrective to Humanist assumptive logic. It provides a theoretical apparatus that allows Black people to *not* have to be burdened by the ruse of analogy—because analogy *mystifies*, rather than clarifies, Black suffering. Analogy mystifies Black peoples' relationship to other people of color. Afropessimism labors to throw this mystification into relief—without fear of the faults and fissures that are revealed in the process.

Let me put it another way: Human Life is dependent on Black

---

* Nakba: In 1948, "Al-Nakba," "The Catastrophe," was the mass exodus of at least 750,000 Arabs from Palestine in 1948 when the state of Israel was violently established. Its legacy remains one of the most intractable issues in ongoing peace negotiations. Sand Creek Massacre: On November 29, 1864, more than 230 peaceful Southern Cheyenne and Arapaho Indians were massacred by a band of Colonel John Chivington's Colorado volunteers at Sand Creek, Colorado.

death for its existence and for its conceptual coherence. There is no world without Blacks, yet there are no Blacks who are in the world. The Black is indeed a sentient being, but the hobble of Humanist thought is a constitutive disavowal of Blackness as social death, a disavowal that theorizes the Black as a degraded human entity (for example, as an oppressed worker, a vanquished postcolonial subaltern, or a non-Black woman suffering under the disciplinary regime of patriarchy). The Black is *not* a sentient being whose narrative progression has been circumscribed by racism, colonialism, or even slavery, for that matter. Blackness and Slaveness are inextricably bound in such a way that whereas Slaveness can be disimbricated from Blackness, Blackness cannot exist as other than Slaveness.

The essential antagonism, therefore, is not between the workers and the bosses, not between settler and the Native, not between the queer and the straight, but between the living and the dead. If we look closely we also see that gender itself cannot be reconciled with a Slave's genealogical isolation; that, for the Slave, there is no surplus value to be restored to the time of labor; that no treaties between Blacks and Humans are in Washington waiting to be signed and ratified; and that, unlike the settler in the Native American or Palestinian political imagination, there is no place like Europe to which Slaves can send back Human beings.

CHAPTER SIX

Mind the Closing Doors

I was thirty-three in the summer of 1989 when I moved to New York City. Black, yes, but a Midwesterner, from Minneapolis, and a young Black Minneapolitan is ominously younger than a young Black New Yorker. Quite literally, New York blew my mind in a way my hometown never could. The seismic shift was mostly internal—I found my voice as a writer. I developed as a theorist too, which means I learned how to compare systems of thought, not just what was inside them. But the so-called Big Apple was expensive, in both the cost of living and what it cost my soul. I came to see in New York things I had only read about or heard mentioned on the news: impulsive cruelties, straight-no-chaser. Yet I knew when my studies ended there'd be no way I could go back to Minneapolis; even though the longer I lived in New York City the poorer I became: moving from a swanky high-rise on Ninety-Sixth and Riverside Drive, to a flat I shared with two other grad students in Harlem, to a ramshackle dwelling that the rats were kind enough to share with me in Washington Heights.

. . .

I TOOK THE A TRAIN from Greenwich Village to 168th and Broadway, my stop in Washington Heights. I was formally enrolled in the MFA Fiction Writing Program at Columbia, but I was also taking night classes in fiction writing from Marguerite Young at the New School for Social Research. She taught stream-of-consciousness writing. It washed the minimalist taste of Columbia's daytime fiction writing workshops from my mouth. As I read her hypnotic novel *Miss MacIntosh, My Darling*, it pulled me into the sway of the train, and swathed its rock and tumble and the clatter of the rails in velvet. The glare of the subway car's carriage lights dimmed in my mind's eye. No longer was I in New York. Nor was I underground in a train tunnel, but on a night road in rural Indiana that laced through cornfields and oceans of wheat, and there was "a sleeping couple, a pair of lovers, boy and girl, the only other passengers. They had gotten on at a dust-colored pottery town." I watched them as they "tried to sleep through languorous, creaking miles of a too familiar landscape." A farm boy fleeing with his strawberry-faced girlfriend who was pregnant and slumbered on his shoulder. "The bus-driver was whistling, perhaps in anticipation of his wife . . ."

It wasn't the bus driver. Nor was it a whistle. It was a voice on the speakers above the handrails announcing the Forty-Second Street/Port Authority stop. I hadn't noticed any subway stops between Washington Square and Forty-Second Street. *Mind the closing doors!* came next. I kept reading but was distracted by the rush of legs that jostled toward the exit. This annoyed me. Forty-Second Street wasn't my stop and these people had broken my spell. A pair of faded brown pants stopped in front of me. They were corduroy. A smirk itched in the corners of my mouth. *Who wears corduroys anymore*, I thought, *and in this heat!* Then one leg rose, and as it rose a voice yelled, "Jer, c'mon, man!" from somewhere near the closing doors. The leg and the shoe that it held snapped out like the low half of a whip. My book dropped out of my hands. I felt my head snap backward. I was so dazed I didn't see the corduroys dash away. Like an echo, I heard what had come with the kick. "Fuckin' towelhead!" Jerry was gone, but his voice still splintered the air. "Fuckin' towelhead!" Pelham Bay in the Bronx or Bensonhurst, Brooklyn, was where I felt the voices of both Jerry and the guy at the doors were from. Watchful enclaves, where porcelain faces and hair black as stone nod and hate trespassers.

I was fine. No broken teeth. No skin torn.

The man beside me was bleeding. A turban, not a towel, was wrapped around his head.

He didn't want help from anyone around him. I asked him again if he wanted a doctor or even the transit police. The next stop was Fiftieth, and he got off there, though I'm sure it wasn't his stop. Our pity was more than he could bear. As the platform where he stood, wiping his mouth, glided past our window and the tunnel darkened around us, I thought, *He's a Sikh, not an Iraqi. A Sikh, Jerry*—as if accuracy in racism were the issue here.

When his bleeding face faded, when the screech of iron wheels grinding to a halt at Forty-Second Street faded as well, I still saw that shoe snap up and out from corduroy cuffs, and the cry, *Fucking towelhead!* still pealed in my brain. I carried the Sikh's face with me for days.

By now it was early winter, January 1991. The first war in Iraq was under way. By September of the previous year, George Herbert Walker Bush had deployed half a million troops to Kuwait to drive Saddam Hussein from that country, despite the fact that Bush's ambassador told Saddam in the summer of 1990 that the U.S. would look the other way if such an invasion took place.

The day after the incident on the A train I sat in Professor Edward Said and Professor Jean Franco's Cultural Studies Project class at Columbia. Said and Franco had chosen twenty-five students from an applicant pool of one hundred. I was a novice at critical theory, and not for one moment did I believe I would be admitted. When I was told that the list of one hundred had gone down to fifty people who would be asked for a writing sample and a personal interview with Franco and Said, I thought, in my Minnesota way, the registrar had made a mistake.

I would learn that Jean Franco had survived the 1954 CIA-driven Guatemalan coup d'état that had deposed the democratically elected Guatemalan President Jacobo Árbenz and ended the Guatemalan Revolution of 1944–1954. Her name had not always been Franco. She was British and had taken the name of her husband, a Guatemalan left-wing cabinet minister, whom the CIA's surrogates had killed in the coup. Not only was she a nimble-minded critical theorist, but she wrote fiction, and outside of the Cultural Studies Project sessions, she and I spent several afternoons in her Upper West Side apartment workshopping our respective manuscripts. Before coming to Columbia, Franco had been the first professor of Latin American literature at the University of Essex in England.

It was a prized opportunity for me to study under Edward Said as well; a man I didn't even think I would meet when I came to Columbia; and doubly-so because there were only two students in the class who were not in the comparative literature's Ph.D. program, and I was one of them—a fiction writer (and not a Ph.D. student in comparative literature or philosophy) from the other side of the quad. The other interloper was a Sri Lankan grad student of international affairs who still bore the blotchy skin of two bullet wounds in his neck. A Sri Lankan soldier had shot him as he covered the Tamil conflict in his country, but he had lived, somehow, and managed to escape to

Zimbabwe, where the bullet wounds healed and he lived under a false name for two years before he came to Columbia.

Though I had read the works of Frantz Fanon and studied existentialism at Dartmouth, my eight prior years as a stockbroker had nuked my brain cells. Wholly unprepared was I for the rigor, the breadth of theoretical reflection, and the level of abstraction at which Franco and Said conducted their seminars. The simple and (as I told a fiction professor) simple-minded literature courses we were required to take in the MFA program never scratched the surface of interpretation that I experienced in the Cultural Studies Project just across the quad. We never discussed power, or violence, or the way a text labors in the School of the Arts. We were there to see how fiction was made, not what fiction meant or whose lives it enhanced or how it greased the wheels of death for others.

Edward Said was tall, urbane, and handsome—a concert pianist who, after the Nakba, was sent to boarding school, where he met Omar Sharif, whom he called a "head-boy and a bully." Until I met Said I hadn't met a professor who took the stakes of his profession as seriously, even though I was surrounded by academics as a child. Later, I understood that this was not some sort of shortcoming on the part of my parents or the Black scholars who were their friends. If their scholarship had been as open about its implications for Black liberation as Edward Said's was about the implications for revolution in Palestine, they would have been killed long before they could raise me. Edward Said was a public intellectual, and a founder of the academic field of postcolonial studies. He came to class in what were surely three-hundred-dollar or five-hundred-dollar suits; an even grand if, in addition to his tailored tweeds and handmade shirts, one considered the blended wool trench coats he wore in winter. He was a "controversial" member of the Palestinian National Council, the legislative body of the PLO, because he publicly criticized Israel *and* the Arab countries, especially the political and cultural policies of Muslim regimes that acted against the national interests of their peoples; and because, at least in class and during office hours, if not on every public stage on which he appeared, he was steadfast in his conviction that the state of Israel had no place in an ethical world.

First Martin Luther King, then the Black Panthers, then Frantz Fanon, and the literature of Toni Morrison and Toni Cade Bambara had tutored me. Edward Said and his aphorisms came after all of that. He was far more important in my life than I was in his. When I met Said, at the age of thirty-three, I was primed, intellectually, for a great leap forward. And in the two short years that I knew him, my ability to explain relations of power did just that, it grew by leaps and bounds.

The Palestinian National Council had been run out of Lebanon by the Israeli Defense Force. They set up shop in Tunis. After one of Said's trips to Tunis, I dropped by during office hours and told him of rumors I'd heard that he was on a hit list. This was nothing new; U.S. Zionists, he said, threatened to kill him all the time. But this was Abu Nidal's hit list. Abu Nidal, in addition to being the commander of the PFLP, the Popular Front for the Liberation of Palestine, was also a fellow parliamentarian on the Palestinian National Council, the government-in-exile. I sat at the end of the student queue outside his office and, when it was my turn, tried tricks Scheherazade would have envied to make the time with him last.

I told Said that I'd heard he and Nidal had argued in Tunis about whether or not the PLO's armed wing should target civilians. Said told Nidal that the PLO should not resort to bombing buses and killing people who were not conscripted by the Israeli Defense Force or police. Nidal was purported to have mocked Said's expensive threads and the safety of his life in New York; and to have reminded Said how difficult it was for an under-resourced guerrilla organization like the PFLP to get next to targets of a military nature; and, finally, to have also reminded him that the Israelis don't engage in this kind of hand-wringing when the lives of Palestinian civilians hang in the balance. The argument ended with my professor being added to Abu Nidal's list of targets.

It was late in the day and the corridors of Philosophy Hall were silent, not even the echo of dust. I was fortunate to have been the last student outside of his office, behind a long-haired, taciturn music theory doctoral candidate who went in before me to discuss his dissertation on tonal harmony in light of Adorno's critique of tonality as an automatic system from which one must escape (but from which nobody can escape). He was gone now and there were no more students in the corridor queue. It did not occur to me that Edward Said had a wife and children that he might want to get home to. And since he didn't throw me out after the customary ten to fifteen minutes, I stayed.

I can't say with any certainty that he confirmed the story about his row with Abu Nidal. Whether it was true at all or if the details amassed like a snowball rolling downhill as it moved among the graduate students, he never let on. He smiled obliquely as I spoke. With his elbows on his desk where dust-flecked light fell on unmarked papers, he steepled his fingertips and touched them to his lips. Then he said:

"Abu Nidal and I aren't friends, but the fact that he might want to kill me doesn't mean we're antagonists."

Edward Said placed his palms on his desk. He told me that, unlike him and Abu Nidal, he and Yasser Arafat were in fact friends; that they sat together and talked for long hours and ate cornflakes drenched in orange juice in the old days, in Beirut when the Israeli Defense Force laid siege to the city and cut off its supply of milk. They were lifelong friends. They were also political antagonists.

"Nidal and I don't have a substantive disagreement, although," he added with a chuckle, "my death at his hands would be substantive from my perspective. On the other hand, Arafat and I have a substantive disagreement. Nidal and I want the same thing, the dismantling of the state of Israel (not just a two-state solution, although that might have to be the first step); and, in its place, the establishment of a secular and economically ethical nation—neither a caliphate nor a Jewish state, but a country where ethnic identity and religion play no part in the distribution of wealth and political capital. Nidal and I share a strategic orientation. We both have what's known as strategic rigidity."

Said stressed the importance of knowing the difference between strategy and tactics. His view was that, yes, armed struggle was necessary in order to bring the Israeli state to an end. "No nation has fallen by plebiscite," he noted. But killing civilians at this point in the struggle was *tactically* ill-advised and would hurt his efforts in the West. While he, Said, was *tactically* engaged in counter-hegemonic struggles, appearances on liberal news programs, speaking at massive teach-ins on university campuses, lobbying U.S. politicians, submitting editorials to the *New York Times*—in other words, while he was in the West engaging in a Gramscian War of Position to win the hearts and minds of liberals—it would be counterproductive to the Palestinian cause if Abu Nidal was bombing Israeli school buses. "What exists, Frank, is a fierce disagreement, granted, but not one which is of political, which is to say strategic, significance. It's a heated debate about tactics." He brought Yasser Arafat back into the conversation. Arafat, Said declared, didn't know the meaning of "strategic rigidity." In other words, he didn't have a vision of what absolute liberation for Palestinians meant, and so he would be satisfied with a squatter camp on the border of Israel "as long as we had our own flag." Nidal and Said, he said, were tactically flexible and strategically rigid. Arafat, in stark contrast to Nidal and Said, he explained, was strategically flexible *and* tactically flexible as well. What this said to me was that, their violent disagreement notwithstanding, Said and Nidal were revolutionaries, whereas Arafat was, at the end of the day, a bourgeois reformer.

I was learning something about the precise nature of language in the service of critical theory and revolutionary praxis. I had always used *antagonism* colloquially, but I hadn't known that I was doing so. Therefore, it never occurred to me that just because an interlocutor wanted to kill you, it did not mean that your relationship with that person was antagonistic. The lesson I learned at dusk in Edward Said's office would see me through harrowing moments of internecine violence months later, when I finished my MFA at Columbia and left New York and moved to South Africa and joined the African National Congress.

A desire for the complete dismantling of a paradigm; that was the essence of strategic rigidity: desire into discourse: discourse into praxis. Tactical flexibility was the awareness that there was more than one way to skin a cat; but there was only one cat, not two or three. The cat was the understanding that revolution cannot be reconciled with reform. Again, the idea of strategic rigidity was not Said's original thought. Said was a student of Fanon's works. And we read Fanon's *The Wretched of the Earth* in the Cultural Studies Project yearlong seminar that Said and Jean Franco taught. Early on in that book, Frantz Fanon provides the sinews of strategic rigidity when he writes:

> To break up the colonial world does not mean that after the frontiers have been abolished lines of communication will be set up between the two zones. The destruction of the colonial world is no more and no less tha[n] the abolition of one zone, its burial in the depths of the earth or its expulsion from the country . . . As far as the native is concerned, morality is very concrete; it is to silence the settler's defiance, to break his flaunting violence—in a word, to put him out of the picture.

On this passage Said and Nidal could agree: this passage from Fanon is the cat; but how to skin the cat? That's where they fell out. Arafat, I was learning from Said via Fanon, was a reformer—the fact that he engaged in armed struggle did not change his political orientation; he was no revolutionary because, unlike Said and Nidal, he (Yasser Arafat) had accepted the existence and legitimacy of the state of Israel. Edward Said and Abu Nidal were neither violent nor nonviolent, meaning neither man elevated tactics to the level of principles in the way that Gandhi did.

The Frantz Fanon of *Black Skin, White Masks* differs from the Frantz Fanon of *The Wretched of the Earth* on the question of violence. It is my steadfast conviction that this difference should be thrown into relief in order to understand how the Black, the Slave, suffers in ways that cannot be reconciled with the suffering of oppressed Humans, such as the postcolonial subject.

The Frantz Fanon of *The Wretched of the Earth* makes two points concerning violence. The first point is that violence is a precondition for thought, meaning that without violence the reigning episteme and its elaborated social structures cannot be called into question paradigmatically. Without revolutionary violence, politics is always predicated on the ensemble of existing questions (and these questions are in service to reformist, not revolutionary, projects). The second point is that this absolute, or in Afropessimist parlance *gratuitous*, violence is not so absolute and gratuitous after all—not, that is, in Frantz Fanon's Algeria or in Edward Said's Palestine. It comes with a therapeutic grounding wire, a purpose that can be articulated: the restoration of the native's land. One can read Fanon's second gesture as either an alibi for or a concession toward his hosts, the Algerians; it doesn't matter. What matters is that there is an irreconcilable difference between the violence that positions and is performed on the Slave in social death and the violence that positions and is performed on the (non-Black) native in civil society. The vulnerability of the native is open, but not absolute: materially speaking, she carves out zones of respite by putting the settler "out of the picture," whether back to the European zone or into the sea. There is no analogy between the native's guarantee of restoration predicated on her need to put the settler out of the picture—the Fanon of *The Wretched of the Earth*—and the Slave's guarantee of restoration predicated on her need to put the Human out of the picture—the Fanon of *Black Skin, White Masks*.

By way of contrast, the Frantz Fanon of *Black Skin, White Masks* hits upon (but is never quite comfortable with) the idea that the violence Black people face is a violence of a parallel universe. In short, Black people and non-Black people do not exist in the same universe or paradigm of violence, any more than fish and birds exist in the same region of the world. It is not the violence of economic exploitation and alienation, although most Black people are members of the working class and they suffer, at some important level, economic exploitation as a result of alienation from what is, presumptively, their labor power. I say *presumptively* because Black labor is not the possession of Black people any more than we possess our bodies. Nor are we dispossessed of land like the Irish or the Native Americans or Said and Nidal's Palestinians; notwithstanding the fact that, save Ethiopia, all of Black Africa has been colonized at one time or another. The antagonist of the worker is the capitalist. The antagonist of the Native is the settler. *But the antagonist of the Black is the Human being.* I could not explain all of this when I knew Edward Said, but I *felt* it, this rejoinder, like an unscratched itch. My friendship and solidarity with Sameer, another Palestinian activist, whom I worked with in Minneapolis during the First Intifada (in 1988, a year before I went to Columbia and met Edward Said) had surrendered to the force of his unconscious when grieving the death of his cousin in Ramallah. "The shameful and humiliating way the soldiers run their hands up and

down your body," he said. Then he said, "But the shame and humiliation runs even deeper if the Israeli soldier is an Ethiopian Jew." The
itch was becoming a spike wound; so much so that as the years passed
by I saw more dissonances than resonances between Sameer Bishara's
and Edward Said's Front for the Liberation of Palestine, and the Black
Liberation Army, whose cadres Stella and I had once held dear.

. . .

ON OCTOBER 22, 1970, the Black Liberation Army (BLA) detonated
a timed-release antipersonnel bomb at the funeral of a San Francisco
police officer. This, according to the Justice Department and BLA-
sanctioned literature, was the first of their forty to sixty paramilitary
actions launched between 1969 and 1981. Even though nationwide
they probably never numbered more than four hundred insurgents
working in small, often semi-connected cells, their armed response to
the violence that enmeshes Black life was probably the most consistent
and politically legible response since the slave revolts that occurred
between 1800 and 1840.

Twenty years after the Black Liberation Army launched its first
attack on the state, Toni Morrison, appearing on Bill Moyers's PBS
talk show *A World of Ideas*, was queried about the moral ground that
Sethe, the protagonist of her most famous novel, stood on when she
killed her child, Beloved, in order to save her from slavery. What right,
in other words, did she have to offer her child death as a sanctuary
from bondage? Herein lies the paradox of political engagement when
the subject of politics is the Slave. "It was the right thing to do," Toni
Morrison said, "but she had no right to do it."

The analogy between on the one hand, Sethe and Beloved, and,
on the other hand, insurgents from the Black Liberation Army is a
structural analogy that highlights how both the BLA insurgents and
Toni Morrison's characters are void of relationality. In such a void,

death is a synonym for sanctuary. When death is a synonym for sanctuary, political engagement is, to say the least, a paradoxical undertaking. When I sat on that grassy knoll at the Walker Art Center with Sameer Bishara and, later, when I went to Columbia and met Edward Said, this paradox was something that I disavowed.

At the time I believed in the analogy between Said's and Sameer's much-loved Popular Front for the Liberation of Palestine and my much-loved Black Liberation Army. But when the force of Sameer's unconscious confessed that being frisked and molested by Black Jews was more humiliating and of a greater threat to the psychic life of Palestinians than being frisked and molested by White Jews, my dream of solidarity and redemption went into free fall. It was 1988, and I was only thirty-two, without the toolbox of critical theory needed to explain my sudden disorientation, even to myself. To be honest, my conscious mind tried to ignore the clench in my gut; it clung to a dream of a global, multicolored revolutionary army that would liberate us all. Internationalism was a talisman that I could not let go of. I would not allow my rational mind to say what my unconscious was telling me: that a new Palestinian state would be just as anti-Black as the Israeli state and the U.S., in fact, as anti-Black as the world. This was a thought that hurt too much, so it remained repressed until the turn of the twenty-first century, when it blathered out in spittle and howls beneath the bright lights of a psych ward at UC Berkeley.

Since the murder of Michael Brown* occurred on August 9, 2014, in Ferguson, Missouri, it has become common for radical activists to compare Ferguson with Palestine. Comparisons such as these are based on an empirical comparison of cops killing a Black youth in Ferguson and IDF forces killing Palestinian youths in the West Bank and in Gaza. If we use

---

* Michael Brown, an unarmed Black teenager, was shot and killed on August 9, 2014, by Darren Wilson, a White police officer, in Ferguson, Missouri, a suburb of St. Louis.

our *eyes* the two phenomena have a lot in common. It stands to reason, by extension, revolutionaries in Palestine, such as the largely secular and Marxist Front for the Liberation of Palestine, and revolutionaries in the U.S., such as the largely secular and Marxist Black Liberation Army, could be seen as fighting different factions of the same enemy (capitalism and colonialism), in different countries. But this is not the case.

Most revolutionary theorists try to show how the bond of *political interests* among people of color who are struggling against state domination is of primary importance: we are all anti-capitalists, is a cry commonly heard, or we are all anti-colonialists, or we're all anti-sexist. But this alliance of the conscious mind fails to account for the way the unconscious mind refuses to calibrate with political interests. This is the pitfall of most leftist thinking.

The Black Liberation Army's relationship to state violence is *not* analogous to other insurgent organizations' relationship to violence. Ferguson is not Palestine. Ferguson is a threat to Palestine, a threat far greater than that of Israel's occupying army. At the heart of this *structural* antagonism between like-minded revolutionaries is the difference between two irreconcilable modes of vertigo. Subjective vertigo and objective vertigo.

The guerrilla war that the Black Liberation Army waged against the United States in the late 1960s, the 1970s, and the early 1980s was part of a multifaceted struggle to redress Black dispossession that has been waged since the first Africans landed in the "New" World. With only small arms and crude explosives at their disposal, with little or nothing in the way of logistical support,* with no liberated zone to reclaim or retreat to, and with no more than a vague knowledge

---

* Especially after 1975, when the Vietnam War ended and the revolutionary White Left, like the Weather Underground Organization, came out of hiding, surrendered to authorities, took the often-meager sentences that courts imposed upon them—often no more than probation—and then returned to the private and quotidian of everyday life.

that there were a few hundred other insurgents,* the BLA launched sixty-six operations against the largest police state in the world. Vertigo must have seized them each time they clashed with agents of a nuclear-weapons regime with 3 million troops in uniform, a regime that could put 150,000 new police on the streets in any given year, and whose ordinary White citizens frequently deputized themselves in the name of law and order. Subjective vertigo, no doubt; a dizzying sense that one was moving or spinning in an otherwise stationary world, a vertigo brought on by a clash of grossly asymmetrical forces. There are suitable analogies, for this kind of vertigo must have also seized Native Americans who launched AIM's occupation of Wounded Knee; and FALN insurgents who battled the FBI; and Palestinians in the PLFP who battled the Israeli Defense Force.

Throughout this book I have argued that the Black is a sentient being though not a Human being. The Black's and the Human's disparate relationship to violence is at the heart of this failure of analogy. The Human suffers contingent violence, violence that kicks in when he resists (or is perceived to resist) the disciplinary discourse of civil society's rules and laws. But Black peoples' saturation by violence is a paradigmatic necessity, not simply the performance of contingency. To be constituted by *and* disciplined by violence, to be gripped simultaneously by subjective and objective vertigo, is indicative of a life that is radically different from the life of a sentient being who is constituted by discourse and disciplined by violence when he breaks with the ruling discursive codes. When we begin to assess revolutionary armed struggle in this comparative context we find that Human revolutionaries (workers, women, gays and lesbians, postcolonial subjects)

---

* In *Assata: An Autobiography*, Assata Shakur emphasizes the decentralized, nonhierarchical structure of the BLA—whether by design or desperation. Marilyn Buck, one of the few White "task force" members of the Black Liberation Army, told me this as well, when I visited her in prison.

suffer *subjective vertigo* when they respond to the state violence with revolutionary violence; but they are spared *objective vertigo*. This is because the most disorienting aspects of their lives are induced by the struggles that arise from intra-Human conflicts over competing conceptual frameworks and disputed cognitive maps, such as the American Indian Movement's demand for the return of Turtle Island vs. the U.S.'s desire to maintain territorial integrity, or the Fuerzas Armadas de Liberación Nacional's (FALN) demand for Puerto Rican independence vs. the U.S.'s desire to maintain Puerto Rico as a territory. But for the Black, that is, for the Slave, there are no cognitive maps, no conceptual frameworks of suffering and dispossession that are analogous with the myriad maps and frameworks that explain the dispossession of Human subalterns.

The structural violence that subsumes Black insurgents' cognitive maps and conceptual frameworks *also* subsumes my intellectual and creative efforts as a writer. As a Black writer I am tasked with making sense of this violence without being overwhelmed and disoriented by it. In other words, my writing must somehow be indexical of that which *exceeds* narration, while being ever mindful of the incomprehension the writing would foster, the failure, that is, of interpretation were the indices to actually escape the narrative. The stakes of this dilemma are almost as high for the Black writer facing the reader as they are for the Black insurgent facing the police and the courts. For the intellectual act of embracing members of the Black Liberation Army as beings worthy of empathic consideration is terrifying. One's writing proceeds with fits and starts that have little to do with the problems of building the thesis or finding the methodology to make the case. As I write, I am more aware of the rage and anger of my reader-ideal (an angry mob as readers) than I am of my own desires and strategies for assembling my argument. Vertigo seizes me with a rash of condemnations that emanate from within me and swirl around me. I am speaking to me but not *through* me, yet there seems to be no other way to speak. I am speaking through the voice and gaze of a mob of, let's just say it, White Americans; and my efforts to marshal a mob of Black people, to conjure the Black Liberation Army, smack of compensatory gestures. It is not that the BLA doesn't come to my aid, that they don't push back, but neither I nor my insurgent allies can make the case that we are worthy of our suffering and justified in our actions and not terrorists and apologists for terror who should be locked away forever. How can we be worthy of our suffering without being worthy of ourselves? I press on, even though the vertigo that seizes me is so overwhelming that its precise nature—subjective, stemming from within me, or objective, catalyzed by my context, the raging throng—cannot be determined. I have no reference points apart from the mob that gives no quarter. If I write, "Freedom fighter," from within my ear they scream, "Terrorist"! If I say, "Prisoner of war," they chant, "Cop killer"! Their denunciations are sustained only by assertion, but they ring truer than my painstaking exegesis. No firewall protects me from them; no liberated psychic zone offers me sanctuary. I want to stop and turn myself in.

The Black psyche emerges within a context of structural or paradigmatic violence that cannot be analogized with the emergence of White or non-Black psyches. The upshot of this is that the Black psyche is in a perpetual war with itself because it is usurped by a White gaze that hates the Black imago and wants to destroy it. The Black self is a divided self or, better, it is a juxtaposition of hatred projected toward a Black imago and love for a White ideal: hence the state of war. This state of being at war forecloses upon the possession of elements constitutive of psychic integration: bearing witness (to suffering), atonement, naming and recognition, representation. As such, one cannot represent oneself, even *to* oneself, as a bona fide political subject, as a subject of redress. Black political ontology is foreclosed in the unconscious just as it is foreclosed in the court, for the "black ego, far from being too immature or weak to integrate, is an absence haunted by its and others' negativity. In this respect the memory of loss is its only possible communication." It is important to note that loss is an effect of temporality; it implies a metonymic chain that absence cannot apprehend. Put differently but no less to the point, "loss" indicates a prior plenitude, "absence" does not. Loss is an impoverished and inaccurate concept when deployed to think about Black suffering. And the paucity of its explanatory power is also part and parcel of the paucity of the analogies politicos draw between Black insurgency and the insurgency of other oppressed beings. This is not about playing oppression Olympics, as some would have it; it's about making critical assessments of what have heretofore been insufficiently comparative analyses of the multiracial wretched of the earth; specifically, what has been missing is sufficient comparison between the gratuitous violence of social death and the contingent violence of colonial, class, and gendered subjugation: a comparative analysis of the dead and the living.

In short, *all sentient beings*, Humans and Blacks, bond over the imago of the Black phobic object, that we might form a psychic "community" even though we cannot form political community: When I was twelve, my cheers were among the loudest when the Indians called Dad a "nigger man." Recall that moment in *Black Skin, White Masks* when Fanon sees himself through the eyes of a White boy who cries in terror, "Look, a Negro!"

David Marriott writes, "Symbolically, Fanon knows that any black man could have triggered the child's fantasy of being devoured that attaches itself to a fear of blackness, for this fear signifies the 'racial epidermal schema' of Western culture—the unconscious fear of being literally consumed by the black other. Neither the boy nor Fanon seems able to avoid this schema, moreover, for culture determines and maintains the imago associated with blackness; cultural fantasy allows Fanon and the boy to form a bond through racial antagonism."

This phobia is composed of affective responses, sensory reactions, or presubjective constellations of intensities, as well as representational responses, such as the threatening imago of a fecal body that portends contamination. And this affective/representational performance is underwritten by paradigmatic violence; which is to say, the phobic fantasy secures "its objective value" because it lives within violence too pervasive to describe. "The picture of the black psyche that emerges from" this intrusion "is one that is always late, never on time, violently presented and fractured by these moments of specular intrusion." The overwhelming psychic alienation that emerges from the literal fear and trembling of the White boy when Fanon appears is accompanied by foul language that plunders and traumatizes the Black psyche. One learns, for example, that when one appears one brings with one the threat of cannibalism. "What a thing," Fanon intones, "to have eaten one's father!"

Again, though this is a bond between Blacks and Whites (or, more precisely, between Blacks and non-Blacks), it is produced by a *violent intrusion that does not cut both ways*. Whereas the phobic bond is an injunction against Black psychic integration and Black filial and affilial relations, it is the lifeblood of White psychic integration and filial (which is to say, domestic) and affilial (or institutional) relations. For whoever says "rape" says Black; whoever says "prison" says Black; and whoever says "AIDS" says Black—*the Negro is a phobogenic object*: a past without a heritage, the map of gratuitous violence, and a program of complete disorder. If a social movement is to be neither social democratic nor Marxist, in terms of its structure of political desire, then it should grasp the invitation of social death embodied in Black beings.

If we are to be honest with ourselves, we must admit that the "Negro" has been inviting Whites, as well as civil society's junior partners (for example, Palestinians, Native Americans, Latinx) to the dance of social death for hundreds of years, but few have wanted to learn the steps. They have been, and remain today (even in the most anti-racist movements, like anti-colonial insurgency) invested elsewhere. Black liberation, as a prospect, makes radicalism more dangerous to the U.S. and the world.

This is not because it raises the specter of an alternative polity (such as socialism, or community control of existing resources), but because its condition of possibility and gesture of resistance function as a politics of refusal and a refusal to affirm, a program of complete disorder. One must embrace its disorder, its incoherence, and allow oneself to be elaborated by it, if indeed one's politics are to be underwritten by a revolutionary desire. *What other lines of accountability are there when slaves are in the room?*

There is nothing foreign, frightening, or even unpracticed about the embrace of disorder and incoherence. The desire to be embraced, and elaborated, by disorder and incoherence is not anathema in and of itself. No one, for example, has ever been known to say, Gee whiz, if only my orgasms would end a little sooner, or maybe not come at all. Few so-called radicals desire to be embraced, and elaborated, by the disorder and incoherence of Blackness—and the state of political movements in the U.S. today is marked by this very Negrophobogenisis: Gee-whiz, if only Black rage could be more coherent, or maybe not come at all. Perhaps there is something more terrifying about the joy of Black than there is in the joy of sex (unless one is talking sex with a Negro). Perhaps coalitions today prefer to remain inorgasmic in the face of civil society—with hegemony as a handy prophylactic, just in case.

If, through this stasis or paralysis, they try to do the work of prison abolition, that work will fail, for it is always work *from* a position of coherence (such as the worker) on *behalf* of a position of incoherence of the Black: radical politics morphed into extensions of the master's prerogative. In this way, social formations on the Left remain blind to the contradictions of coalitions between Humans and Slaves. They remain coalitions operating within the logic of civil society and function less as revolutionary promises than as crowding-out scenarios of Black antagonisms, simply feeding Black people's frustration.

Whereas the positionality of the worker (whether a factory worker demanding a monetary wage, an immigrant, or a white woman demanding a social wage) gestures toward the reconfiguration of civil society, the positionality of the Black subject (whether a prison-slave or a prison-slave-in-waiting) gestures toward the disconfiguration of civil society. From the coherence of civil society, the Black subject beckons with the incoherence of civil war, a war that reclaims Blackness not as a positive value, but as a politically enabling site, to quote Fanon, of "absolute dereliction." It is a "scandal" that rends civil society asunder. Civil war, then, becomes the unthought, but never forgotten, understudy of hegemony. It is a Black specter waiting in the wings, an endless antagonism that cannot be satisfied (via reform or reparation), but must nonetheless be pursued to the death.

But lest we forget, this is not a question of volition. It is not as simple as waking up in the morning and deciding, *in one's conscious mind*, to "do the right thing." For when we scale up from the terrain of the psyche to the terrain of armed struggle, we may be faced with a situation in which the eradication of the generative mechanism of Black suffering is something that is not in *anyone's* interest. Eradication of the generative mechanisms of Black suffering is not in the interest of Palestinians and Israelis, as my shocking encounter with my friend Sameer, on a placid hillside, suggests; because his anti-Black phobia mobilizes the fantasy of belonging that the Israeli state might otherwise strip him of. For him to secure his status as a relational being (if only in his unconscious), his unconscious must labor to maintain the

Black as a genealogical isolate. "The shame and humiliation runs even deeper if the Israeli soldier was an Ethiopian Jew."

The Israelis are killing the Palestinians, literally; but psychic life, Human capacity for relations, is vouchsafed by a libidinal relay between them and their common labor to avoid "niggerization" (Fanon). This relay is the generative mechanism that makes life *life*. It is also the generative mechanism of Black suffering and isolation. The end of this generative mechanism would mean the end of the world. We would find ourselves peering into the abyss.

This trajectory is too iconoclastic for working-class, post-colonial, and/or radical feminist conceptual frameworks. The Human need to be liberated *in* the world is not the same as the Black need to be liberated *from* the world; which is why even their most radical cognitive maps draw borders between the living and the dead. *Finally, if we push this analysis to the wall, it becomes clear that eradication of the generative mechanisms of Black suffering is also not in the interests of Black revolutionaries.* For how can we disimbricate Black juridical and political desire from the Black psyche's desire to destroy the Black imago, a desire that constitutes the psyche? In short, bonding with Whites and non-Blacks over phobic reactions to the Black imago provides the Black psyche with the only semblance of psychic integration it is likely to have: the need to destroy a Black imago *and* love a White ideal. "In these circumstances, having a 'white' unconscious may be the only way to connect with—or even contain—the overwhelming and irreparable sense of loss. The intruding fantasy offers the medium to connect with the lost internal object, the ego, but there is also no 'outside' to this 'real fantasy' and the effects of intrusion are irreparable." This raises the question, who is the speaking subject of Black insurgent testimony; who bears witness when the Black insurgent takes the stand?

Who is writing this book?

CHAPTER SEVEN

Mario's

1

Eleven years had passed since Stella and I drove down Hennepin Avenue in the dead of night, and three years had passed since we parted. I had won a literary award that sent me to South Africa to research a novel that was never written, two six-week trips in 1989 and 1990. Between these trips to South Africa I lived in New York and had studied with Edward Said. Now I was married to a South African named Khanya. We met in Johannesburg in 1989 and were married in New York at City Hall in the summer of 1990. She was a law student from Bophuthatswana—a scattered patchwork of enclaves spread across what was then the Cape Province, the Orange Free State, and the Transvaal. The land in between was called "South Africa" and it tended to be more fertile than Bop, a Black Bantustan run by Black proxies for their Pretoria paymasters. Khanya, at the time, was ambivalent about law school; her dream was to make films. Khanya had a daughter, Reba, who was two years old when I met her in 1989, during a state of emergency. Reba lived, not in Johannesburg with Khanya, but in Bop with her grandparents. She would live there until we were settled and financially sound enough to send for her.

By the summer of 1991, the summer of my graduation, I thought we'd be on a houseboat in Amsterdam, where I would write fiction and poetry when I wasn't waiting tables or teaching creative writing; and where Khanya would be in film school. In the evenings, we would string a speaker out to the deck and listen to soft jazz ballads and smoke the best weed and gaze at the languid and bittersweet Dutch as they cycled home along tranquil canals.

Immigrating to South Africa where Black people couldn't be out and about anytime and anywhere they pleased, couldn't get a meal at any restaurant they wanted, and ran the risk of being stopped at checkpoints that would choke the city like weeds without warning was not my idea of a plan. Why not just stay in the States? Which was not an insignificant sentiment lurking beneath what happened, for Khanya suffered from the shock of seeing America show its true face of racism. The war in Kuwait/Iraq began that winter and I came home one night and told her of the Sikh who had sat beside me and was kicked in the teeth on the subway.

"Why," she had asked one cold February morning in the moldy flat we shared with rodents on a hill in Washington Heights, "should I trade one South Africa for another, when my family isn't even here?" I often wonder if she would have stayed had I had the presence of mind to say, "I'm your family." I hadn't told her what had happened to me and Stella in 1980. Why we left Minneapolis and went to Dartmouth. I didn't think she could take *that* vision of America. As she left for the travel agent to buy a ticket, I told myself that I had been right not to tell her. Had I told her that story she might not have come to the States at all. Khanya left in February 1991. I graduated and followed her.

From my time of arrival in 1991 to the first nonracial elections in 1994, in which I voted, as permanent resident, for Mandela, I struggled alongside thousands of others to topple the apartheid government, to bring the ANC to power, and to crush White hegemony and capitalism in South Africa. (Not everyone in the ANC shared the latter goal; nor were White hegemony and capitalism destroyed.) Not since my adolescence had I lived through a political context in which the word *revolution* was used without irony; a context in which the dream of toppling a racist regime was a matter of "when" and "how," not "if." During those years, I did everything and anything that was asked of me to make this dream a reality, from legally sanctioned political organizing to insurgent tactics that would make a "pacifist" cringe. *Pacifist* is in scare quotes because the same person who condemns guerrilla warfare will pay their taxes without pause or thank a military veteran for his service. In the first instance the "pacifist" disavows her identity as a mass murderer; in the second instance, she applauds in one person the behavior she condemns in another. Armed with Edward Said's mini-lecture on strategic rigidity and tactical flexibility, I went to South Africa unencumbered by this mendacious mind-set.

In the gray zone between organizing and insurgency, I worked for the ANC Regional Peace Commission; which also served as a cover for gunrunning weapons to squatter camps and townships. At the ANC Peace Commission I wrote reports for Amnesty International and for Human Rights Watch. But, as I said, we were also engaged in gunrunning. And we had to hide this fact in our reports, of course, because you have to be a "pure" victim to get support from these Western NGOs. So there was a series of disinformation initiatives that we were engaged in. In other words, we came face-to-face with the awful liberalism of Human rights discourse and how it acts as a drag on revolutionary activity.

In addition, I also conducted political education workshops on Gramsci and other theorists for members of a clandestine uMkhonto we Sizwe unit; and supplied the commander with "political scenarios": what-if documents on the gain or loss of political capital that might result from insurrectionary initiatives. There were three theaters of insurgent tactics that this unit, as well as other units, focused on.

1. Secret propaganda: Creating an information context or a disinformation context in the press that advanced the work of aboveground mass movement structures; and the production of political broadsides that could not be attributed to MK.

2. Psychological warfare: Mainly in the university-industrial complex where our targets were English-speaking liberals, rather than Afrikaners. The endgame was to force liberals to openly wield the violence that sustains them. The overarching objective was to isolate and emasculate White liberals (English-speaking South Africans) who were in key positions of power, and who were against apartheid, but not in favor of a socialist dispensation. These individuals wanted an evolution from apartheid capitalism to laissez-faire capitalism. Ultimately our goal was to turn the commanding heights of the university-industrial complex into liberated zones. This would help to weaken the overall structure of racial capitalism in South African.

3. Covert operations: The violent response to Inkatha and the state security forces, which often meant simply gunrunning to ANC-aligned Self-Defense Units in the townships. The people I reported to were students at the University of Witwatersrand, where I taught when I first arrived; students who had been

trained in the Soviet Union or in secret guerrilla bases *inside* South Africa. When the Soviet Union was dissolved, our supply of arms from the Soviet Bloc began to dissolve as well. Unconventional and creative ways of obtaining arms were developed. Such as bilking Western NGOs by working with a dedicated comrade on the inside to create a fantasy project and then funneling the bulk of the money to purchase weapons for armed struggle in the townships and squatter camps.

In the "daylight" realm of political organizing, I was seconded to the ANC Subregional Executive—a five-person group of political commissars for Johannesburg and the sixteen surrounding townships. And Nadine Gordimer, the South African novelist who won the Nobel Prize in Literature in 1991, nominated me to take her seat as projects coordinator on the Regional Executive Committee of the Congress of South African Writers.

But none of the activities mentioned above happened overnight. I went to South Africa reluctantly, intending to stay only long enough for Khanya to finish her law degree. More disappointments and reversals were bundled into the first six months of our life in South Africa than I had known since the first six months of my life with Stella eleven years prior, in Minneapolis. Had I been an Afropessimist and not a Marxist at the time, I might not have been so broken by it all; I would have known that the world is one big plantation.

I went to work in a dreamy trattoria called Mario's in a suburb of Jo'burg not far from where Khanya had returned to law school. White English-speaking South Africans called "Wits" the "Harvard of the South."

Shortly before I arrived, the government confiscated Khanya's identity documents. She was stateless, now, in the place of her birth. And her passport was revoked. Even if she changed her mind we couldn't leave. The dream of Amsterdam was receding swiftly. Nor could I get permanent residency through her status as a citizen of South Africa. Khanya and I were collateral damage. Her older sister, Rebone, had been fired from her job in the Finance Department in Bop. Rebone's partner was an insurgent in the Azanian People's Liberation Army, the armed wing of the Pan Africanist Congress (PAC), and he was wanted by the South African intelligence community for the transport of arms and munitions from Zimbabwe to South Africa. So Rebone was fired and placed under house arrest and Khanya's identity documents were confiscated as well.

None of this fazed me when I arrived, for I had a glowing letter of recommendation from Edward Said. Within days I had landed a job as a junior lecturer in comparative literature.* Khanya and I thought our problems were solved. But on the day before classes began, I was fired. I went to the office of the dean to sign my contract. Instead, I saw that she had a copy of my letter of recommendation from Edward Said on her desk next to a copy of the syllabus for my graduate seminar, Intellectuals and the State. The dean was aloof and pushed for time. She had no contract for me to sign. Instead, the dean told me a story: Edward Said had given a public lecture at Wits, a few months before I emigrated. "Our Jewish students," as she called them, "rioted." She told me how they tore through campus overturning dustbins and disturbing the peace; the kind of thing "we" are used to from "our Black students." Apparently, *her* Jewish students had not agitated on campus prior to Said's visit. Employing me, she said, ran the risk of all that happening again; especially when the contents of the syllabus—she slid

---

* Equivalent of an assistant professor in the United States.

it across the desk to me—got out. I pleaded with her. But she stood up and offered me her hand.

It was January, the hottest month in Jo'burg, the coldest month in New York. I didn't go home for several hours. How would I break this news to Khanya? I read a newspaper in the dining room of Wit's Great Hall, across the street from where we lived. The headlines gave no indication that our lives had been turned upside down. The Soviet Union had dissolved into the Russian Federation, which meant Cuba was now the ANC's only source of tactical support for the armed struggle; President George H. W. Bush ate something bad on a state visit to Japan and vomited on Prime Minister Kiichi Miyazawa's lap; a cleaning woman found photos of Texas millionaire John Bryan sucking the toes of the Duchess of York; Paul Simon's tour opened in South Africa; and serial killer Jeffrey Dahmer pled guilty but insane. Not one article on the manhole I fell into that morning.

The professors in Comparative Literature were appalled by the dean's reversal of their decision to hire me. Graduate students had already signed up for my seminar, which was to start tomorrow. I said I would teach for free. But Ulrike Kistner, a professor who (I later found out) worked in the underground and was a dedicated Marxist, said that would be unethical. She persuaded the chair of the department to pay my salary from Comp Lit's annual outside-speakers budget. It came to less than what I would have earned had the dean not fired me, and there were no health benefits, nor would there be employment documents that I could take to Home Affairs to get permanent residency. Finally, at term's end, I'd be out in the cold again. But it was better than nothing. I also waited tables at Mario's several noon and night shifts a week. And I taught an evening creative writing workshop for Wits' extension, but that, I was soon to find out, would also come to an early end.

2

On the evening of June 1, 1992, as my journal records, I went straight to class from the aftermath of a massacre in Phola Park.* I looked around the table at fifteen alabaster faces and said to myself, *I can't do this. I really can't do this. Not tonight. Pretend that their stories and their vignettes are meaningful—or that they're ethical! Pretend that I care about them. There's Huntley Bridge, the diamond jeweler from Parktown; primed and ready to go with fifteen copies of his turgid memories of the bombing of London when he was a boy. And beside him, Grace Kensington, mummified in enough makeup to open a Revlon franchise. Last week we had to slog through a tea party for the wives of silver mine managers ten years ago in Zambia. And young Jimmy. Why can't I ever recall his last name? Jimmy Deadhead, that ought to do. How are we doing today, Jimmy? Not too coked-up, I hope. If only he knew how much I loath science fiction. Okay? And Muriel Mendelssohn, sweet little Muriel, she's in her mid-thirties, like me: Muriel who writes sunflower and poppy vignettes about life in a White boarding school just outside Harare, when Zimbabwe was still that quaint land called Rhodesia.*

They vibed off of me. There's no better feel-good than praise from a Black man. I'd become their first Black friend (besides their domestics). Grace invited me to Sandton for tea. Muriel wanted my help

---

* The details are complicated, in that the South African Defense Force maimed and shot people, and destroyed many shacks in Phola Park (the day before my creative writing class), in their search for the weapons we had smuggled into Self-Defense Units (SDUs) in the squatter camp; while, almost simultaneously, Inkatha Freedom Party paramilitaries (*impimpis*) had carried out a massacre of people who lived in a township—not a squatter camp—that was just a soccer pitch away from the Phola Park squatter camp.

with her jazz collection. Huntley Bridge had a deal on diamonds for me. Jimmy, bless his heart, wanted to know if I got high.

I had dreaded walking into that workshop. How could I have gone there after going to Phola Park? I could have called in sick. Now I'm out of a job. I was emotionally unable to workshop Huntley's piece on English children in the air raid. I told them we'd get to it after a preliminary exercise. I passed around fifteen copies of a newspaper article on the massacres. I asked them to get out their Gabriele Rico book, *Writing the Natural Way*, and review the section on clustering and mind-mapping as a means to producing a more engaging vignette. Not the first time I'd started the session like that. But it was the first time when the word I asked them to cluster (once it was *fear*, once it was *love*, another time it was *loss*, last night it was *violence*) was put deliberately in context of the here and now.

"Why are we doing this?" said Grace. "I thought we were going to work on Huntley's story."

"We are. But I want us to do this now—I'll do it with you."

Huntley said, "She asked you why."

"Because three hundred people are being killed each month in this country and more than half of them within a twenty-mile radius of this university. I can't for the life of me understand why you're not affected by that, seeing as how you're so deeply affected by deaths that happened two thousand miles away and more than fifty years ago."

Huntley hissed, "I lived through that!" slapping the table with his manuscript.

"You're living through *this*. Granted, you might not know how you're living through it. That's what the clustering helps you find out."

"I didn't come here to find out."

Then young Jimmy, ever the chilled-out peacemaker, chimed in, "Hey, china, like, I'm affected by it, and I'm sure Huntley is too. But what we're trying to say is that it's just not in our writing. Like, my writing isn't even about countries, china, it's all about other worlds."

"Don't call me 'china,' you're not Black, you're a White Led Zeppelin–head from the suburb of Norwood."

We'd crossed the Rubicon. The lines were drawn. All that was left was to fight it out. Huntley told young Jimmy that he didn't have to take that, "not from him." My back stiffened at his "not from him." Grace nodded. Muriel looked distressed. The rest of the class sat absolutely still.

Huntley and Grace, the elder statesman and stateswoman, gave me a thorough working-over. Grace said it was a violation of etiquette to bring politics into the classroom: This is neither a Boer campus nor is it a Black campus; we're neutral at places like Wits. She said she had a mind to report me to the extension school director. Huntley followed with a tirade on how he'd survived Hitler's firebombs but "my mother did not!" He told me how he'd spent such a long time in the countryside only to come back to London and find his mother had died. "Do you have any idea what a shock that was? I was eight years old at the time. My father brought us here to get away from that. Not to rush headlong into it again. I'm nearing retirement. I want peace, and peace starts with peace of mind."

It was like group therapy, where I was both the trauma and the cure.

"Okay," I said at last, "now that you've had your say, let's scan the news clipping and the images, then write the word *violence* in the center of an unlined sheet of paper, cluster and mind-map the word; then write your vignette. As usual, we'll take fifteen minutes for the whole exercise. Whoever wants to share when we're done can share; it's okay if you don't."

Huntley balled up my newspaper clipping and threw it behind him.

"You haven't heard a word we've said. I don't even read the bloody newspapers! My days are hard enough. Do you know what's happened to my diamond sales during all these years of the sanctions? I'm a British subject. I'm not a Boer. This violence has nothing to do with me. I've always said live and let live."

"You're a diamond seller, Huntley." I folded my hands on the table and very calmly told him, "You've got blood all over you. The rest of you pay apartheid taxes and vote. What more of a connection to these massacres do you need?"

Huntley rose to his feet. He snatched the copies of his manuscript from the people around him and stuffed them into his satchel.

Muriel Mendelssohn had been listening in distress, as though she were reliving some horrible scolding from the headmistress in her Rhodesian boarding school. Now her voice cracked as she spoke. "We were all happy in your class. Now look what's happening. You came here with an agenda. Like *you're* having problems so you're going to impose your neurosis onto us."

"I *came* here straight from Phola Park, where—"

Slowly, Huntley sat back down. "What were you doing in Phola Park?"

"I work for the ANC Peace Comm—"

"I bloody well knew it," Huntley cried.

"He wants to brainwash us," said Grace Kensington, looking around for confirmation.

"I'm leaving," Huntley said, but he remained seated. "This fellow can't help us with our writing."

Muriel said, "After tea, we can all come back and be sensible."

"Tea is going to be delayed for the fifteen minutes it takes to do this exercise," I told them.

Grace was incredulous. "No tea? Rubbish. First you turn our creative writing class into a communist reeducation camp; then you inflict tea deprivation. We are not your slaves!"

I started laughing.

"You think I'm funny? I'm a joke to you?"

"You live in Sandton, don't you, Grace?"

"Don't answer that, Grace," Huntley scoffed. "The man's a sophist. Where she lives has nothing to do with *tea*."

"How many other people live in Sandton?" I went on. Four of the fifteen students lived in Sandton. The rest of them lived in other rich White suburbs near to Sandton, such as Rosebank and Parktown (where Nadine Gordimer lived)—well-policed enclaves for the British. Those under forty lived east, in Yeoville, Norwood, or Bellevue East, where apartments could be found.

I told them some things they knew already: that no more than a thin highway separated Sandton from the Black township of Alexandra. "Alex" had a population of four hundred thousand residents living in one of the most densely populated areas in the world. Sandton had wide boulevards, sprawling parks, a five-star shopping mall, and houses the size of citadels. Did anyone know what percentage of the people in Sandton had electricity? They scoffed at the ridiculousness of this question and said one hundred percent. Right, well, what was it in Alex? No one knew. Twenty percent. That meant three hundred twenty thousand out of four hundred thousand people—or more than a quarter of a million people who lived right across the street from them—didn't have electricity.

"Still don't see how this gets back to tea," Huntley said lazily.

"Since they don't have electricity it's safe to assume that they don't have the elaborate burglar alarm systems on their shacks that you all have. There's no early warning system when they get killed in the night. Not that anyone would come if there was. How is it that the electricity that you take for granted can't cross the street? And why is it that the massacres they take for granted won't cross the street to *your* homes?"

Grace insisted that the people of Sandton were not responsible for the lack of electricity in Alexandra and that they were certainly not responsible for the violence.

"The violence is Black-on-Black. Zulu against Xhosa," she said. "You don't see White men hacking each other with pangas."

Would she agree, I asked her, that since July 1990 Inkatha *impimpis* have been streaming into the Transvaal in record numbers? She told me *impimpi* was a derogatory term; how would I like to be called "nigger"? I decided to ignore that and changed the word to *warriors*. She insisted upon *migrants*; and, rather than ask her if she moonlighted as Gatsha's publicist,* I agreed on *migrants*.

"More than a hundred thousand of them have streamed in here over the past two years. You don't need to read the papers to know this, just look outside your window."

"Yes," she conceded.

"Have they been attacking—let me rephrase that, have they been at the center of this violence?"

"Yes."

"Do they burn down the houses of township residents, do they shoot and maim people in their sleep, do they abduct women from the trains?"

"I have no knowledge of that."

---

* Mangosuthu "Gatsha" Buthelezi was chief minister of the KwaZulu Bantustan when I worked at Mario's. He was also the founder and president of the Inkatha Freedom Party.

"Grace, you don't have to be a rocket scientist. All you have to do is open your window and look across the street. They've run the multi-ethnic workingmen out of the hostels. They kill the residents and anyone they think supports the ANC. The police give them arms and take them wherever they want to go in huge vans."

"Fine. What's your point?"

"The Sandton City Council pays the rent for those hostels; which means *you* pay their rent. That's my point. But you say the violence has nothing to do with you. Doesn't sound like Black-on-Black violence to me—not when the guns are White, the logistical support is White, and the money is White."

Huntley stood up. "All those in favor of tea, follow me." With the expeditionary zeal of a tour guide in Trafalgar Square he led all but four of them from the room. With moist eyes, Muriel Mendelssohn approached me.

"You must think we're really repressed," she said.

I didn't know what to say.

A day later, the director of University Extension telephoned. She had received a complaint from the head of the Sandton City Council. She said she did not approve of an adjunct at Wits slandering the Sandton municipality. (I had also received a phone call from another member of the city council who demanded I present myself at the council's next meeting and retract statements that I made implicating them in the violence. She said that if I didn't pitch up at the next council meeting they would initiate civil and perhaps criminal proceedings against me—that if I wasn't prosecuted, I could be detained.) The university traded on goodwill, the director of University Extension intoned. I was hired because I had an MFA in fiction, not a Ph.D. in political science. They would not need me to teach creative writing in the next term.

Now Mario's Trattoria was all I had left.

3

Mario's restaurant sported a sunken dining room. When patrons and waiters inclined their heads to look out the long, slender windows that ran along the upper reaches of Mario's inner walls, they glimpsed a pageantry of smartly creased pants cuffed above business shoes and the trendy pumps or high heels of White women bustling back and forth between the sneakers that Black women wore or the scuffed work shoes of Black men, who worked in the same suburban office buildings (serving tea, cleaning toilets, mending pipes, and guarding the front door against people who looked just like them). The dining room itself was small, but a floor-to-ceiling mirror yawned across the far wall, giving the room the feel of a candle-lit cavern that opened to a moonstruck sea at night.

Two or three times a night, Dean Martin's rendition of "Volare" played in the loop of romantic ballads that pulsed from the speakers in the corners of the ceiling. I loved to watch the faces of the patrons when this song came on. I could always tell the patrons who were there for the first time from those who had been there before. The newcomers' first response was always one of astonishment—as if they wanted to ask why everyone stopped talking. Why, they seemed to ask themselves, are these businessmen's heads cocked and poised with the stillness of hunting hounds? Why had the wedding table's toast been triaged? Why did lovers lean away from each other as the bars of the intro were played? I once saw a throng of Nadine Gordimer's dinner guests look at the Nobel Laureate as though she'd lost her mind when she cut the conversation and held her index finger aloft. Her friends' sense of confusion lasted less than two seconds. Just long enough for the first two syllables of "Volare" to leave Dean Martin's lips. Then all the voices in Mario's ascended in a blue whale of sound.

Let's fly way up to the clouds
Away from the maddening crowds

Even newcomers caught by surprise swayed in their seats and sang along. Everyone loved Mario's. Mario and his cousin, Sandro, had come to South Africa in the recent flow of Southern and Eastern Europeans: the Portuguese who crossed the border with Mozambique, licking their wounds from having lost the war; Romanians, Czechs, and Germans from the GDR with dust from the demolished Berlin Wall still on their shoes; Greeks and Italians like Sandro and Mario.

Two Romanians in their early thirties, both with engineering degrees and no outlet for their knowledge in the rubble of COMECON, where the old was dying but the new had not been born, worked as waiters. Two Africans, who also worked as waiters: one a man without papers who hailed from Zimbabwe's Matabeleland, the other one at least fifteen years older than all of us, which put him in his late forties or early fifties, came from Venda, the Bantustan in the far northern corner of South Africa, just this side of the border with Zimbabwe. DeNight was the name of the man from Zimbabwe, who was an illegal immigrant, like me. The older man from Venda, who sent his pay back to his wife and kids in the Bantustan, was called "Master" by everyone, including Mario and his wife, Riana. We were a patchwork assemblage from the land of misfit toys serving penne, fettuccini, and eggplant lasagna to bankers, businessmen, professors, and tourists under the watchful gaze of little Napoleon standing on the landing beside his long-legged Josephine. Riana was a tall, striking woman of Afrikaans descent, born and raised in a *klein dorpie*, a wide spot on a tarred road somewhere in the Karoo. We were all new to Jo'burg: Mario, Sandro, DeNight, Master, the two Romanians, and me.

The alcove between the dining room and the thick, two-way

swinging doors to the kitchen was my hideaway. A counter ran along the half wall separating this dimly lit snug from the rest of the dining room. Plastic, compartmentalized crates, each holding twenty-five water glasses, were stacked four feet high at the far end of the counter. It was the job of the waitstaff to see to it that the fifty glasses in the top two racks were turned right side up and filled with ice water. I could stand behind those porous crates and survey the entire dining room, even the seven steps that led to the landing with the cash register and menus stand.

In the evening, the ceiling lights were dimmed and candles burned romantically on the tables. Dean Martin sang "Volare" and the diners sang as well. As a meeting ground for the major White intellectual and political actors who were part of the seismic shifts the country was embroiled in, Mario's was an embarrassment of riches. I saw Roelf Meyer, F. W. de Klerk's former minister of constitutional development, dining in the candlelight with his wife. When I arrived in South Africa in 1991 and began working at Mario's, De Klerk had just appointed Roelf Meyer minister of defense as successor to Magnus Malan. The generals didn't like him; and other hard-liners on the right called him a *"verligte Nat"* (a "liberal" or "enlightened" National Party politician) who didn't harbor the proper sentiments toward communism and the *swart gevaar,* or "black threat." He lasted at that job about as long as I lasted at Mario's, and from the alcove where I watched him dine I could see why. His dinner guests spoke English, not just to me and the other waiters but among themselves; which meant that they were English, genealogically; or they were members of a new breed of Afrikaners who emerged from the shadows in 1989 when De Klerk came to power—urbane Boers, self-conscious about world opinion. Roelf Meyer was the poised and polished poster boy for this new breed. The only Black patrons that I recall were celebrities, the likes of stage and screen stars Jon Kani and Thembi Mtshali.

The evening crowd was better dressed and more relaxed than the hurried noonday business diners.

What surprised me was the degree to which the people working at Mario's—from Riana to Mario, to the two Romanians, to Master and DeNight, the two African waiters—were clueless about the significance of the clientele, especially when it came to the dinner guests. From White liberal academics who made their names as consultants to COSATU and law professors who advised the moderate faction of the ANC when they weren't lecturing four blocks away at the University of the Witwatersrand, to powerbrokers like Roelf Meyer, famous actors, and the literati, a phalanx of faces known around the world to anyone who kept up with the changes occurring at a staggering pace sauntered down the steps to Mario's sunken dining room and tucked into plates of penne smothered in arrabiata and smoked salmon while washing it down with the best sangria in South Africa. Everyone loved Mario's. But not everyone who *worked* at Mario's knew they were feeding the highly placed notables whose hands were forging their future.

The first time I espied Nadine Gordimer she was dining with her husband and a guest from England. As Riana passed through the alcove where Master, DeNight, the Romanians, and I observed our tables without being seen, I told her that Nadine Gordimer was the last person I expected to be in a room with when I moved to South Africa.

Riana said, "Which one is she?"

I was bowled over. "You're kidding, right?"

She was hurt by this and I was sorry. It was a spontaneous and unintentional put-down. "Three months ago she won the Nobel Prize for Literature."

"Oh, yeah, I read about that," Riana lied.

Master and DeNight agreed that she was a kind White lady who said please and thank you "even to Africans."

The Romanians accused me of making this up.

I asked them who had "watered" Nadine's party. When one of the Romanians nodded, I told him to let me come to the table with him when it was time to take the order. If I was lying about anything I'd just said, I promised to give him my entire haul in tips for the night; but if I was telling the truth, he would give me all of his tips. He didn't like the wager, so I modified it. If I'm lying, I said, you still get all my tips, but if I'm telling the truth, then I'll take her table and her tips. "How do you know her?" he scoffed. I could tell he was getting cold feet, but he had to save face in front of Riana and the others.

Gordimer, I observed, paid more attention to her guest from England than to her husband Reinhold Cassirer. Gordimer was then sixty-eight years old. Reinhold had been one of South Africa's most influential art dealers in the 1970s, and a South African Army captain seconded to British intelligence in Cairo during World War II, still with a strong trace of a German accent. He was a German Jew of substantial means whose family fled Berlin when Hitler came to power. Now he was eighty-three, fifteen years her senior. This Jewish Holocaust-refugee-turned-dashing-spy-turned-art-dealer was, no doubt, the brightest flare in her sky. But all flares dim on the way down. Reinhold, with an oxygen aid, was no different.

Before the Romanian could take their order, I spoke. I introduced myself by telling her how much her work had meant to me as a writer. It wasn't the whole truth, but it got her attention. The truth was that her politics had meant a lot to me. But I was enthralled by the writing of J. M. Coetzee, whom I considered to be a better storyteller and a more profound wordsmith—though I loathed his politics.

"This young man," I said, referring to the Romanian with a tincture of condescension, "as well as Mario and his wife Riana, asked me to offer you our congratulations on winning the Nobel Prize for

Literature." In her eyes I saw the gears of vanity and skepticism turn-ing in on each other. In that thin steel voice I would grow accustomed to over the next two years, Nadine Gordimer asked why they had nominated me to make "this little speech." She didn't flatter easily. In a shrewd pedagogic move, I turned to the Romanian and said, "Good question. Why *did* you all give me the honor?" He was hemmed in by the truth, but determined to escape. Because you taught her work at Columbia, he consented with all the gusto one might have for a pend-ing root canal. Where Said is, she said. I told her that I had studied with him. The Romanian looked like what he was, a man who'd lost a bet. Nadine asked if I could remain as their waiter. She had a project that she wanted to discuss with me.

4

Africans were not allowed to touch money at most high-end (and even some low-end) retail establishments. But what was I in the minds of Mario and Riana? Mario ran the kitchen. Riana ran the dining room. He was a European. She was an Afrikaner. From the landing beside the front door, Riana watched the Black waiters like a barn owl over mice. When guests left their table for the night, she swooped down the steps and scooped up the tips that Master's and DeNight's guests had left. If she wasn't on the landing they would clear an entire table and reset it with cloth napkins, cutlery, and glasses without touch-ing one note or coin. At the end of every shift, Riana divided the tip jar for Blacks between Master and DeNight. Since they didn't know how much they earned each night, they didn't know if she was cheating them.

My first day on the job, I shadowed Master during the lunch and the dinner shifts; so all the tips belonged to him. When I asked him why he and DeNight let Riana take their tips while the two Roma-nians collected their own, he smiled and shrugged and said, "This is South Africa, m'china." I said, "Fuck the dumb shit," and we both laughed. He thought I was playing.

When my first table on my first shift paid the bill, they paid it to me. The man at the table who was paying started to lay the bill I had just given him, along with his wrinkled rand notes, on table, but I held out my hand.

"I'll take that for you?" I said, smiling.

He looked at me as though I'd spoken Serbo-Croatian. I realized that perhaps he had never *paid* an African directly before.

Finally, slowly, he gave me the bill back, and gave me the money too.

"I'll bring your change."

He told me the change was the tip.

My back was to the landing, where, I was certain, Riana was watching. I lingered for a moment with the people at the table. I could almost feel her squirm. On the landing, I gave her the bill and the cash. Her jaw looked as clenched as my stomach felt. I smiled. She counted the notes into the cash register. She kept the change.

"I'll see he gets it," she said.

"It's my tip." I held out my hand. "You can ask him."

She wasn't happy, but she gave it to me.

The first time there was a credit card transaction she cashed the customer out and kept my tip. I walked up the steps to the land-ing. "My tip," I said nodding at the register. My heart raced. Anxiety burned ten years off my life. Riana snubbed out her imported Gaulo-ises cigarette. I had not moved. The cash register chimed and opened. But instead of putting my tip in the African tip jar, she put the money on the ledge beside the register. I put the money in my pocket. She didn't say a word.

5
___

Nicolas and Sipho were both muscular men with hands more callused than any cooks I'd worked with Stateside. They must have been
from the country, I thought, or done some form of hard outdoor work
before they came to Mario's. The only time they came into the dining room was to go home after a shift or to set food on the long staff
table where Mario, Riana, Sandro, and the two Romanians ate their
lunch. On day one, I went to the kitchen with Master and DeNight,
where they ate pap-n-fleece* with their fingers along with Nicolas,
Sipho, and the kitchen crew. Why did the Black waiters eat porridge
and tough meat while the Whites ate penne with creamy salmon and
vodka sauce? I asked them. I settled in to eat with them, when Sandro, Mario's cousin, came into the kitchen. He said Mario and Riana
wanted to know if I cared to join them at the waiters' table in the
restaurant. (Was I Black or was I an American? Perhaps they flipped
a coin to decide.)

I don't know what rankled me more, my invitation as an hon-
orary White, or the sense of pride I interpreted in the smiles of the
kitchen crew (as though their own Jackie Robinson were in the
majors now). I told Sandro to tell Mario and Riana that I was just
fine with the Blacks. Sandro understood immediately: he told me
to stop being a jerk and learn to appreciate what it means to be
accepted. I told him I'd be there in a minute. When he left, I told
Master and DeNight that I would go out there only if they came
too. They looked at me as though I'd given them consecutive life
sentences. They told me how much they liked pap-n-fleece; it was,
after all, Master said, an African dish. You like it better than Italian

_____
* Pap: mealie porridge; fleece: meat.

food? I queried. They nodded. I asked them how much Italian food they'd had since working there. Crickets.

How can you serve food you've never eaten? I asked Master and DeNight. If you can describe the taste of food to a customer and then tell them which of our wines go best with their order, they'll be pleased and your tips will go through the roof. Come on. Let's go out there and eat. All conversation stopped when the three of us entered the dining room. I thought I was going to have to fold Master and DeNight into their chairs, so petrified were they by the look on Riana's face. Mario was trying to be stern, but he didn't have his wife's chops. When they were seated, I served them and then myself. Master and DeNight loved the food! The table was so silent throughout the entire meal that we could hear the voices of pedestrians on the sidewalk beyond the glass.

<h1 style="text-align:center">6</h1>

When the lead cashier quit, several African women entered the trattoria to apply for the job but each one was told the position had been filled. After the third time, I confronted Riana and Mario about this. At the time I believed that I had caught them red-handed in an act of discrimination. Now, through the lens of Afropessimism, I can see that it was more complicated (or, perhaps, more *elemental*) than that. Something else was at stake.

In *Das Kapital*, Karl Marx mentions but cannot or will not theorize the slave. For Marx, the worker is the host upon which civil society feeds. And the worker is also the engine of revolution, the sentient being whose liberation will destroy capitalism and, by extension, the world as we know it. *Das Kapital*, however, suffers from an insufficiently comparative analysis between the position of the worker

and the position of the slave. Marx calls the slave a "speaking implement"—which, I have argued, is indeed an apt description, one that
deserves careful reflection; but Marx makes this observation and
moves on. Marx is as mute and astonished by this speech-endowed
subject who is not a proper subject as Mario and Riana were when I
called them out on the way they treated the Black women who applied
for the cashier's job. Mario and Riana had lived in the midst of Black
waiters, Black cooks, Black women who made salads and desserts, and
the Black dishwashers much as Edwin Epps and his wife Mary Epps,
in the film *12 Years a Slave*, lived among their slaves. It would not
occur to Edwin and Mary to camouflage their ill treatment of their
implements, their slaves. In a toolshed, one doesn't break a wrench and
wonder how the hammer feels about it. True, up the seven steps from
the dining room and out the front door, the world of rational political
change and debate was impinging on Mario's Trattoria. There might
even be a Black president in South Africa before the twentieth century
waned. But Mario's was a dim recess in the skull of the city, not unlike
the unconscious; a realm of what Freud called primary signification,
where relational logic had diminished purchase: there is no time in the
unconscious. There's tenacious fixation, lethal consumption, phantasmagoric couplings, and the shortest path to pleasure, mobilized by
force.

Edwin and Mary discuss the most intimate details of their marriage when they fight in the parlor right in front of their slaves. They
slash each other with aspects of their sexuality and their past that they
would be loath to discuss in front of their closest friends. Yet somehow these slaves, these "speaking implements," are not a threat—they
remain, to paraphrase Saidiya Hartman, "unthought." It is as though
Edwin and Mary are not downstairs in the parlor but upstairs in their
bedroom, alone and unclothed, with only the eyes of the furniture on
their naked bodies. Indeed, they *are* alone. For the parlor is not peo-

pled with interlocutors, but rather is decorated with a menagerie of objects; some of which are animate.

Mario's Trattoria doubled as Edwin and Mary's parlor. They tore at each other in front of the Africans. In front of the kitchen crew, he would yell at Riana with a flurry of hand gestures. He would tell her how she could return to tending drought-hardy cows in the Karoo if she kept complaining about the way he made sexual advances to Sibongile and Liyana, the two women who made salads. And she would remind him that he wouldn't have a visa if it weren't for her— no visa, no restaurant, she'd say as her voice rose an octave.

Mario and Riana weren't so much embarrassed, much less shamed, by my calling them out as they were *startled* by the observation and judgment of one of their implements. Imagine Mary Epps's shock if, the moment after she attacked Edwin Epps's "manhood" in the parlor, Patsey, the slave he raped (with "love") on a regular basis, said, "You are so right, Mary, he's Lothario." (Mary's shock would be short-lived, of course; given all her numerous demands that Edwin whip or sell Patsey, one can't imagine the conversation progressing— for Mary Epps would have Patsey killed.) Mario and Riana had lived the "unthought" of the sentience that surrounded them for years; just as Mary and Edwin Epps had done.

It took them several beats before they could respond to my accusation of employment discrimination. For a moment they both were speechless. I took their aphasia for guilt. I could not have been more wrong. Then Riana did something strange. She smiled. Master and DeNight were setting up their sections and trying not to be aware of what was unfolding. But Master's face tightened with worry lines that made him look much older than the fifty-one-year-old face in the passbook he continued to carry, despite the fact that the Pass Law was repealed. He was a generation older than me. Old enough to have seen before a smile like that made to a man like me by a woman like

Riana. It was not the smile of fellowship. It was not the smile of sex. Master knew his place and he needed to help me know mine. So he asked me to bring him four of my folded linen napkins. I'm running short, he lied.

Riana said that what she told the three Black women about the job being taken was a "white lie," meant to shield "the girls" from a loss of self-esteem. I would have laughed, but Master's tense caution had seeped into me. Riana's voice was edged with condescension. Telling them the job had been filled, she went on, was a lot better for their self-esteem than telling them that they weren't qualified. Mario stood beside her, nodding.

Now I laughed. "You're a class act. A real humanitarian."

Mario thrust his finger at me from his elevated perch on the landing beside her.

"What's so funny?" he said.

"Three white lies for three Black women," I replied

"You laughing at my wife?" The muscles in his neck pulsed.

"You kidding? I admire her compassion."

Master said, "Frank, I'm out of serviettes. Can I have your extras?"

I didn't reach for the napkins or acknowledge his request. I knew damn well he had all the napkins he needed for his section.

Mario started down the steps. Riana grabbed the sleeve of his chef's jacket, which was white with cloth knot buttons.

I pressed on. "Only a clairvoyant would know they weren't qualified before reading their résumés."

A puddle of silence grew between us. In my mind's eye I saw Mario's black windswept hair, his powerful hands seared with rage, his white-vested chest lunging down at me over the railing.

Riana said, "What kind of American are you?" And I laughed again. Mario shook free of her grasp.

"Frank!" Master's voice hammered.

I turned to face him.

"The serviettes, m'china."

. . .

MASTER'S CONCERN for my safety was something I felt at a profound prelinguistic level, so much so that I pressed him to put it into words. He was always the first person to reach the locker room and change from his street clothes to his waiter's uniform. Master had been with Mario and Riana since the beginning. Not even Nicolas and Sipho, two fixtures in the kitchen, had been there as long as Master. The work Master did for Mario and Riana went well beyond his expertise as a waiter. He could fix the air-conditioning; he could break the gas range down and reassemble it; and he liaised with the laundry service that washed the linen, that is, before Sandro, Mario's cousin, immigrated from a village near Naples and was paid to do what Master had done for free. This diminished his pride; and he responded by smiling even more. But he hadn't smiled when he saw me on the bench violating his space and solitude. Everyone knew that this time belonged to Master; and everyone but me seemed to respect that. Even Sibongile and Liyana, the two women who made salads, slathered butter on warm garlic bread, and helped the dishwasher when he was slammed, timed their arrival to the interval between Master's arrival and the arrival of male kitchen crew and waiters. In this way, Master could have the time that everyone except me knew that he needed, and Sibongile and Liyana could change before the men arrived to witness them disrobing.

I waited on the bench to the side of the door so that I could see him a few seconds before he saw me when he entered the locker room. As the door opened and he came into view, I saw his shoulders sag with the weight of a day that had not yet begun. He was muttering, a soft, anxious splutter of English and Venda that he spoke into his neck. The door closed behind him. It was too late by the time he saw me. Too late to change, like Clark Kent in a phone booth, into his superhero smile. I had heard the reluctant heel-to-toe shuffle of his shoes on the cement floor. And I had tasted the rot, resignation, and regret in the ruins of words. The expression on his face was one that I had never imagined he was capable of. It was an expression of anger, almost hatred. I wondered if anyone in the world, even his wife and children in Venda had ever seen Master's face like this, without that eternal white smile pressed into the landscape of his glowing, onyx-colored face. He blinked. Then he smiled. The world was set right again. I felt a jolt of shame. I apologized.

"For what?" he asked, in a voice that was reassuring. "You belong here as much as I do."

Even though I wasn't sure I meant it, I thanked him for trying to defuse yesterday's confrontation. He turned his back to me and spun the dial on his combination lock.

"I wanted to ask you about that," I said.

"Master was in need of serviettes," he told me, speaking of himself in the third person. "Master didn't mean to give problems, Bra Frank." He flashed that infuriating, inscrutable smile.

This annoyed me. I was not his age-mate. According to tribal custom, he was an elder. Master had no cause to show deference to me, by calling me "Bra" (for Brother or uncle) as though I were his elder. *This Negro's signifying,* I thought with bitterness. *Yesterday he called me "Frank" with the urgency and command one would use on a subordinate; now he becomes an inscrutable African and treats me like a man twice his age or like a White man, someone to be lied to with respect.* I wanted to tell him to forget it and then walk out. He made eye contact with me in the mirror as he clipped on his bow tie. What he said next surprised me. It had nothing to do with the words I had exchanged with Mario and Riana. Master sat down on the bench across from me.

With seriousness I would have thought him incapable of, Master said, "Do you having any idea where you are?"

At the ass-end of the world, I wanted to say, when I could be in Amsterdam, laid back with a blunt.

"Where am I, Master?"

"South Africa," he said firmly.

Then he told me that Mario had a short fuse. Nothing I didn't know. He said he didn't want Mario to assault me, which he might have, had I kept insulting his wife. I said that she was insulting my intelligence; and I asked him if he thought I couldn't handle a man as small as Mario. Master waited a moment, as if deciding if I was worth the candle of his wisdom or if he should go out and start setting up the dining room, let me find the land mines on my own. That's when he told me that he had been afraid not of what Mario would do to me but what Nicolas and Sipho might have done.

"They might have killed you," he said.

I looked at him as though he had said he'd just returned from vacation on the moon.

"The chef and the sous chef?" I said in disbelief. "They're *Black*." I said maybe he was the one who didn't know where he was. "Nicolas and Sipho are Black men, who Mario uses as doormats. Why would they come to his aid," I implored, "when I was standing up for three Black women?"

I took advantage of Master's wordless expression to remind him of my efforts to organize a union at Mario's. I reminded him of the African National Congress pamphlets and brochures that I regularly slipped into the hands of the workers when Mario, Riana, the Romanians, and Sandro's backs were turned. Whenever a massacre occurred in the Transvaal, whether it was the forty-six people killed in the Joe Slovo squatter camp or ten people killed in Mapetla, the crew in the kitchen as well as he and DeNight could count on me to come to work the next day with literature explaining the political implications of the paramilitary alliance between the IFP and the South African Security branch.

I had begun my political work in the ANC the second week I arrived in South Africa, and I was steadfast in my conviction that one must organize where one lives. I did not want to mimic the lives of immigrants I had seen in the U.S. who had either cobbled their new lives together on the backs of Black Americans, who were less likely to be employed than a disciplined and grateful newcomer, or who had simply done their best not to bear witness to the suffering around them.

Within a month of my arrival I had become active in aboveground political structures of the ANC, like the ANC Peace Commission, which monitored and tried to prevent the rash of massacres that the police, the SADF and the Inkatha Freedom Party carried out in the townships surrounding Johannesburg.

Of course, I never told the workers at Mario's that the ANC Peace Commission was also a handmaiden of the ANC's armed struggle— secreting weapons into squatter camp Self-Defense Units—but Master reminded me that I had distributed a position paper written by a midlevel MK operative which argued that the liberation movement should not get hoodwinked by the liberal argument that all violence was unethical: that the violence of the apartheid government and its surrogates in Inkatha was not to be equated with the revolutionary response of the liberation movement. All of which, I told Master, with a tone of finality and resolve, should make perfect sense to any Black person who's worked at this restaurant, this miniature plantation, for five minutes.

"Of course," Master said, surprising me with a level of sarcasm I would never imagine his open, smiling face was capable of, "that explains why Nicolas chased Fana with a knife in the kitchen because he caught him reading a book you gave him."

Fana was the dishwasher, a teenage boy who said he was eighteen but looked like he was fifteen. Fana probably wasn't his name; it means "boy." But that's what he was called.

I knew the answer to the question I didn't need to ask. But I asked it anyway.

"Why would Nicolas do that?"

Master shook his head and started to leave.

"You're saying Nicolas and Sipho are Inkatha supporters?" I felt cold and moist. For weeks I had ordered food from and chatted with men with knives who were members or supporters of the IFP. I had had the gall to assume that they wanted what I wanted out of the mass struggle waging in the streets; the height of such insolence was the fact that I had deputized myself on their behalf and I didn't even know who they were. Nicolas and Sipho were livid with me—and their rage had simmered for weeks without my having the slightest inkling.

Nicolas and Sipho may have come to the Transvaal from their homes in KwaZulu-Natal. Their migration from the Indian Ocean to the roiling killing fields of the Jo'burg townships might have coincided with the influx of an estimated hundred thousand Zulu contra forces that F. W. de Klerk had mobilized to move to Jo'burg's townships and put a black face on the apartheid government's aggression. Only a fool would try to organize them into a union aligned to the ANC. I was that fool.

But why hadn't Nicolas and Sipho confronted me when I first started? I asked Master this question, but he just shrugged. Then I asked him, What happens next? He shrugged again. But he said it wouldn't be hard for them to deal with me and not pay the price for it if they said they were trying to protect a White man and his wife.

I stayed in the locker room after Master had gone. I was embarrassed. And, when that wore off, I was scared.

7

To my surprise, Riana and Mario hired an African woman for the cashier position. Her name was Doreen. The contrast between Doreen and Riana could not have been greater. Riana's only certification was what in the States would be a junior college degree in hotel management, whereas Doreen held a B.S. in business and accounting from the homeland University of Bophuthatswana. Nor could there be greater dissonance between the way they dressed and carried themselves. Riana flounced through the restaurant in jeans so tight she might have been poured into them. In the summer months, December and January, she wore retro hot pants from the 1970s. She smoked imported Gauloises cigarettes that she often snubbed out and abandoned after a single drag. Doreen, on the other hand, did not smoke Gauloises or anything else, nor did she drink alcohol. Her skirts were pleated, as though she played field hockey at Vassar, and her blouses were buttoned above any hint of décolletage. Doreen found it hard to look Riana in the eye, even though Riana made an exaggerated performance of trying to make Doreen feel welcome.

On Doreen's first day, Riana seized her hand and led her down the steps to the dining room. We would not open again until dinner. It was time for the dining room staff to eat. Riana did not let go of Doreen's hand until Doreen had agreed to sit near the head of the table where Riana and Mario always sat. Riana was giving Doreen Sandro's seat. He shrugged and took an empty chair at the far end of the table, nearer to me, Master, and DeNight. Doreen protested. She said she would be just fine eating pap-n-fleece in the kitchen with the dishwasher, the salad makers, and the chefs.

Doreen implored Riana to let her go and eat in the kitchen. Riana shot a look of victory at me, as if she was saying, Doreen just wants to be with her own kind, it's called *community*. Doreen turned to go to the kitchen.

"Sit down, Doreen," Riana commanded. "This is the new South Africa."

8

Several days later, the cash register ran out of the paper that printed receipts. Doreen leaned over the railing and asked Riana where the replacement spools were kept. She had looked in the cupboard under the register but hadn't found any there. Riana was on the floor speaking with the Romanians. Before Riana could speak, Mario, who was at the bottom of the steps checking a wine order that had just been delivered, told her to look again. What happened next was over and done within ten seconds.

Mario wore soft-soled shoes that made no sounds when he crossed the floor made of redwood imported from Oregon. Doreen didn't hear him as he sprang up the steps in three silent bounds. Nor did she see him, for she was bent over, searching the cupboard one more time. Mario came at her from behind. Surely, I thought, days later when I still couldn't shake what had happened from my mind, she must have sensed air as it shifted behind her, a new warmth from the sudden presence of his body—he was so close to her I thought his groin had brushed her backside. With two or three backward and forward movements, he thrust his pelvis perilously close to her. His eyes were closed orgasmically, as though pesto aromas had drifted in from the kitchen. Riana, Sandro, and the two Romanians burst out laughing.

Doreen turned to find herself so close to Mario that she could have smelled his aftershave. Now his face was creased with concern.

"Here," he said, gently brushing her aside. "Let me help you." When he stood up, he said, "You were right, it's not here. Where the hell is that paper, Riana?"

9

I averted my eyes and slinked past Riana and the two Romanians. I headed for the kitchen. Riana called Mario a naughty boy. Master and DeNight cleared the tables in their section in an effort to unsee what they had seen. I almost knocked Sandro down when I entered the kitchen through the wrong side of the swinging doors. Sandro sucked his teeth and shot a death stare at me as he tried to steady the tray he was carrying.

"Watch where you're going!" I snarled.

The bright lights and bouquet of aromas in the kitchen was no refuge. For some time, Nicolas and Sipho had begun a ritual of chopping mutton or carrots or anything that could be chopped when I came into the kitchen. The sound was a chorus of guillotines. On these occasions they didn't look at me; but I heard my neck being hacked in rhythm to the Zulu songs they sang as they cut the meat.

Fana, the young dishwasher, was the only one who nodded when I came in. Sibongile and Liyana washed lettuce in an open sink beside him but did not turn around. When I first began at Mario's Trattoria, Nicolas and Sipho raised their voices in Inkatha war songs as they guillotined hunks of meat when I came into the kitchen. I didn't know they were war songs, nor did I know they were meant for me.

But since Master's lesson in the locker room, my blood grew cold when I came into the kitchen and heard them singing. But not this time. This time I was grateful to them. This proxy execution of the meat expiated my guilt. What kind of coward would stand by while Mario did what he had done to Doreen?

10

Doreen lasted all of one week. Toward the end of the week, she had left immediately after lunch to run some errands before the evening meal. The restaurant was all but empty. I was alone in the alcove. I watched Riana as she sat in a chair on the landing, chatting with a woman named Fiona. Fiona and Riana were longtime friends from the same *klein dorpie* in the Karoo; and Fiona had also been the cashier before Doreen. Riana lifted the cash register an inch and slid an envelope out from underneath.

"Christmas?" Fiona smiled. "You already gave me my back pay."

"It's two hundred rand, ducky," Riana said. "I'll want it back in a few days. Best if you don't know more than that. I'll explain then. Promise."

"You're a woman of mystery," Fiona said.

Riana lit a Gauloises cigarette, exhaled, and extinguished it. Then Riana pecked Fiona on the cheek and bade her farewell.

11

Later, I saw Riana and Doreen by the cash register where Riana had pecked Fiona on the cheek. There was an adding machine between them on the table where the menus were kept, and receipts from the lunch hour as well. Riana punched the keypad and looked up at Doreen, shaking her head. Now she came down the steps. She entered the kitchen. When she came out she was with Mario.

Mario snagged a chair from the dining room on his way up the steps and the three of them sat close together, facing each other. Riana spoke. Doreen's gasp was almost audible from where I was on the floor. She put her hand over her mouth. Mario shrugged with his palms to the ceiling. Riana put a hand on Doreen's shoulder.

12

Now Doreen was in the alcove, with me. Riana and Mario had remained on the landing, speaking to each other quietly. Doreen was dazed. Her eyes were moist. I gave her a glass of ice water from the tall stack of plastic crates filled with ice-water glasses. I inched nearer to her. The two Romanians were singing "Volare," off-key, as they set the tables in their sections. DeNight and Master were also preparing for the evening meal. They told jokes to each other in a blend of Ndebele and English.

"They're bastards," I said, taking for granted she knew I meant Riana and Mario.

Her voice faltered. "You know?" she said.

"Yes," I said. "What are they talking about up there?"

"Madam wants to fire me. *Meneer** says I should have another chance."

It was just a few days ago that Doreen had felt the ease to use their first names. Now things were back to normal.

"Madam promises a reference with no mention of it." Now she

---

* *Meneer* is Afrikaans for mister.

was crying, trying not to let her sobs carry beyond the alcove. "I didn't take the money."

13

Doreen was revived by the paramedics. They had moved her from the alcove to the dining room, where they ministered to her as she lay on a stretcher. Her eyes were open but unfocused. And she had not spoken since she had fainted. The side of her left hand was bandaged. She'd cut it on a shard of glass from the water goblets that smashed on the floor when she and I fell.

One minute she and I were standing side by side in the alcove, whispering. I told her how Riana had given the former cashier two hundred rand from the register. Although I had not seen Riana actually take the money from the cash register, I *had* seen her slide an envelope from underneath the register. I saw her give the envelope to Fiona and I heard her tell Fiona it contained two hundred rand and that she, Riana, wanted it back in a week or so. They framed you, I told Doreen. It was a setup from the beginning. Now they can say, *You can't trust Africans with money*, I told her. I was going to tell her that we could fight this. I was going to say, I hate these people. I was going to tell her she could count on me, that I had her back (though I wasn't going to tell her why Riana and the Romanians laughed at her when Mario took her, in a manner of speaking, from behind, or how I had slinked away) when I saw her hand sliding listlessly toward me, along the counter where we stood.

For an instant I saw how her mouth opened; how her eyes pitched back into her skull. Her body slammed into mine. We were reeling backward now, she and I. She must have weighed thirty pounds less than me, but when she passed out her body was a mass of dead weight that fell against me with a force twice what I weighed. I couldn't hold on to her. Nor could I break her fall. We crashed into the column of water crates together. Ice and water showered us like stinging hail and rain. Her blouse was soaked. Her hand was bleeding. My hair was wet and matted. I could not lift her off the floor.

The sound of wet whiskered brooms whispered in the alcove behind me as Master and DeNight swept ice and broken glass. Two paramedics knelt beside Doreen. One of them stuck her with a finger prick to read her blood sugar level. Doreen's eyes were completely open now, as she stared up at a fresco of faces, Riana, Mario, the paramedics, and me. Riana was asking Doreen what had happened. The paramedic with the finger prick said she fainted, in a tone that suggested he thought this was obvious. But Riana ignored him and asked the question again. Doreen looked at me. But what did she want me to say? Did she want me to say anything? What could I say that wouldn't make matters worse?

"These Africans," one of the paramedics said, speaking to Doreen in the third person, plural, "they must *eat*. You hear me, *sisi*?* Your blood sugar is too low." He looked at Riana. "That's why she fainted."

Riana shot Mario a glance as if they knew the real reason why Doreen had passed out. It wasn't low blood sugar.

14

I ran to the window that was pitched at street level. All that could be seen from the dining room were the shoes and the lower legs of passersby. But the stretcher was low enough as the paramedics prepared to hoist it into the ambulance that I could see Riana bent low to the

_____
* Sister.

ground. Doreen was speaking to her now. When she finished, Riana nodded and stood up. The only thing I could see were Riana's smooth, bare legs close to the white chef's trousers that belonged to Mario. Now his legs turned and sprinted to the door. Instinctively I backed away, deeper into the dining room.

15

From the landing, Mario yelled one word: *Poison!* As he pounded down the stairs he shouted, "Poison! Poison! Poison!"

I kept walking backward, but he was closing on me.

"You spread poison everywhere!"

We were toe-to-toe. His breath was one with my breath now. I felt the mist of his saliva.

Riana was yelling from the top of the landing, but I couldn't comprehend what she was saying. Just words, isolated words and her high-pitched rage. Now I knew what she was saying. Riana was saying that Doreen had told them everything I had said in the alcove just before she fainted.

For some reason I had put my sunglasses on when Mario hurtled down the steps. Why, I have no idea. Now I took them off. I didn't want plastic shards embedded in my face or eyes if Mario threw a punch. My arms were so weak. It was as though the bones in my body had disappeared. I had every right to push Mario away. Riana was yelling that it (what I had told Doreen) was all a lie. She would sue me for slander. Mario inched closer, as if that were even possible. I threw my sunglasses on the floor. The plastic frame cracked like the spine of a rat.

In my peripheral vision I saw the kitchen door swing open. Nicolas, the executive chef, and Sipho, the sous chef, slipped through; but they advanced no farther than the lip of the alcove. Now Fana oozed through the door, followed by Sibongile and Liyana, and two more from the kitchen crew. I wanted to ignore the stab of panic in my chest but I couldn't. *If the Zulus fight me in support of Mario*, I thought, *I'm dead*. Even at that moment, with broken bones, arrest, prison, deportation, and death in the balance, the critic in me chided my thoughts for having let the word *Zulu* shimmy to the surface. It was bigoted and wrong. *Not all Zulus are Inkatha Freedom Party* impimpis; *there are Zulus in the ANC*, a voice inside admonished. Panic fought a turf war with my shame.

Every slight Mario had felt since I had started working there spewed from his lips like emerald vomit. The litany of abuses he had suffered at my hands surprised me, not because I didn't know what he was talking about or because I thought he was lying, but because I'd always assumed that only his wife, Riana, had the capacity to explain innuendo and subtext. I had been wrong about him. He spoke in clipped, spit-speckled bursts. A battlefield of verbs and nouns with prepositions and conjunctions often triaged and left for dead. He said I thought the patrons who dined there were *my* guests, not his customers. In stunning detail, he described how I swanned through *his* restaurant entrancing *his* guests with élan, "including those who not even seat in your section! You aka like this-a your *house*! Like your name's on the door, not Mario's."

(Indeed, some of Mario's regulars had begun to come to the restaurant and ask for me by name. Nadine Gordimer was chief among them. She and I had hit it off the first night I met her with Reinhold. Soon she returned on her own and we discussed literature and South African politics as I served her. She had invited me for afternoon tea (which was not tea but wine) at her house in Parktown, where she had asked me to join the ANC-aligned Congress of South African Writers.

She and I would spend several months creating a series of dramatic readings by various township members of COSAW, which took place at traditionally White, high-tone venues, like museums and concert halls. Mario and Riana were no match for the charm and charisma I slathered the candlelit room with. I had learned, from years and years of watching my parents at their cocktail parties, how to work a room; how to compliment a White man's wife without either of them thinking it was sexual; I'd waited tables in private clubs, and knew how to ask them both if they wouldn't mind if I ordered for them, followed with a guarantee that the meal was free if anything I brought them was not to their satisfaction; how to introduce an article I might have read in the newspaper about any of Mario's famous patrons without sounding like a supplicant or an autograph hound. I made them feel as though it were an honor for them to speak with me. I made them feel alive. I made them feel safe. Mario and Riana had the boot of apartheid pressed down on my neck. But the heel of my ego was dug into theirs. I didn't believe that this balanced the scales. Still, I loved to tell a three-minute story to a party of *his* regulars and look up at the landing, at *his* face cracked with anguish as *his* guests roared with delight. I felt the satisfaction of a boy sitting cross-legged in the grass plucking the wings off flies. *Eat your homunculus heart out, Mario.*)

Specks of saliva sprinkled my face as he raged. He said I had caused Master and DeNight so much pain when I pressured Riana to let them eat at the break table outside the kitchen. (In this, he turned apartheid segregation into a healing balm that I had deprived my African brothers of.) But when he said he knew all about the ANC literature I thought I had so discreetly passed to members of the kitchen crew and to Master and DeNight, my sense of amusement at his outpouring turned to panic. I let myself look away from him, just long enough to take in what I could of Nicolas and Sipho. From their demeanors I had no way of knowing if the two of them would enter the fray.

Mario told me to take back what I had told Doreen about Riana: that she stole the money to frame Doreen. He demanded that I tell everyone in the dining room that it was a lie. The problem was this: no one but Mario and Riana knew what I had said to Doreen because she made her confession outside, right before the paramedics slid the stretcher into the ambulance. My silence enraged him. He told me it was one thing for me to disrespect him but quite another for me to disrespect his wife. He gave me one more chance to apologize. Instead, I turned to face Master, DeNight, Sibongile, Liyana, Fana, Nicolas, and Sipho. Like a record spinning at seventy-eight rpms, I told them Riana stole two hundred rand from the till and hid the money in an envelope under the till. Then Riana made a show of helping Doreen balance the till, I said as fast as I could, but the fix was in.

That's when Mario slugged me.

16

From the landing Riana was screaming at the top of her lungs. She yelled at Mario to stop fighting. When a glass broke or a dish landed on the floor, she became even more animated, as though the well-being of the tableware were what was at stake. "What kind of American are you?" If she only knew that I didn't know. If anything as comprehensive as a thought entered my mind as Mario charged at me like a bull, head-butting me in the solar plexus, it was the irony of her question. Riana's shrill screams shredded the air like shrapnel. Mario drove his head into my stomach and drove me back into the railing just below where Riana stood.

Mario was shorter than his wife, Riana, a five-foot-seven former *stofbak** beauty queen. I was three inches taller than her. I had thought that it would be easier to fight a short man than a tall one. I was wrong. His low center of gravity gave him an advantage as he drilled his forehead into my torso and pinned me to the railing. I pummeled his ribs with a pendulum of blows but he kept holding on. He caught me with an uppercut to the chin. I felt my bottom teeth cut the inside of my lip. Blood beetled down my chin.

One of the Romanians got into the mix. He was a thin coat-hanger of man, with the eyes of a startled squirrel. He grabbed my arm and tried to pull me off of Mario. I tossed his narrow ass like salad. The edge of a table spiked his back. He grimaced in pain and drunk-walked to the alcove, groping his back.

Mario pulled me down from behind and we fell to wrestling. We rolled on the floor in each other's arms. Two panda bears making love. Our brawl lacked the bull-stunning fisticuffs, the flying chairs, of an action film. No denouement decided the winner.

17

We are both on our feet now. Sandro, not Mario, is in tears and standing between us. Riana tells me Black Americans have dined at Mario's and none of them were like me. They're clever and civilized, she is saying. Mario is pointing his finger in my face from behind Sandro's back, telling me I'm fired. I'm fired, I reply, when you put it in writing.

He says, "Fuck you, I'm not writing you shit!"

---

* *Stofbak*: Afrikaans for dustbowl.

18

Our flat was on the corner of Ameshoff Street and Jan Smuts Avenue, a five-minute walk from Mario's. Rebone, Khanya's older sister, was in the living room when I walked in. My bloody lip, my knuckles, my ribs, and my pride were too bruised for me to register the meaning of Rebone's presence. She was in Jo'burg; not in Mmabatho under house arrest almost two hundred miles away. (Did this mean that the police had captured her lover, the insurgent in the Azanian People's Liberation Army?) Khanya was seated next to her on the sofa. A tray of tea and scones was on the table in front of them.

My shirt was torn. My bow tie was god knows where. I was so ashamed of the way I kept crying. I shook and snorted like a freezing horse. Khanya and Rebone begged me to tell them what had happened.

"I'm . . ." I couldn't speak. Something large and empty like the belch of a walrus burst in my chest. "I'm going . . ." Again, nothing came but convulsive sobs. I looked at the ceiling. "I'm going to kill that White man!"

Rebone raced to the double doors that opened onto the balcony and closed them. Only in its absence was I aware of the ambient sound from the street below, the scat of horns and laughter swathed in silence now. I said it again. "I'm going to kill that White man." Rebone did something she had never done before. She snapped her fingers at Khanya. Then she pointed at me. It broke the trance Khanya was in; she was beside me now. Her palm bore down on my mouth as I tried to say it again. Her hand clasped my jaw with a strength I had never felt from her in the three years that we had been together. Rebone bolted the front door.

In the bedroom, Khanya had me strip down to my drawers. It was almost comical, the way she drew the covers over me so high they almost hid my head. I could talk without crying now. I told her everything. She listened with neither surprise nor disbelief. "This is South Africa," she said. Then Khanya closed the curtains and the room dropped into darkness. She took my clothes and, upon leaving the bedroom, she said, "You'll get another job."

19

The room was so dark when I awoke that I thought it was the middle of the night. I panicked. The clock on the sideboard said 3:53 and I wondered what Khanya was doing out of bed at this hour of the morning. Then I saw a long blister of light where the curtains came together. I went to the closet and put on a new white shirt with a collar and black pants.

20

I won't go down like this. Hell. Fucking. No.

21

Khanya pleaded with me not to go back to work the dinner shift at Mario's. With her iron-fist-in-a-velvet-glove voice, the same voice she had used to give directives to her younger sister, Rebone said, "There's no habeas corpus here. You'll just be disappeared."

22

When I walked through the front door Riana scampered down the steps ahead of me and disappeared into the kitchen. She came out with her husband in tow. They watched me from the alcove. My intestines roiled. My chest clenched. I tried to ignore them as I set the tables. Now, Mario was upon me.

"Didn't I fire you?"

Riana hurried up to the landing and dialed the telephone.

23

Mario's older brother, Angelo, entered the restaurant, and was solemnly greeted by his sister-in-law and Mario.

The three of them spoke in hushed tones on the landing. In a voice meant to be heard by them, Master said I was setting the tables all wrong. This gave him an excuse to come to my table. In that grandfather's voice of his he admonished me as he pretended to rearrange my table settings.

"Anti*pas*to. Soup. Pasta. Entrée. And *then* the salad fork," he said, as he laid the cutlery.

Now he whispered, "He's not a violent man," referring to Angelo. Was my fear that transparent?

I replied, "They're gonna take me out back and beat the shit out of me." The only thing I didn't know was if Nicolas and Sipho would join them. Would it be two-on-one or four-on-one?

24

In Mario's office a baseball bat leaned against a chipped filing cabinet. It was a cramped utility room with a desk, a filing cabinet, and on the wall a calendar of nude women on top of cars. My first inkling that Angelo was running the show came when I saw Mario seated, not behind his own desk but in one of the two chairs meant for visitors. His older brother, Angelo, sat behind his desk. Now Angelo rolled Mario's chair from behind the desk and sat on it next to Mario. The chairs had been arranged so that when we sat down our knees almost touched. Unlike Mario, Angelo never raised his voice. He let Mario yell his "poison" mantra and report all the "lies" I had spread without so much as a twitch. He looked at me, even when Mario spoke, and I never saw him blink. Finally, he silenced us both by holding up his hand.

"You came to this country with a six-months' tourist visa, am I right?" he said.

I didn't answer.

"You had no money, no work permit. Fresh off the boat. You think that we don't understand? We understand. The same was true for us. We could be brothers."

The thought of the three of us as brothers didn't seem to sit well with Mario. He frowned.

Angelo nodded toward Mario. "So, here, your brother hires you right off the boat. Am I right? He asks you for papers? No. He says, 'Where are your references'? No. You walk in off the street. My brother doesn't know you from any other paisano in the street, does he? *But he gives you a job.* And how do you repay him?" He sat back and laced his hands across his stomach, as if we were somewhere other than a moldy utility room with a baseball bat in the corner. Then he said I sowed dissent and spread lies, trying to turn the kitchen against his brother, accusing his sister-in-law of stealing just to fire a woman that *she* herself had hired.

"We're at the end of our rope, my friend," Angelo informed me. "You're going to have to leave. No, do not shake your head. Do. Not. Shake. Your. Head. You are going to leave now, paisano."

"No."

"Angelo," Mario insisted, "we open in twenty minutes. We need to—"

Angelo said, "Quiet, Mario."

"He's busting our balls!" Mario cried. "We didn't come all the way from Napoli to have our balls busted by some—"

Angelo cut him off with a look before he could say the word. But I would have traded Angelo's death stare to be called the N-word by Mario. Now Angelo changed his tone. He spoke to me with the tenor of someone offering me a job rather than giving me the boot.

"What's it going to take? Huh? Tell me."

"I want it in writing," I said. "I'm not disputing your right to fire me, but I need it in writing. You have to say why."

Angelo leaned in so close to me that for an instant our knees touched. I heard the faint sound of air funneling in and out of his nostrils. He tapped his finger on my knee. A low-voltage current jagged up my thigh to my heart. I hated myself for not slapping him into next week. As Angelo tapped me he said, in what can only be described as a whisper, "You're going to leave or our friends in La Cosa Nostra will break your kneecaps."

When Angelo finished telling me how long I would be in traction in the hospital after the Mafia busted my knees (six weeks before I could stand, six weeks of physical therapy, a hobbled existence even after I walked), he said, "What's it to be, door number one or door number two?"

Run, a voice inside was saying, *run.*

"Fine," I said.

Angelo smiled and leaned back in his chair. He extended his hand to me and said, "No hard feelings?"

25

"You get the Mafia to bust my kneecaps and I'll get uMkhonto we Sizwe to bust yours and Mario's." I could feel the sweat pasting my shirt to my underarms. "We might be in the same hospital if it's multiracial. And I'll use my time of recovery to write op-ed pieces about how bloody racist this place is. Maybe get Montshiwa Moroke of the *Star* to do an exposé. Do you know his byline? Of course not, you don't read." I wanted to tap his kneecap with my index finger, but my hands were moist with perspiration; he would know I was bluffing. Then I said, "Wait till your regulars, like Nadine Gordimer, read this. Did you know she's a member of the ANC? No, you don't even know where you are. *This is South Africa*. You're surrounded. Fifteen million of you. Forty million of us. You're surrounded. Wait till it spreads from Mario's restaurant to your string of beauty parlors. How many White women from Parktown are going to jostle through a throng of picketing Africans just to get their hair done at your salons? Did you know that Nadine Gordimer lives in Parktown? No, you didn't even know who she was."

After a beat, I asked if we were finished. Angelo snorted. I left without turning my back to them. In the hallway I heard the scamper of work shoes on the concrete floor. When I turned at the corner where the alcove was, I saw the kitchen door swaying lazily. Someone from the kitchen had been listening outside Mario's office.

In the dining room, the Romanians and Riana looked at me as though they were seeing the second coming of the Mummy.

Riana turned the outdoor lights on, removed the CLOSED sign, and unlocked the front door. When she turned her back I hurried to the men's room. I wanted to use the farthest stall in case an early guest came in, but I wouldn't make it that far. I dropped to my knees, held on to the toilet seat as though it was a life preserver, and I retched so hard I strip-mined the walls of my stomach.

I washed my face and wondered when the mirror would stop quivering my lips.

"Don't you cry," said the twisted prune in the mirror. "Don't you fucking cry."

26
—

The Black people who worked at Mario's had little in common politically: Master and DeNight kept their politics to themselves, as did most of South Africa's thirty-five million Black people when they were at work; this was also true of Sibongile and Liyana. Nicolas and Sipho were IFP members, sworn enemies of the ANC, the South African Communist Party, and the Congress of South African Trade Unions (COSATU). Fana, the dishwasher, was a dedicated comrade. All of these differences mattered in *important* ways. None of them mattered in ways that were *essential*. We were all positioned in the same place paradigmatically. We were all, in other words, the antithesis of the Human. We were all implements on Mario and Riana's plantation.

From the Arab slave trade, which began in AD 625, through its European incarnation beginning in 1452, everyone south of the Sahara had to negotiate captivity. At a global level of abstraction we can see how Africa has been carcerally contained by the rest of the world for more than a thousand years. *There's no habeas corpus here.* Captivity overdetermined the condition of possibility for *everyone's* life. How people *performed* on a carceral continent was as varied as the "choices" made by us at Mario's.

Some fled the coast and trekked deeper into the interior to avoid notice and, with any luck, capture—the way DeNight kept to the corners of the restaurant where no one was likely to speak with him when he wasn't serving his tables. Some made themselves indispensable (for as long as possible) to the White slavers by becoming slave hunters—like Nicolas and Sipho, and *impimpis* of the Inkatha Freedom Party. Some wore their prowess and pride on their sleeves and lashed out without a plan or foresight—like me. Some confided in the mistress in the hope, perhaps, of attaining some form of sanctuary, or for reasons they themselves could not fathom—like Doreen. The essential Afropessimist point rests not in a *moral judgment* of the choices they made, but in an *ethical assessment* of the common dilemma they all shared—the questions that haunt the slave's first waking moments: What will these White people do to my flesh today? How deep will they cut?

Some were captured and refused to live. Some sent their children to a different death, as in *Beloved.* The dreams of all these different captives could not be reconciled, but their place in the paradigm was the same. They woke up each morning with a deeper anxiety than the proletariat, the worker. The proletariat wakes up in the morning wondering, How much will I have to do today and how long will I have to do it? Exploitation and alienation morphed into an early morning ulcer. How much will the capitalist demand of me and how long will I have to do it?

Again, the Slave wakes up in the morning wondering, What will these Humans do to my flesh? A hydraulics of anxiety that is very different than exploitation and alienation.

If a can of tuna or a bucket of nails could speak, their essential questions would not revolve around how their labor power is being exploited, or how they are alienated from the value that they produce. Exploitation and alienation are not the grammar of their suffering. (How can one exploit an implement?) And the value that a tool helps produce never accrues to the tool. For the Slave, the implement, exploitation and alienation are trumped by accumulation and fungibility. Slaves *themselves* are consumed, not their labor power. Slaves are implements, not workers. What Marx called "speaking implements": Mario and Riana's speaking implements. Our response to captivity was as varied as the myriad choices that our ancestors made hundreds of years ago on that continent. But the question was the same: What will these White people do to my flesh? And the answer is the same: Anything they want.

There is no habeas corpus here, Rebone warned. She didn't know how right she was: for Black people there is no habeas corpus anywhere. Doreen knew this better than any of us. She negotiated her captivity by fainting: her unconscious attempt to save herself by throwing herself overboard. When she came to, she was staring up into the faces of all her masters, and me, a fellow slave. Freelance pallbearers took her body to the ambulance. She would live, when what she really may have wanted was to follow death into freedom; to jump ship before it docked. Who wouldn't tell them what they wanted to hear? *There's no habeas corpus here.* Doreen and the rest of us lived (if *lived* is the word) in a paradigm of violence that bore no analogy to the violence of exploitation and alienation suffered by the worker.

Doreen was the first Black person specifically hired, and officially sanctioned, to handle money with her Black hands. White South Africans had hired her to break their libidinal laws—to violate the mainstays of their collective unconscious. Then some trickster in the alcove whispers in her ear what her intuition had not let her think out loud: that it was all a setup.

The Black people who worked at Mario's were different ages, ethnicities, and genders. But these differences at the level of identity did not alter our sameness at the level of position. One does not position oneself in the world; one is born into a name that's been chosen. Perhaps there was a moment of solidarity sparked by a common acknowledgment of our common position within social death. If there was such a moment, it was splintered: The stern way Master schooled me in the locker room and the flickers of kindness he showed in the tensest situations, gestures that put his wife and his children in Venda, to whom he sent money each month, at risk. The way Nicolas and Sipho did not hurt me, or worse, when they had the chance; a deed for which they would have been exonerated and rewarded.

27

I finally quit Mario's in late June; in early winter, when one could be sopped without warning by a midday rain. I said my warm goodbyes to Master and DeNight. Riana blew the smoke of a Gauloises cigarette to the side and wished me all the best. The Romanians and Sandro nodded. To my surprise, Mario shook my hand. Had I really been here for the better part of six months? I thought. Outside the rain drummed the awning and laid siege to the front door. I'd left my umbrella at home. I didn't want to run a quarter of a mile in this weather, but nor could I endure the awkwardness of being in Mario's once I'd said my goodbyes.

Then I remembered I had not said goodbye to Fana, the dishwasher, or to Sibongile and Liyana, the two women who made salads and buttered warm garlic bread. *It's just the decent thing to do*, I thought. But it also meant facing Nicolas and Sipho, two Inkatha supporters if not outright *impimpis*. A chill ran over my flesh at the memory of my having pressed MK pamphlets in Nicolas and Sipho's hands. A bigger fool had never been born. I told myself that I didn't owe Sibongile, Liyana, and Fana goodbyes. They weren't my friends. We worked together. I should leave out the front door and forget this place. But I knew that I was lying to myself. I was simply afraid of encountering the Zulus whom I still feared and, most of all, whom I made a fool of myself to without knowing I'd done so. I looked at the clock and realized that it should be safe to go into the kitchen. Nicolas and Sipho would be long gone. Sibongile, Liyana, and Fana might be there, cleaning up.

At the door, I heard the sound of butcher knives melting through mutton and thumping the block. It matched the thumping in my heart. It was Fana, Sibongile, and Liyana who were gone. Nicolas and Sipho had their backs to me. I turned to leave before they saw me.

"Frank!"

Too late.

They had traces of mutton blood on their hands and aprons. They stood together at the butcher-block table. They still had their knives in their hands. I thought of the story Master had told me about how Nicolas had chased Fana around this room with a knife, telling Fana he would meet his mother if he was caught with more of "Frank's pamphlets and books."

Nicholas put his knife down and wiped his hands on a towel. "We heard you're leaving," he said. Sipho said nothing.

"Yes . . . yes . . . lunch was my last shift."

"To do what?" Nicolas insisted.

"Well . . . I . . . I teach at Wits. That's why I'm not here on Mondays; and I teach creative writing there at night. But those jobs are over now. I have a more permanent teaching position somewhere else."

"Teaching what?"

"It's like English," I lied.

In point of fact, I was hired to be the second-in-charge of an NGO project working with township organizers (the very people who were fighting Inkatha). For the next year, I would write training materials and facilitate workshops for Civic leaders from the Black townships surrounding Johannesburg. The workshops were on everything from strategic planning for grassroots social movements; the theory of civil society elaborated by the Italian communist Antonio Gramsci; political organizing; office work and division of labor; and writing. But I couldn't say this to them. The Civics were the townships' version of the Paris Commune—organs of people's power aligned with the ANC.*

Nicolas's eyes lit up. Sipho nodded to him as though he'd won a bet. "That's why you speak perfect English," Nicolas said.

"Fellas, there's no such thing as perfect English. That's a racist myth. In fact—"

"You speak it like the Whites," Sipho said, as though that settled it.

"You must teach me, m'china," Nicolas implored. "I ask Mario to wait tables. He says my English is bad, I would scare the customers. He says my head is wood."

As Nicolas spoke, my compassion for him grew, which confused me. *This man is a state lackey; what am I doing talking to him?*

"I want to be clever, like you. But I don't have my Standard Four."

You held my life in abeyance for four months without my knowing it; I'd say that's pretty clever.

---

* For a better understanding of the Civics and the role they played in the struggle, see Mzwanele Mayekiso, Patrick Bond, ed. *Township Politics: Civic Struggles for a New South Africa* (New York: Monthly Review Press, 1996).

The character of the encounter was so contrary to anything I could have imagined for a wet afternoon alone with these two in a cold cave-like kitchen that I was tongue-tied. I rattled something non-committal, like, Wits has a school for workers, and then again there's the Workers Library; and, well, of course, I'd love to teach you, but we'll have to get together and work out the time and place and of course you can come by my office anytime and we can see if—but then again I'm rarely in my office, but I'm sure we can work something out. I can't recall an encounter in which I've been that baffled, afraid, and ashamed.

Nicolas spread his fingers on the butcher block and said, "I'll miss you, Frank."

For months, ever since I had learned he was member of the IFP, I had wanted to feel hatred for him and Sipho, hatred toward them for the hundreds of people per month that their cohorts, and maybe even they themselves, had hacked to pieces, shot to death, and burned alive.

I walked, gingerly, over to the butcher block and shook both their hands. "I'll miss both of you as well." Then I turned my back on them, without the dread of days gone by.

I looked down from the landing at the silent dining room. I had heard the blue whale of sound ascending, all the candlelit faces singing "Volare," for the last time.

Epilogue

The New Century

⚬⚬⚬

The term "nervous breakdown" is sometimes used by people to describe a stressful situation in which they're temporarily unable to function normally in day-to-day life. If you have a primary care provider, talk to him or her about your signs and symptoms or seek help from a mental health professional.

DANIEL K. HALL-FLAVIN, M.D.

They cannot love themselves as black but are made to hate themselves as white . . . What do you do with an unconscious that appears to hate you?

DAVID MARRIOTT

1

Elsewhere, I have written about the dissolution of the revolution in South Africa after Chris Hani, the chief of staff of MK, was assassinated; how Nelson Mandela's moderates consolidated power and purged the ANC of its most prominent revolutionaries, such as Winnie Mandela; how Khanya and I parted; how President Mandela's intelligence czar put my name on a list of "ultra-leftists" to be "neutralized." I won't rehearse that here. Toward the end of 1996, I returned to America, the plantation of my birth.

In Compton, where I worked as a substitute teacher in grade schools, middle schools, and high schools, I was gobsmacked to see the police using tactics on Black children that I thought I'd left behind in the schools of Soweto. The next year I went north to Berkeley to get a Ph.D.; and equilibrium seemed to return to my life. But the year 2000 came and, one day, I cracked. In the nineteen years since my breakdown I have not been able to pinpoint the cause. One day I was attending seminars and political rallies, the next day I was groaning on a gurney in the student health psych ward. The absence of an origin story unnerves me to this day.

• • •

THE DOCTOR AND THE NURSE at the UC Berkeley clinic pressed me for answers. What brought this on? How did I get to the clinic and (if they released me) how would I get home? They peered at my car keys in my hand, as though it were a dangerous weapon in the hands of a child. I shook my head and told them I had taken the bus.

Now the pain was not only in my heart, but also in my rib cage and my arms. *If the antagonism was not between the haves and the have-nots, as Marx had claimed, nor between the man and the woman, or the*

311

gay and the straight, as I had learned in my graduate seminar on psycho-analysis, but if the essential antagonism was, instead, between the Black and all others, then to free the world was to free the world of me.

> *for Halloween I washed my*
> *face and wore my*
> *school clothes   went door to*
> *door as a nightmare.*

When I left my apartment to come there, I had looked down the seven steps from my door to the street as though I were staring into a ravine. I thought I would pass out. My Honda Civic dozed at the curb like a blue sleeping lizard. My keys had scratched the wrought-iron railing as I stumbled down the steps. Threads of saliva spooled on the hood of my car. "Somebody help me," I groaned. But I didn't want my neighbors to see me like this, let alone come to my aid. My neighbors in Berkeley, like my neighbors in Kenwood, were White. It would take ten reincarnations to free me from their debt. *You don't want to owe them*, something deep within me had said. But how could I explain all of that to this doctor and this nurse? I told them the truth, that I took the bus there. But I didn't tell them why. *Make them feel safe.*

They sent me home from the UC Berkeley clinic with pills. SSRIs, which sounds like a branch of the military, when in point fact it stands for selective serotonin reuptake inhibitors, uppers for depression, and chlordiazepoxide, which, I was pleased to hear, was not a rare form of leprosy but a pill for panic attacks. We normally don't prescribe anti-depressants and anti-panic drugs together, the doctor confessed, as though gilding his conscience by being up-front with me.

For several weeks after I left the clinic, I sought Black therapists, thinking they could help me best. They were no saner than me; which is not to say that like me they were falling apart. For the most part these therapists reminded me of my parents, who were both psychologists. Sharp as tic-tac-toe. They cared like none of the White therapists I had sampled cared ("A mind is a terrible thing to waste"* kind of care). Without realizing it, we worked hard together in order to help me solve all the problems I *wasn't* having, to lead me from the gully of despair, and to keep me from going crazy again. But I hadn't *gone* crazy.

Many people do *go* crazy and many of them are not healed, but none of them are Black. (One can go crazy only if one has been sane. The time of sanity is not a temporality that the Slave has ever known.) To a fleeting eye their madness looks like mine. They go crazy from the pressures of racism, sexism, homophobia, and colonial rule. The external forces of aggression become too much for them and they too find themselves being gaped at on a gurney. But their tensions are bundled in the question, How does it feel to *have* a problem? My tensions (and those of the Black therapists who tried to heal me) are bundled in the question, How does it feel to *be* a problem? There's no analogy between having and being.

Every story of despair has a three-point progression. *Equilibrium*: the status of the mind free of psychic trauma. *Disequilibrium*: the intrusion of a wounding trauma, which indeed all but destroys equilibrium. *Equilibrium restored, renewed, or reimagined*: the therapeutic cure in psychology or the end of analysis in psychoanalysis. But if the mind has never known the first point on that progression, if madness (even low-grade and as-yet-unexpressed madness) is your status quo, then time stands stills, for you cannot possess your own image as your ego ideal. You cannot love yourself as Black, but are *made* to hate yourself as White. And it is the word *made* that throws a wrench in the works of recovery; for your self-hatred is the product, not of

---

* Slogan from the United Negro College Fund ad campaign launched in 1972.

your personal neurosis, but of violence so vast it birthed your other, the Human being. If the talking cure is a cure for Humans, what is your cure? *You are not the subject of your own redemption.* You are, as Cecilio M. Cooper explains, "a vector through which others can accomplish themselves."

You marry White. It doesn't change. You change your slave name. You turn your White Jesus to the wall. It doesn't change. You marry Black. It *still* doesn't change. For it to stop, it would have to have started. You go through life not knowing your desire from theirs. Like a man being lynched and forced to eat his severed penis while telling the lynchers lording over him how good it tastes, you see yourself as a phobic object in need of self-destruction for someone else's safety—that someone is you but also not you. What do you do with an unconscious that *appears* to hate you?

After reading David Marriott's *On Black Men*, the word *appears* crushed my skull like an elephant's foot. Some days, the weight kept me from getting out of bed. On one such day I was slumped on the floor beside my bed. My first class had already started. But that word, *appears* had its foot on my neck. Did it mean that my unconscious hates me every time it comes into view? That to glimpse my unconscious is to glimpse the desire for my own destruction? Or did *appears* suggest doubt—as though my unconscious only *seemed* to hate me? The quandary made it hard for me to move my body, to rise from the floor and get dressed for my seminar. For if self-hatred was a constitutive element of my unconscious, then the talking cure of psychoanalysis (and most certainly of therapy) was no more than high-grade snake oil. The Black was a static imago of abjection. But this stasis was productive for the Human: against Black abjection Humans could know *themselves* as agents of change as well as agents who *could* change. A Marxist like me, I told myself at the time, can't believe this. But several months into the twenty-first century, a Sacramento lawyer, who co-authored Proposition 21, let me know that I was wrong. I woke up in the morning with that phone call on my mind.

I had been doing political organizing in the San Francisco Bay Area to persuade people to vote against Proposition 21. I had called a lawyer in Sacramento who was a member of the inner circle of lawyers at the state capital who had authored the proposition. Under Prop 21, many children as young as fourteen years of age charged with committing felonies would no longer be eligible for juvenile court and prosecutors would be allowed to directly file charges against juvenile offenders in adult court without having to get the permission of juvenile court. I could not believe any rational person would want to send a child to a place like San Quentin. A lawyer, I thought, was a rational being.

When he answered I told him my name was Jay Walljasper (a prominent left-wing activist and journalist). This was the test. If he knew the name, the jig was up. But he didn't know the name. So I compounded the lie by saying that I was a freelance reporter for William F. Buckley's *National Review*. As a stockbroker I'd been trained to *feel* smiling vibrations in the voices of people I cold-called. I could *feel* this Sacramento lawyer was grinning ear to ear. I congratulated him and people like him across the country who were putting propositions on state ballots to crack down on juvenile crime. Proposition 21, I beamed, was a trailblazer. I had every bit of confidence that the *National Review* would accept my story because the editors there were as incensed with this pandemic as he and his colleagues were. I had to be a good journalist, however, and ask him some difficult questions. He told me he understood.

The law, if passed, I reminded him, would also let prosecutors and judges decide if a child of fourteen could be tried as an adult for a felony.

"That's not a problem for most people in California," I continued, "but the touchy-feely liberals of the Bay Area will say that the guidelines for sending children to adult court and then to San Quentin or Folsom are just veiled strategies for instructing prosecutors and judges on how to weed kids who are Black from those who aren't."

The silence on his end of the line was too long. For a moment I thought he knew what I was up to—which would put him two steps ahead of me, because I did not know what, exactly, I was up to. But when he spoke, he asked me if I had any children. So the game wasn't up; we were still talking White-to-White. My daughter's thirteen, I confessed, without also saying she's a beautiful South African girl with glowing onyx skin, almond eyes, and a hint of mischief in her smile.

I have two boys, he said. He then said that he and I both knew something. I started to sweat: I didn't know what he and I knew. We know that our children are not those children. *Those* children are "animals." We are, he informed me, categorically *not* sending fourteen-year-old children to San Quentin, we're sending "animals" to San Quentin. I was so dazed that when he said, "It's been a pleasure, Mr. Walljasper," I didn't know whom he meant. A new century had begun but nothing essential had changed.

I sat on the floor of my Berkeley apartment with no will to move. A riot of memories ransacked my brain: from Celina Davenport's interrogation ("How does it feel to be a Negro"?), to Sameer Bishara's reverie ("The shame and humiliation runs even deeper if the Israeli soldier is an Ethiopian Jew"), to Riana's question ("What kind of American are you"?), to the man I had just spoken with on the phone, with whom I had condemned my own child ("Our children are not those children").

2

Mom, you once called me a glutton for punishment; said I'd rather beat up someone's fist with my face than find a way to live in harmony. Well, here I am, my flesh in bits and pieces. Hoisted by my own petard. The cold part about my phone call with the lawyer is that the lawyer wasn't just talking about the "super predator" that Hillary Clinton alluded to. He was talking about the women who give birth to them; the reproductive labor of Black women who give birth to beings that are not Human. I am floored by what he said about *you*. Did he not know how you nurtured the children of Kenwood as their mothers cannibalized yours?

Had you done to Elgar Davenport what his mother, Celina Davenport, did to me, those mothers would have shown you no mercy. Mom, not only did you *not* treat their children as fodder in a proxy war, but their memories of you are often fonder than their memories of the women who gave birth to them. Women without half your education; and not a trace of your compassion. *Three Coins in a Fountain* ingénues who stewed their minds in martinis. Women who never lectured on early child development in China and Germany, only to come back to the States and be called "gal" in Macy's. Women who could not conceive of the roads you'd traveled, as when you and Dad pierced the jungles of Belize to post bail for study-abroad students being held in a mud-and-metal jail. Women who, well into their forties, stayed free, white, and twenty-one. They worked crosswords in their pearls. They could hurt you through your child. But all their children loved you.

You showed Elgar Davenport that a mother's love was more than Celina Davenport's smoke rings and ridicule. The extra scoops of ice cream that he couldn't get at home; the reassurance that his weight and his wandering eye and the Coke-bottle glasses did not make him a freak; "You're your own kind of special, Elgar, like any child," you told him. All my friends felt at home with you. Well into adulthood they recalled how you folded newspapers into gunboat hats that you painted red, white, and blue on the Fourth of July; and the way you cheered them on and lit their sparklers as they marched up the hill past our house. You made them feel loved. *You made them feel safe*, as their own mothers twisted your stomach into knots; as a scrum of lawyers wrote your children and your children's children into the criminal code. Give me one good reason, Mom, why you think I should get up and go to class.

I fought battles in South Africa that I wasn't sure I would live through. But had I died in South Africa, I would have at least died with the illusion that I had died a Human death, a worker's death; a death of universal meaning. I wish I had died there, Mom. How can I go on without that illusion? There's only one way; but it's a million miles over rough terrain from the floor beside my bed to the medicine cabinet with the pills I need to freeze-dry my pain.

When I was feeling low-down, as a boy, you didn't give me psychotropic drugs. Instead, you told me, "You're of good Louisiana stock, and you have a strong mind." I'm immune to that tonic now. When did your wisdom stop working for me? When did you and I grow so far apart? It must have been in 1968, when your mother and I cheered the looters on TV in the days after King was killed. It must have been that summer, when birds strafed the sun like a fist of pepper in the last good eye of God, and you sliced through a crowd of rusty-butt boys to stop Luke from bleeding Reg. Do you remember that hangdog look I gave you all summer after you saved that White man's life? Surely you recall how I got my revenge despite the fact that I was only twelve years old.

3

My mother was at the kitchen table making flash cards of French verbs. Dad stood at the stove making roux for gumbo. With the reverence of a choirboy I entered the kitchen.

"Mommy, I want to go to Vietnam," I said as piously as I knew how at the age of twelve.

"Whatever for?" she asked.

My father, who had not a cunning bone in his body, didn't know that I saw the don't-look-a-gift-horse-in-the-mouth glance he exchanged with her.

"I want to do my part," I said.

She was pleased and worried, at once. She didn't like war, but she was a patriot and she wanted me to be one too.

It was too good to be true. Her darling boy had returned to her without the help of an exorcist. She touched my cheek the way she used to do when I lay on the living room floor in Minneapolis imbibing her choir's Gregorian chants. She said the war could be over when I turned sixteen. But you can join the Coast Guard, Dad offered, as the roux thickened. Or the Peace Corps, she added. Then she told me how before I was born her bags were packed and her plane ticket was in hand; she was going to Guam to live and teach English for a program not unlike the Peace Corps, when my father asked her to marry him.

"The rest," Mom said with a chuckle, "is history—the rest is *you*, son."

I let the two of them bask in the glow of our reconciliation.

Then I said, "You don't understand me. I didn't mean the White man's army, I meant the *Viet Cong*."

And so it began, our decades of strike and counterstrike, a mother-child dyad that took no prisoners.

"Have you voted for Obama?" she said forty years later. "You know, the polls are closing in California."

"I voted for Mandela in 1994. One milquetoast Negro is enough."

"How will you explain it to your daughter, my granddaughter, if you miss this historic moment?"

" 'Your daddy wasn't no fool.' "

"Sarcasm is the last refuge of the weak, son."

"Would you hold a ticker-tape parade for the first Black man to drop an atomic bomb?"

"Your point being?"

"What's a U.S. president? That's my point."

"Frank, when will you say something good about this country instead of tearing it down?"

"When it's no longer this country."

"Where's your Christian forgiveness?"

"I'm a communist, Jesus sends me hate mail."

When I lived in New York and studied at Columbia, when I lived in South Africa and fought against apartheid, when I went to Berkeley to earn a Ph.D., and even when I finally left and became a professor in Southern California, I was always glad to be on the other side of the world or across the continent where I could be free of your patriotism, your debutante balls, your Lady's Auxiliary of the Knights of Columbus, your Jack and Jill conventions, your God. When I was fifteen I moved to the attic, where I could smoke weed undetected, read Mao and Fanon, and make-believe all the cretins on the floors below were no kin of mine.

Not once in forty years did I say, I love you; nor did I hear it from you.

But you saved my life when I was in fifth grade. Kenwood Elementary School had crushed my resolve like an anvil dropped from a great height. My only sanctuary was the cold, clammy bed I wet so many nights. At first you counseled me the way you counseled your clients in your private practice. But I was too depressed for words. Then, when they told you they would hold me back a grade, you took the switch to me. But I was too numb for pain.

Finally, you came in one morning and pulled me out of bed. But there was no switch in your hand. In your Macy's nightgown and your robe you dropped and did push-ups on your hands and knees. I laughed and said, "You do push-ups like a girl."

In between your counts, you said, "At least *I* can do them, Mr. Defensive Lineman who's still in bed. You're a boy on the Peewee football team whose mother does more push-ups than him. Wait till they hear—"

That was all you had to say. I was on the floor beside you, and not on my knees. We did push-ups, together, you and I. Twenty. Then we did sit-ups.

"Get the endorphins going," you huffed and puffed. Then you left to stuff my pee-stained sheets down the dirty-clothes chute before my siblings woke up. After I washed and got dressed, you stooped and looked me in the eye. "You're of good Louisiana stock and you have a strong mind." Over Easter vacation, I finished six months of missing math and reading assignments; and I made it to sixth grade.

Even in the Seattle summer of my discontent, you taught me. I became a writer by watching you earn your Ph.D.; and by memorizing those long, epic poems you made me memorize. You made me study them with flash cards the way you absorbed French and statistics. When you passed your qualifying exams and were ABD (all but dissertation), I asked you if you were finished. You smiled at me and said, "No, it's only the beginning. The writing comes next." "And after the writing?" I asked you. "After the writing is the rewriting."

I marveled at the way you hunkered down to write your dissertation. I watched you feed IBM punch cards into the mouths of Godzilla-sized computers that chewed raw data like cud—from ideas in your head to holes in punch cards; magic made into meaning; meaning molded into theses; theses typed onto pages; pages that became your black-bound book. You spun dross into gold. The next day they called you "Doctor"; but to me you were a wizard.

I asked you if I would ever write, and you told me, yes, I would. I asked you what I should write about, and you told me to write what I know. So I wrote horror stories in which some of my teachers were unlucky. But they made you frown. Yet I might not have made it to the point where you would frown at my writing had I not knelt on the floor beside you, with ashy legs in pee-stained pajamas.

As a child I used to think life would be so much better in the year 2000. Flying cars, Dick Tracy watch-phones, Ponce de León's fountain of youth boiled down into pills anyone could buy; and Kenwood would be buried in an archaeological dig. I never dreamed that Kenwood was everywhere; that you and I would still be "animals" when the new century was born. I was no Afropessimist when I was a child.

4

My seminar on Lacan would start in ten minutes. It was a half-hour bus ride to campus and I had not moved. *What's the use, Mom? Give me one good reason to get up off the floor.*

I shifted from my butt to my stomach. *One push-up, Mom*, I said inwardly. *One's all you get.* It was no use. My muscles didn't care. I glimpsed silos of dust beneath my bed. I knew what you would have said: How can you attain the good, the beautiful, and the true if your bedroom isn't clean?

One push-up turned into one hundred. I even did some sit-ups. I went to the bathroom. Juiced with just enough endorphins to open the medicine cabinet. There they were, selective serotonin reuptake inhibitors and chlordiazepoxide, my two best friends in orange-brown bottles. I flushed them down the toilet.

I was committing to make madness my refuge; to face the fact that my death makes the world a decent place to live; to embrace my abjection and the antagonism that made me Humanity's foil. I would make my home in the hold of the ship and burn it from the inside out.

I washed my face and wore my school clothes and went to my class as a nightmare.

5

Nine years later, in 2009, I was a tenured professor at UC Irvine, in Orange County, four hundred miles down the coast. Alice and I lived in an ample, high-ceilinged condo across from the campus. I had just turned fifty-three. The aleatory fits and starts that had characterized my life's journey made me noticeably older than most professors at the rank of associate professor. In November, Alice would be seventy-five. She'd retired from teaching up in Santa Cruz and moved to Orange County. We both were fond of saying we were in Orange County but Orange County wasn't in us. Until moving to the Irvine–Newport Beach area I had seen only two Rolls-Royces in my life. Now we lived four miles from a Rolls-Royce dealership and we saw one (at the mall, on the boulevards, at the gas pump, at the drive-up window of Starbucks) three to four times a month. Frequent sightings of half a million dollars on wheels in the most banal and quotidian locations. The poverty line for the county was eighty thousand dollars a year. This wasn't Berkeley. Alice and I were slow to make friends.

Up until the Race Rave conference in 2001, at UC Santa Cruz, when the White people in her group attacked her for insisting that they talk about themselves in terms of their common structural position, rather than in terms of their gendered identities or cultural heritage, Alice and I had not only embodied the antagonism between us (the irrevocable divide between species), but we had performed it as well. Those were rough years in which love was laced with hate. During the ten years before she retired, however, she had also begun to teach the works of Black radical thinkers, in particular the thinkers who, by 2009, would be associated with Afropessimism. And her intellectual commitment had spilled over into action. It was this willingness to throw her body against the institutions that had been the foundation of her entire life, as well as the glue that held her most dear relations together, that unburdened our love affair of much of its inner turmoil and tension.

Over the course of two years, she fought the anti-Black racists at two Santa Cruz colleges where we taught; among them were her lifelong friends and her daughter who taught at one of the colleges. Even though I love her, I hesitate to give her props for doing what she should have been doing before we even met. Why am I so chary with my praise in writing, when I am much more appreciative and not nearly as miserly at home? Because I fear the sense of relief a White reader might imbibe from such praise; that dewdrop of hope in a liberal's heart when they see a Black-and-White couple in love. There are, indeed, bonds of affection, often deep and profound, between a master and her slave, but that doesn't make it a relationship—structurally. Structurally, there is no relationship between Black and Human lovers. But nor is there an *intra*-Black relationship, even though here too we often find bonds of deep, profound affection. A captive who marries his captor remains a captive. This was the brutal truth of what, for lack of another word, we called our *love*. Just as two captives who share the same bed under the roof of what, for lack of an honest word, they call their *home*, are still captives—not captives to each other, but to a mesh of masters, from their White neighbors to the FBI. In 1980, Stella and I learned this the hard way when we fled, first our "home," and then the state of Minnesota.

The saw "Love conquers all" makes us disavow a violence that has always already conquered love.

. . .

THERE IS NO INTERRACIAL REDEMPTION. There is no Afrocentric redemption. Redemption is the narrative inheritance of Humans. There is no denouement to social death.

But now Barack Obama had been sworn in three months prior and there seemed few auditors for such an unflinching lens of analysis as Afropessimism in the academic circles Alice and I traveled in. At the campus yoga studio, one of Alice's White female friends, Henrietta, rejoiced at how wonderful and filled with hope the world was again.

"You and Frank must feel it," Henrietta said knowingly.

"Feel what?" Alice asked. Alice knew exactly what Henrietta meant; that even though she, Alice, was well beyond childbearing age and therefore could not make her own little baby Obama, she and I had been sanctioned as a couple in the personage of the most powerful man in the world. Henrietta was nearly reduced to stammering by the discord in Alice's voice.

"Well . . . well . . . you know what I mean," Henrietta pleaded.

"No, what do you mean?" Alice said.

"Then why on earth *did* you vote for Obama?"

The door to the yoga studio opened. Alice stood, gathered her bolster and her yoga mat.

"I didn't," she replied.

Henrietta was apoplectic.

"You voted for *McCain*?"

"I don't vote, Henrietta. I stopped voting some time ago. If you knew more about this country you'd stop voting too. There are other ways to fight for change."

Rather than ask what those other ways were, Henrietta recoiled, as though Alice had said, I don't bathe, Henrietta. I stopped bathing long ago. If you knew more about hygiene you'd stop bathing too. (Later, Alice told me she'd never dismiss a Black person's investment in voting. Henrietta, however, was a different story.)

The election of the first Black president seemed to give my parents renewed vigor in the cold war we'd fought since I was twelve. Dad was seventy-eight. Mom was seventy-seven. They both were retired and, like Alice, who was seventy-five, they had more time on their hands. This meant (to my outer welcome and my inner dread) they came to California more often, to visit my brother in Los Angeles and me and Alice fifty miles south on coastal Highway 1.

. . .

WE DINED AL FRESCO on a marble terrace with tall terra-cotta columns on a cliff overlooking the sea in Newport Beach. Mom's hair was well-coiffed and perched with sunglasses, which gave her a cool, just-back-from-Club-Med-for-Seniors look. Dad was better dressed than I had been even when I worked as a stockbroker. Alice and I were dressed in solid black, as though we had come not for lunch on a cliff above the sea, but to carry their bags. There were precious few guests on the terrace. It was spring. The summer-season droves of tourists had yet to arrive. A squadron of double-crested cormorants laid siege to a boulder a mile out from the shore; and when the conversation lulled one could hear the sound of suicide being practiced by waves on the rocks below. Soon the conversation ran aground as well.

Alice and I had shown a little too much enthusiasm when we told them how high school students sometimes called us during the dinner hour to ask questions about Afropessimism. I think Mom was a bit incredulous at the idea that high school students were reading this material. But we explained that these students were high school debaters who read critical theory as part of their training. College debate coaches were also calling the house to ask questions and request Afropessimist seminars ever since a Black debate team from Towson University in Maryland beat Harvard in a national debate tournament. They did so, I explained, by refusing the question of the tournament, rather than arguing pro or con within the logic of the question: It's unethical to insist that Slaves argue *within* the logic of a world that defines itself in opposition to them. So they *interrogated* the question's assumptive logic. Black students were mobilizing my claim that civil society was a murderous juggernaut for the Slave, not a terrain of consent balanced by coercion; and mobilizing Saidiya Hartman's argument that "the slave is the object or the ground that . . . by negation or contradistinction, defines liberty, citizenship, and the enclosures of the social body."

My parents, especially my mother, were impressed by the social-uplift narrative of Black students beating Harvard students in a game of wits. They were, however, underwhelmed by the strategies and, I suspect, were inwardly alarmed that this was becoming a national trend.

Alice chuckled. "It's gotten to the point where White parents want to hire Frank to teach Afropessimism to their White children so that they can beat Black students in future tournaments."

"Some professors and debate coaches," I chimed in, "want to impose a rule that would disqualify students who interrogate the question. We're witnessing the *blackening* of a major intercollegiate 'sport.'"

Mom sighed. "I don't see how Afropessimism can help these Black children become good citizens. What can it do to get Black people from point A to point B?" she opined with her characteristic logic, not in the least dulled by age.

Out at sea, a large skiff of whale watchers skipped across the water, alarming the double-crested cormorants. They scattered like buckshot off the boulder. The main plates were cleared and we ordered coffee and dessert. We were down to brass tacks, my mother and I.

She said, "What's the use of Afropessimism? What *practical* use does it have?"

I said, "It's not a tractor, it can't mow your lawn, if that's what you mean. But it makes us worthy of our suffering."

She said, "How's suffering going to make me a good citizen?"

I said, "I can't believe you're a Black psychologist who's read Fanon."

She said, "I read the funnies, but I don't *quote* the funnies."

I said, "Don't patronize me."

Dad tried to change the subject by noting how lush and green the headland looked. Alice said California had seven growing seasons. They chewed that bit of trivia like cud. I told Mom that it was common for most people to feel like they'd been mugged by Afropessimism. It was a shrewd move on my part, for I knew how she hated to think of herself as a victim.

"That's why most people don't take the time to understand it," I said. "They're too afraid."

She scoffed. "Afraid of what?"

"Afraid of a problem in which everyone is complicit and for which no sentence can be written that would explain how to remedy it. Most people, Mom, even profound intellectuals like you and Dad and Alice, and myself, if I'm to be honest, are emotionally unable to wallow in a problem that has no solution. Black suffering is that problem. And a suffering without a solution is a hard thing to hold, especially if that suffering fuels the psychic health of the rest of the world. But that's what it means to be a Slave, to be the host of that parasite called the Human."

Mom rejoined that she wasn't anybody's slave, and that even when our ancestors were slaves they were Human beings.

"Being Human isn't anything to aspire to," I said. "Just ask Alice."

Though we all laughed, the laughter was uneasy. This was the elephant in the room: my marriage to Alice; her presence and place in what the conversation implied. No one asked me to defend the thinly veiled claim that Alice was both my wife and my master. But everyone, including me, especially me, flinched when I told that joke. We all knew what I meant. We were all academics. And that's how the conversation was supposed to stay, *academic*, if we were going to have it at all. *Say what you want, but don't bring it home.* I had broken that unspoken rule, but it got their attention (and Obama had not been shot by them across the bow).

Every time Alice spoke I witnessed a slight delay of comprehension in my mother's eyes—like someone paused at a green light—as though Alice's words were chasing the faces they went with. Faces my mother had seen years before in Kenwood. The countenances of White women Alice surely conjured when she spoke; a sonic boom of faces from the past. *All the masters in the world*, Mom must have thought, *rolled into my son's wife as he drones on about our suffering.*

Martin Luther King was killed a year after Celina Davenport wounded Mom by wounding me; and in the same year the White housewives of Mom and Dad's fair housing workshops shut her down and exiled her to the marble foyer of a mansion. Six days after King was gunned down, Mom made me and my sister trudge through the slush of a winter-touched spring and stuff those women's mailboxes with an open letter she had written.

"Here in Kenwood, a sharp struggle for better human relations for our community and city," Mom wrote . . .

> . . . has been raging during the past few months. If you haven't heard about it or haven't been called by someone, pro or con, just ask your neighbor.
>
> The most vicious aspect of this struggle is not that one plan or another has been considered or not considered, but that the minds of so many are closed, so obstructive to anything which challenges or tends to alter the "uniqueness" of Kenwood, whatever that is. (That there are only two black homeowners in Kenwood, and that these purchases were made in spite of deliberate impediments and undue difficulty is a fact. Is this the uniqueness of Kenwood?)

Perhaps I was channeling the memory of that day we "mailed" her letter, when we all ate lunch by the sea. It helped me understand why Mom seemed to tense and withdraw when Alice spoke. Alice wasn't one of the women from her past but, *structurally*, she was. This made Mom an Afropessimist par excellence. But to show it, she'd have *to bring it home*.

· · ·

A FEW WEEKS BEFORE my parents came out to California, a young Black woman came to my office hours and said she wanted to drop my class. She said she was having difficulty with the reading material and the effort was taking too much of a toll on her. I couldn't fathom this, since her midterm exam and her paper demonstrated mastery (an unfortunate word!) of the material. She understood critical theory at levels exemplary of the most advanced graduate students, and she was still a senior in college. I told her that the thing that prevented most students from getting their heads around Afropessimism was the fact that it described a structural problem but offered no structural solution to that problem.

"To suffer like a White woman or Native Americans or postcolonial subjects would be heaven for us, because the suffering of the Slave would have Human resonance. And that Human resonance would lend itself to very Human answers to the question, What is to be done? or What does freedom look like? We could launch coherent liberation campaigns. However, that would be disastrous for the Human race. This is why Afropessimism has no prescriptive gesture: because the end of our suffering signals the end of the Human, the end of world. But you know all of this," I assured her. "You should be holding office hours for me!"

"It's not that I don't understand," she said. "This class has turned my head around. It's explained things that I only saw before in my peripheral vision."

"Then what's the problem?" I asked.

"It hurts," she said. "It hurts so bad."

She began to cry, first softly, then like an uncontrollable torrent. I told her that I had forgotten—no, I corrected myself, I had *repressed*—how much it hurts. This made her laugh. I was glad to see her smile but I didn't think what I said was funny.

"I don't believe you," she said. "You teach with such composure and your voice never cracks. And here I am bawling in your office."

"You might not believe this," I confided, "but only nine years ago I had a nervous breakdown when I was a graduate student. It was a doozy! Snot all drippin' down my mouth, mixed with tears. I was a sho' 'nuff embarrassment to the race!"

She was shaking her head and laughing now, as though watching an act on the Chitlin Circuit.

"Lawd have mercy, there were mornings when I rolled out of bed, onto the floor, and ate balls of dust for breakfast. I could stay there for hours. That's how broke down I was."

She laughed again and said I was lying. It was good to see her come out of her funk.

"I kid you not. I was a slobbering fool. A graduate student in his forties, who'd fought a revolution in his thirties. The *stakes*, the *implications* of what it all meant for the dissertation I was writing. What it meant for Black life! I'm telling you, uppers and downers were my two best friends. And my wife is White, you dig? Afropessimism ain't exactly an aphrodisiac in an interracial love affair. 'Hey, baby, how 'bout we smoke a little structural antagonism before we make love?' Shoot. It's a wonder I ain't cross-eyed."

She grinned ear to ear and said it seemed strange to laugh at her professor. Then she asked if she could tell *me* something personal. I nodded. She said that her father was Black and her mother was White; and she added that her boyfriend was Asian American.

"My mom is the master of my father and of me; and so is my boyfriend," she went on. "I can see it clearly now, in the symptoms of our relationships. Professor, it hurts. It hurts so bad because I also see things in me that *I've* repressed: the way I love my mom but hate her so, so much. The way I love my boyfriend and hate him as well. I hate them not for what they do, because they're both loving and sweet. I hate them because of what they *can* do. And they don't want to talk about it."

"Human capacity." I nodded. "It's your mother's inheritance but she can't pass it on to either you or your father. And if you and your Asian partner have kids, they will follow your lack, and not his plenitude. It's a lot to take in."

"It seems like I've loved them and hated them forever," she said.

I told her that my first book was about this very problem, a duel in the heart, for which no denouement is possible. She was adamant, however, about dropping the class because it was too painful to discuss social death and Black suffering in a multiracial classroom. It was then that I realized what needed to be adjusted in the way I presented the material in class. The spotlight has been too much on us, I admitted, and not enough on them—how they are who they are because we are who they have *made* us; how anti-Blackness reproduces them as Human beings. So I made her a deal. For the rest of the quarter I would focus on how the Human functions and thrives as the parasite of the Slave. We would do a close reading on how Human capacities are manifest in specific genders and cultures. The course needed balance. I would *explain*, not merely assert, how and why the Human is unethical, whether she is a communist and a feminist, whether he is a fascist and a misogynist. They are all the embodiments of capacity, and capacity is an offense. I asked her if she would give me two weeks of teaching to make good on my promise. She was laughing again.

"Now what's so funny?"

"The non-Black students will complain and the administration will fire you."

"Would admin fire a non-Black professor if the Black Student Union complained?" I asked. She shook her head. "Then to hell with the administration. You're risking your sanity to stay with me for two more weeks. The least I can do is risk my job."

6

It was going on three and my parents needed to drive up the coast to my brother's house in Los Angeles ahead of the afternoon traffic. I paid the bill and the four of us, Alice, Mom, Dad, and me, filed out of the open-air dining terrace and made our way through the enclosed part of the establishment to where their driver was waiting for them. Alice and Dad led the way, speaking amicably. Mom and I trailed in silence. Then she stopped. She let them sift away from us. Now her hand was on my heart.

"I want you to manage your time better," she said.

Defensiveness coursed through my veins. *Just leave me alone.* I braced myself for one of her criticisms. When my first book came out, she wrote me to say: With degrees from Dartmouth, Columbia, and UC Berkeley, you could have been president, like Obama, but you had to do *this*. Why can't you put your talents to use in a way that contributes to America's reform, instead of tearing it down all the time? I'd heard this since I was twelve, it looped in my brain like Muzak in an elevator stuck between floors. *Just go to L.A. and see my brother, he's a good citizen.*

"I could tell from our conversation at the table," she said, "that you have two more books in you. Don't take on undue administrative responsibilities, and every class you teach doesn't have to be perfect. Manage your time so you can write those books. You've got a good head on your shoulders."

I laughed, not at her but in relief. Of all the things she could have said, this was the most unexpected.

"Why are you laughing?"

" 'You're of good Louisiana stock, and you have a strong mind.' "

"Well, that too. That too."

"I'm still doing push-ups."

"Push-ups?"

"Never mind." We were both smiling. "Dad and Alice are waiting."

"Write those books, you hear?" She patted my chest again. "I'm proud of you, son. I love you."

They say that the flutter of a butterfly's wing can trigger a monsoon somewhere else in the world. That's what happened when she touched my heart and said what she said. Forty years of strike and counterstrike, a war of attrition we'd fought since she'd saved Reg's life in that Seattle parking lot, had ended. I told her I was proud of her too, and I said I loved her.

For the next ten years we each made an effort to say these things to each other. I praised her for her leadership roles in sororities and social clubs, even Jack and Jill, and in religious orders I had heretofore been disdainful of. I praised her for all the people's lives she had healed in the private psychology practice she and Dad maintained. I even told her I was proud of what a good citizen she was. I said it like I meant it, and I really did. And for her part she kept encouraging me to write, without lambasting my politics. We always parted, whether on the phone or on our rare face-to-face encounters, with the words, "I love you." We had ten good years before her stroke, her heart failure, her dementia—that is, before she lost my name and died.

The last time I saw her she was sitting in the memory unit, the lockdown ward, of a nursing home. A polite but no-nonsense German-looking woman called her Miss Ida as she straightened the bedclothes and watered a plant I had sent her. Mom cast a raised eyebrow of caution my way and whispered, "We call her Il Duce." The woman heard this, and I realized from Mom's smug demeanor that she was meant to. I apologized profusely on Mom's behalf and found out that her name was really Angela.

"Miss Ida, you're a hoot."

"Owls hoot," Mom said flatly. Adding, "You should show less cleavage. Who are your people?"

Angela said she wasn't leaving until Mom ate some of the food she hadn't even touched.

"Fascism is alive and well," Mom observed.

My mother's arms, wrists, and hands made me think of prisoners in a concentration camp. Her dexterity was no match for the simple tasks of holding her utensils. I offered to help her but Angela said that, difficult as it may be, she could do it, and she did it yesterday, and that she had to get her strength back. The fork fell to the floor. Mom pushed her plate away. "I told her," she said, as though speaking to herself, "I'm not interested in food." Then she asked me if I had just come from the Washington Monument. When I said no, we're in Minneapolis, not in D.C., she said I never did have a sense of direction, no wonder I'd come late for my sister's recital.

"What recital," I wanted to know, "where?"

Angela's two-way radio called her to an emergency, and she left. When Angela was out of earshot Mom said she was sure Angela was tapping her phone. I didn't argue but asked where the recital was.

"What do you mean, where? The *Jack and Jill* convention, down the hall in the ballroom, silly." She asked me when my father and Dr. Johnson (a longtime psychology colleague of theirs) were returning from wherever they went. I wanted to remind her that Dad was in a nursing home on the other side of town, but she held up her index finger. "Listen. Your sister plays beautifully."

The Jack and Jill convention must have been in 1970, and my sister had not played the piano for almost forty years. But I sat with Mom and listened until the end of the concerto, or was it an étude? Then came an ice age of silence in which she said nothing and seemed not to notice I was there. Snowplows groaned in the street below her window. The branches of trees were bare and starred with frost. Where was the woman who danced slowly in her stocking feet with my father in the living room at night, Johnny Hartman on the hi-fi and not a worry in the world? The woman who said my stock was good and my mind was strong. Where was she, the woman who made me want to write?

Her hair was as white and thin as dandelion puffs. But there was a natural beauty to it that I had not seen when I was a child and she used to press it, then. Lizard tracks lined her face drawn thin as her wrists, thin as the last rail of garden sculpture. She was humming now. She had not spoken for a while. Then, as if she'd been reading my mail, she sat up straight as a washboard. Her bony hands seized the arms of her wheelchair. Like Harriet Tubman staring down a gun barrel, she looked at me. "Didn't I tell you, boy, people have to die? I know I told you that."

Then she fell back into her eyes.

I went into the hallway so she wouldn't see me cry. When I returned to the room, she asked me who I was.

· · ·

SHE DIED IN A POLAR VORTEX. It was forty-nine degrees below zero in Minneapolis. Pyramids of snow mobbed the margins of the highway from the airport to the funeral home. The wind swept torrents of snow off the mounds along the highway. I saw it coming but it was too late. I was driving too fast. It rose in a cyclone and dropped, suddenly: a massive white wall erected over the highway. It made anything more than a foot in front of me impossible to see. The rental car plunged into this white wall at sixty-five miles an hour. The car skidded and hydroplaned as I frantically pumped the brakes. Would I kill or be killed as I rammed another car from behind? I wondered. *There are no atheists in foxholes*, Mom used to say. For an instant she was right.

Then, without warning it lifted; the road was clear for miles, and I was still alive. It was four-thirty and the sun had set. I had fifteen minutes to get to the funeral home, but I had to slow down.

The viewing rooms at the funeral home were closed for the night, but the mortician was kind enough to roll her body into a utility room. The hallways were adorned with pictures of Martin Luther King and Malcolm X. This was Estes Funeral Chapel on the north side of town. She did not want to be buried in Kenwood.

For a long time my knees wouldn't take me to the side of the room where she lay. I stood just inside the room, sobbing, begging her to wake up.

You can't die, I told her. I asked her how she could leave me without saying goodbye; why didn't she wait for me? The mortician was a brother thirty years my junior but he led me over to her body like I was a baby learning to walk. I kissed her hard, cold cheek. I begged her to wake up until I was hoarse. I told her I would be the good citizen she always wanted me to be. I would do anything she ever wanted me to do.

At a gathering of family and friends that took place after her funeral I told the story of what she did when we walked out of the restaurant on the precipice in California, how she placed her hand on my heart and said she was proud of me; how that changed our relationship in a way that I could never have imagined possible. How we said, "I love you," to each other for the first time in forty years. Then I read a poem I had written for her.

> *Civil Rights*
> *Mother never spoke of slavery*
> *Not New Orleans doctors who cut without pain*
> *killers the privates of female slaves in their Mad Hatter*
> *quest to cure incontinence*
> *Not the lash of whips upriver*
>
> *But when they killed Dr. Martin Luther King she wrote every*
> *blue hair blonde eye*
> *a letter*

Like any spring of no reply
winter was late in leaving and we were her
only postage
my sister and I walking end to end

through the seep of slush and the push
of wind
no one dabbed a crystalled eye for
she would have no crying

On the way to the airport for my flight back home I don't know why, but I bought a blank card. It lay open on my tray table for the entire flight. I didn't know what to write. Who buys a greeting card for the dead? The Newport Beach coast, where we had dined al fresco, was coming into view. I looked down at the card. It was wet with tears. Now the flight attendant told me, again, to stow my tray table. As the plane surrendered to the pull of the earth, I wrote what time allowed.

Dear Mom,

I don't know if you're in heaven with your Jesus, or sailing the cosmos with Shango, or if your soul has gone to rest in the consummate hands of gifted musicians. But wherever you are please wait for me, that we might spend eternity as we spent the last ten years. I miss you so much.

With all my love,

Your son, Frank

BREMEN, HUDSON, IRVINE, *2014–2019*

NOTES

I

1 **"I came into the world":** *Black Skin, White Masks*, trans. Charles Lam Markmann (New York: Grove, [1952], 1967).

1 **"I'm prized most as a vector":** Cecilio M. Cooper and Frank B. Wilderson III. "Incommensurabilities: The Limits of Redress, Intramural Indemnity, and Extramural Auditorship," in eds. Hunter et al., "Co-presence with the Camera," special issue, *Performance Matters* (April 2020).

Chapter One: For Halloween I Washed My Face

12 **Blackness is a locus of abjection:** David Marriott, *Haunted Life: Visual Culture and Black Modernity* (New Brunswick, NJ: Rutgers University Press, 2007).

12 **a sentient implement to be joyously deployed:** David Marriott, *On Black Men* (New York: Columbia University Press, 2000).

13 **"responsible for all the conflicts that may arise":** Frantz Fanon, *Black Skin, White Masks*, trans. Richard Philcox (New York: Grove, [1952], 1967), 169.

13 **libidinal economy:** Jared Sexton describes libidinal economy as "the economy, or distribution and arrangement, of desire and identification (their condensation and displacement), and the complex relationship between sexuality and the unconscious." Needless to say, libidinal economy functions variously across scales and is as "objective" as political economy. Importantly, it is linked not only to forms of attraction, affection, and alliance, but also to aggression, destruction, and the violence of lethal consumption. He emphasizes that it is "the whole structure of psychic and emotional life," something more than, but inclusive of or traversed by, what Gramsci and other Marxists call a "structure of feeling"; it is "a dispensation of energies, concerns, points of attention, anxieties, pleasures, appetites, revulsions, and phobias capable of both great mobility and tenacious fixation."

13 **"The slave is neither civic man":** Saidiya V. Hartman, *Scenes of Subject: Terror, Slavery, and Self-Making in Nineteenth-Century America* (New York: Oxford University Press, 1997), 65.

13 **"a point of undecidability":** William Harmon, *A Handbook to Literature*, 12th ed. (Upper Saddle River, NJ: Pearson, 2011), 65.

16 **"economy of disposability":** Jared Sexton, "Unbearable Blackness," *Cultural Critique* 90, no. 1 (Spring 2015): 168.

16 **"social death":** Orlando Patterson, *Slavery and Social Death: A Comparative Study* (Cambridge, MA: Harvard University Press, 1982).

17 **"difference between ... something to save":** James Baldwin, *Nobody Knows My Name: More Notes of a Native Son* (New York: Vintage, 1993), 172.

Chapter Two: Juice from a Neck Bone

40 **"deathliness":** David Marriott, *Whither Fanon? Studies in the Blackness of Being* (Stanford, CA: Stanford University Press, 2018), 63.

46 **"the hidden structure of violence":** Jared Sexton, "Afro-Pessimism: The Unclear Word," *Rhizomes: Cultural Studies in Emerging Knowledge*, no. 29 (2016), https://doi.org/10.20415/rhiz/029.e02.

47 **"Imagine the black man":** David Marriott, *On Black Men* (New York: Columbia University Press, 2000), 11–12.

47 **"I am a marked woman":** Hortense J. Spillers, "Mama's Baby, Papa's Maybe: An American Grammar Book," in *Black, White, and in Color: Essays on American Literature and Culture* (Chicago: University of Chicago Press, 2003), 203.

47 **the Black family:** This report was known more simply as the "Moynihan report," by Daniel Patrick Moynihan, "The Negro Family: The Case For National Action (1965)."

Chapter Three: Hattie McDaniel Is Dead

58 **"During his stay in Trinidad":** Federal Bureau of Investigation, NW#: 60158/DocId: 34295707, July 12, 1976.

58 **"The FBI legal attaché":** See the Federal Bureau of Investigation's web page "International Operations," accessed March 20, 2019, https://www.fbi.gov/about/leadership-and-structure/international-operations.

67 **blow the lid off COINTELPRO:** In March 1971, anti-war activists broke into an FBI office in Media, Pennsylvania. "Among a huge stash of confidential documents the group retrieved were secrets about the FBI's blanket surveillance of the peace and civil rights movement, the tactics of disinformation and deception the bureau used to silence protesters and even an attempt by agents to have Martin Luther King commit suicide." See Ed Pilkington, "Burglars in 1971 FBI Office Break-In Come Forward After 43 Years," *Guardian*, January 7, 2014, https://www.theguardian.com/world/2014/jan/07/fbi-office-break-in-1971-come-forward-documents. In the FBI's own words, "The FBI began COINTELPRO—short for Counterintelligence Program—in 1956 to disrupt the activities of the Communist Party of the United States. In the 1960s, it was expanded to include a number of other domestic groups, such as the . . . Black Panther Party." See "The Vault," accessed March 20, 2019, https://vault.fbi.gov/cointel-pro.

68 **the Gerson Method:** Gerson therapy is a complex regimen that has been used to treat people with cancer and other diseases. Key parts of the Gerson Method are a strict diet, dietary supplements, and enemas.

73 **"The westward movement":** Ira Berlin, *Remembering Slavery: African Americans Talk About Their Personal Experiences of Slavery and Emancipation* (New York: New Press, 2000), xxv.

93 **"Mistress [Mary] Epps," he writes:** Solomon Northrup, *12 Years a Slave: And Plantation Life in the Antebellum South*, ed. Sue Eakin (Lafayette, LA: Lafayette Center for Louisiana Studies, University of Louisiana at Lafayette, [1853], 2007), 196, emphasis mine.

93 **can secure his satisfaction in the open:** *Mary Chesnut's Civil War*, ed. Comer Vann Woodward (New Haven: Yale University Press, 1981). The

work of Hortense Spillers and Thavolia Glymph offer insights into the desire and sexual violence of White female slaveholders and Black female slaves. Special thanks to Ellen Louis for her insights as well.

93 **"without discrimination":** Northrop, *12 Years a Slave*, 201.

94 **"laugh . . . and commend him":** Northrop, *12 Years a Slave*, 201.

94 **"It was rarely a day passed":** Northrop, *12 Years a Slave*, 135.

96 **fantasies have "objective value":** David Marriott, *On Black Men* (New York: Columbia University Press, 2000), 11.

102 **"historical stillness":** For more on the "slave" as the "essence of stillness, or of an undynamic human state," see again Hortense Spillers, "Mama's Baby, Papa's Maybe: An American Grammar Book," *Diacritics* 17, no. 2 (Summer 1987): 78.

104 **is organically anti-Black:** Howell Meadows Henry, "The Police Control of the Slave in South Carolina" (Ph.D. dissertation, Vanderbilt University, 1914), and Frank B. Wilderson III, *Red, White & Black: Cinema and the Structure of U.S. Antagonisms* (Durham, NC: Duke University Press, 2010), 79–85, 109–116.

128 **"By 1973–75 . . . Euro-American":** Joy James, ed., *Imprisoned Intellectuals: America's Political Prisoners Write on Life, Liberation, and Rebellion* (Lanham, MD: Rowman & Littlefield, 2003), 109.

141 **"There is no golden age for blacks":** Jared Sexton, "Racial Profiling and the Societies of Control," in Joy James, ed., *Warfare in the American Homeland: Policing and Prison in a Penal Democracy* (Durham, NC: Duke University Press, 2007), 201.

Chapter Four: Punishment Park

148 **clips from *Punishment Park*:** Director Peter Watkins (1971).

150 **McCarran Internal Security Act of 1950:** Martin Gruberg, "McCarran Internal Security Act of 1950 (1950)," *The First Amendment Encyclopedia* (Middle Tennessee State University), accessed March 13, 2019, https://mtsu .edu/first-amendment/article/1047/mccarran-act-of-1950.

151 **Algiers Motel incident:** "On July 26, 1967, the third day of one of the worst riots of the 20th century, the Detroit police ordered five [unarmed] black teenagers and two white women into a hallway of the Algiers Motel, where they forced them to stand spread-eagle facing a wall . . . They stripped the women and then took the men one by one into a motel room, where

they interrogated them. A series of shots were fired. When the incident ended, Pollard, Temple and Cooper [three of the black teenagers] had been killed." DeNeen L. Brown, "Detroit and the Police Brutality That Left Three Black Teens Dead at the Algiers Motel," *Washington Post* (August 4, 2017), accessed June 21, 2019, https://www.washingtonpost.com/news/retropolis/wp/2017/08/04/detroit-and-the-police-brutality-that-left-three-black-teens-dead-at-the-algiers-motel/?utm_term=.8ab9eb9edea7

151 **Fred Hampton was gunned down in his bed:** "Fred Hampton [was] deputy chairman of the Illinois chapter of the Black Panther Party. During an early morning police raid of the BPP headquarters at 2337 W. Monroe Street on December 4, 1969, twelve officers opened fire, killing the 21- year old Hampton and Peoria, Illinois Panther leader Mark Clark." Dwayne Mack, "Fred Hampton (1948–1969)," *Black Past* (April 16, 2008), accessed June 21, 2019, http://www.blackpast.org/african-american-history/hampton-fred-1948-1969/

151 **Jackson State:** The Jackson State Killings took place at Jackson State College (now Jackson State University) on May 15, 1970, in Jackson, Mississippi. Around midnight on May 14, city and state police confronted a group of students and opened fire on them, killing two students and injuring twelve. The Jackson State Killings occurred eleven days after the more widely publicized Kent State University shootings in Kent, Ohio. Samuel Momodu, "The Jackson State Killings, 1970," *Black Past* (September 9, 2017), accessed June 21, 2019, https://www.blackpast.org/african-american-history/events-african-american-history/jackson-state-killings-1970/

155 **Students for a Democratic Society:** Students for a Democratic Society was an American student organization that flourished in the mid- to late 1960s and was known for its activism against the Vietnam War. Tactics included the occupation of university and college administration buildings on campuses across the country.

156 **affilial conflict:** *Filial*: any community one is born into: nation, religion, ethnicity, family. *Affilial*: a voluntary association, a community one chooses to enter. In *The World, the Text, and the Critic*, Edward Said describes affiliation as "the transition from a failed idea or possibility of filiation to a kind of compensatory order that, whether it is a party, an institution, a culture, a set of beliefs, or even a world-vision, provides men and women with a new form of relationship, which I have been calling affiliation but which is also a new system . . . Thus if a filial relationship was held together by natural bonds and natural

forms of authority—involving obedience, fear, love, respect, and instinctual conflict—the new affiliative relationship changes these bonds into what seem to be transpersonal forms—such as guild consciousness, consensus, collegiality, professional respect, class and the hegemony of a dominant culture. The filiative scheme belongs to the realms of nature and of 'life,' whereas affiliation belongs exclusively to culture and society." See Edward Said, *The World, the Text, and the Critic* (Cambridge, MA: Harvard University Press, 1983), 19–20.

158 **"ontological resistance in the eyes":** Frantz Fanon, *Black Skin, White Masks*, trans. Charles Lam Markmann (New York: Grove, [1952], 1967), 110.

159 **"connections, transfers and displacements":** Peter Miller and Nikolas Rose, "On Therapeutic Authority: Psychoanalytic Expertise Under Advanced Liberalism," *History of the Human Sciences* 7, no. 3 (1994): 31.

159 **"characteristics of the family":** Frantz Fanon, *Black Skin, White Masks*, trans. Charles Lam Markmann (New York: Grove, [1952], 1967), 142.

161 **His *"flesh"*** Hortense Spillers, "Mama's Baby, Papa's Maybe: An American Grammar Book," *Diacritics* 17, no. 2 (Summer 1987): 67.

163 **given over, to the power and desire:** David Marriott, *On Black Men* (New York: Columbia University Press, 2000).

164 **"Death is such an essential":** Jonathan Lee, *Jacques Lacan* (Amherst, MA: University of Massachusetts Press, 1990), 92.

165 **"The slave dies, it is true, but he [sic] dies in the master":** Orlando Patterson, *Slavery and Social Death: A Comparative Study* (Cambridge, MA: Harvard University Press, 1982), 98.

169 **"[It] seems counterintuitive":** Jared Sexton, "Race, Sexuality, and Political Struggle: Reading *Soul on Ice*," *Social Justice* 30, no. 2 (2003): 36.

174 **my critique of Antonio Gramsci's assumptive logic:** Frank B. Wilderson III, "Gramsci's Black Marx: Whither the Slave in Civil Society?" *Social Identities: Journal for the Study of Race, Nation and Culture* 9, no. 2 (2003).

174 **"the terrible gap":** James Baldwin, "Black Boy Looks at the White Boy," in *Nobody Knows My Name* (New York: Vintage, 1993), 174.

174 **"[T]he really ghastly thing":** James Baldwin, "Black Boy Looks at the White Boy," 175.

175 **"I am afraid that most of the white people":** James Baldwin, "Black Boy Looks at the White Boy," 172.

176 **affect of hostility and patronizing condescension:** Affect theory explores nonverbal modes of conveying feelings and influence. The "father" of affect theory is the psychologist and personality theorist Silvan Tomkins. He

argued that affects form the biological system that underlies emotions; but they are not the same as emotions. "Affects are the inborn protocols that, when triggered, bring things to our attention and motivate us to act." The Tomkins Institute, accessed June 22, 2019, http://www.tomkins.org/what -tomkins-said/introduction/nine-affects-present-at-birth-combine-to-form -emotion-mood-and-personality/

182 **"the anxiety of antagonism":** Jared Sexton, "Afro-Pessimism: The Unclear Word," *Rhizomes: Cultural Studies in Emerging Knowledge,* no. 29 (2016), https://doi.org/10.20415/rhiz/029.e02."

II

189 **"The slave is the object":** Saidiya Hartman. *Scenes of Subjection: Terror, Slavery, and Self-Making in Nineteenth-Century America* (New York. Oxford University Press, 1997), 62.

Chapter Five: The Trouble with Humans

191 **"extension of the master's prerogative":** Saidiya Hartman, "The Position of the Unthought: An Interview with Saidiya V. Hartman Conducted by Frank B. Wilderson, III," *Qui Parle* 13, no. 2 (Spring/Summer 2003): 188.

193 **In one episode:** Season 4, Episode 5, "About a Boy," directed by Charlotte Sieling, aired October 26, 2014.

193 **overdetermined by mutual consent:** *Overdetermined:* to account for or cause (something) in more than one way or with more conditions than are necessary, for example, "every gesture is overdetermined by cultural form, personal biography, historical contingency, and so on."

194 **White family is the cutout of the state:** The paraphrase comes from *Black Skin, White Masks,* the chapter titled "The Negro and Psychopathology." In espionage parlance, a cutout is a mutually trusted intermediary, method, or channel of communication that facilitates the exchange of information between agents.

194 *She has a limited capacity to marshal:* Jared Sexton, "Race, Sexuality, and Political Struggle: Reading *Soul on Ice," Social Justice* 30, no. 2 (2003): 36. Emphasis mine.

195 **"[E]nslaved men were no less vulnerable":** Saidiya Hartman, *Scenes of*

Subjection: Terror, Slavery, and Self-Making in Nineteenth-Century America
(New York: Oxford University Press, 1997), 81.

195 **"objective value":** David Marriott, *On Black Men* (New York: Columbia
University Press, 2000), 11.

196 **"You better understand White people's fantasies":** From a workshop
Sexton and I conducted for Black undergraduate student organizers at UC
Berkeley in 2000.

196 **"An electoral choice of ten different fascists":** George L. Jackson, *Blood in
My Eye* (Baltimore: Black Classic, 1971, 1990), 72.

197 **"389,000 [that's less than a half million]":** From Lee Ballinger's review
of *The American Slave Coast*: Lee Ballinger, "Slavery is the Root of all Evil,"
CounterPunch 22, no. 10 (2015).

200 **South African woman named Khanya:** The details surrounding my
divorce from Khanya and my partnering with Alice are not as straightforward as this sentence implies, nor do the details present me in the best possible light. I have explored these events and their racial implications in my
memoir *Incognegro: A Memoir of Exile and Apartheid* (Boston: South End
Press, 2008; Durham, NC: Duke University Press, 2015).

204 **N.W.A.:** An abbreviation for Niggaz Wit Attitudes. N.W.A. was an American hip-hop group from Compton, California.

211 **"works at Cal":** The University of California, Berkeley.

216 **"violence beyond the limits":** David Eltis, "Europeans and the Rise and
Fall of African Slavery in the Americas: An Interpretation," *The American
Historical Review* 98, no. 5 (December 1993), 1423.

217 **new, global shift in political economy:** Allen Feldman, *Formations of Violence: The Narrative of the Body and Political Terror in Northern Ireland* (Chicago: University Of Chicago Press, 1991).

217 **"extension of the master's prerogative":** Saidiya Hartman, "The Position
of the Unthought: An Interview with Saidiya V. Hartman Conducted by
Frank B. Wilderson, III," *Qui Parle* 13, no. 2 (Spring/Summer 2003): 188.

217 **"the prehistory and (concurrent) history of slavery":** Orlando Patterson,
Slavery and Social Death: A Comparative Study (Cambridge, MA: Harvard
University Press, 1982), 3. Emphasis mine.

217 **Africa's spatial coherence:** See Achille Mbembe, *On the Postcolony* (Berkeley: University of California Press, 2001); S. E. Anderson, *The Black Holocaust
for Beginners* (Danbury, CT: For Beginners LLC, 1995); Bernard Lewis, *Race
and Slavery in the Middle East: An Historical Enquiry* (New York: Oxford

University Press, 1990); Orlando Patterson, *Slavery and Social Death: A Comparative Study* (Cambridge, MA: Harvard University Press, 1982).

222 **"absolute dereliction":** Frantz Fanon, *Black Skin, White Masks*, trans. Charles Lam Markmann (New York: Grove, [1952], 1967).

226 **"historical stillness":** Hortense Spillers, "Mama's Baby, Papa's Maybe: An American Grammar Book," in *Black, White, and in Color: Essays on American Literature and Culture* (Chicago: University of Chicago Press, 2003).

227 **"It marks stasis and change":** Frank B. Wilderson III, *Red, White & Black: Cinema and the Structure of U.S. Antagonisms* (Durham, NC: Duke University Press, 2010), 339.

227 **"story world":** H. Porter Abbott, *The Cambridge Introduction to Narrative* (New York: Cambridge University Press, 2008).

Chapter Six: Mind the Closing Doors

239 **"To break up the colonial world":** Frantz Fanon, *Wretched of the Earth*, trans. Constance Farrington (New York: Grove, 1963), 41–44.

240 **reigning episteme:** French philosopher and philologist Michel Foucault (1926–1984) used the term *episteme* to indicate the total set of relations that unite a given period. Richard Nordquist, "Episteme in Rhetoric," December 28, 2017, accessed June 27, 2019, https://www.thoughtco.com/episteme -rhetoric-term-1690665.

241 **"out of the picture":** Frantz Fanon, *Wretched of the Earth*, trans. Constance Farrington (New York: Grove, 1963), 44.

242 **forty to sixty paramilitary actions:** The Justice Department–LEAA Task Force report on BLA activity records sixty BLA actions between 1970 and 1976. In the past, this report has been reproduced on BLA-sanctioned websites and, most recently, in a book of essays by Jalil Muntaqim, a Black Liberation Army prisoner of war. The University of Maryland's Global Terrorism Database (GTD) puts the number at thirty-six. Whereas the GTD includes BLA bank expropriations, it does not, unlike the BLA-reproduced Justice Department report, include prison escapes (successful and unsuccessful). See Jalil Muntaqim, *On the Black Liberation Army* (Montreal and Toronto: Abraham Guillen Press and Arm The Spirit, 2002).

242 **"It was the right thing to do":** Television interview with Bill Moyers reproduced in Toni Morrison, *Conversations with Toni Morrison*, ed. Danielle Taylor-Guthrie (Jackson, MS: University Press of Mississippi, 1994), 272.

244 **guerrilla war that the Black Liberation Army waged:** Akinyele Umoja, "Repression Breeds Resistance: The Black Liberation Army and the Radical Legacy of the Black Panther Party," *New Political Science* 21, no. 2 (1999).

245 **sixty-six operations:** This is the number of operations that BLA members acknowledge, presumably because this number is a matter of public record. See Jalil Abdul Muntaqim, "On the Black Liberation Army."

245 **FALN insurgents:** The Fuerzas Armadas de Liberación Nacional was a Puerto Rican clandestine paramilitary organization that, through direct action, advocated complete independence for Puerto Rico. It carried out more than 130 bomb attacks in the United States between 1974 and 1983. "FALN" in Gus Martin, ed., *The SAGE Encyclopedia of Terrorism, Second Edition* (Thousand Oaks, CA: SAGE, 2011): 193–4.

245 **ruling discursive codes:** See Frank B. Wilderson III, *Red, White & Black: Cinema and the Structure of U.S. Antagonisms* (Durham, NC: Duke University Press, 2010); "Gramsci's Black Marx: Whither the Slave in Civil Society?" *Social Identities: Journal for the Study of Race, Nation and Culture* 9, no. 2 (2003); and "Biko and the Problematic of Presence," in *Biko Lives!*, eds. Andile Mngxitama, Amanda Alexander, and Nigel C. Gibson (New York: Palgrave MacMillan, 2008).

248 **"black ego":** David Marriott, *Haunted Life: Visual Culture and Black Modernity* (New Brunswick, NJ: Rutgers University Press, 2007), 219.

248 **imago of the Black phobic object:** David Marriott, *Haunted Life*.

249 **bond through racial antagonism:** David Marriott, *Haunted Life*, 211.

249 **"its objective value":** David Marriott, *On Black Men* (New York: Columbia University Press, 2000), 11.

249 **"picture of the black psyche":** David Marriott, *Haunted Life: Visual Culture and Black Modernity* (New Brunswick, NJ: Rutgers University Press, 2007), 212.

249 **For whoever says "rape" says Black:** Frantz Fanon, *Black Skin, White Masks*, trans. Charles Lam Markmann (New York: Grove, [1952], 1967).

249 **whoever says "AIDS" says Black:** Jared Sexton, *Amalgamation Schemes: Antiblackness and the Critique of Multiracialism* (Minneapolis: University of Minnesota Press, 2008).

252 **"In these circumstances, having a 'white' ":** David Marriott, *Haunted Life: Visual Culture and Black Modernity* (New Brunswick, NJ: Rutgers University Press, 2007), 426.

Chapter Seven: Mario's

256 **MK:** uMkhonto we Sizwe, the armed wing of the ANC.

256 **Inkatha:** The Inkatha Freedom Party, a Zulu nationalist party that worked with the apartheid state to suppress the ANC.

261 **"Because three hundred people are being killed":** Huntley was writing a novel about his childhood in England when he was sent to live in the countryside as the Luftwaffe bombed London.

261 **"Hey, china":** *China* means "good friend," as in, "This oke's my china." It can also mean "bro" or "dude."

265 **"each other with pangas":** A panga is a large, broad-bladed knife used as a weapon.

268 **rubble of COMECON:** The sobriquet of Council for Mutual Economic Assistance (CMEA), established in January 1949 to facilitate and coordinate the economic development of the Eastern European countries belonging to the Soviet Bloc. See "Comecon," *Encyclopedia Britannica*, accessed May 12, 2019, https://www.britannica.com/topic/Comecon.

268 **somewhere in the Karoo:** *Klein dorpie*: a small town. *Karoo*: a semi-desert region six hundred miles southwest of Johannesburg.

276 **"unthought":** Saidiya Hartman, "The Position of the Unthought: An Interview with Saidiya V. Hartman Conducted by Frank B. Wilderson, III," *Qui Parle* 13, no. 2 (Spring/Summer 2003).

282 **SADF:** The South African Defense Force.

302 **had to negotiate captivity:** See Achille Mbembe, *On the Postcolony* (Berkeley: University of California Press, 2001).

Epilogue: The New Century

309 **"The term 'nervous breakdown'":** "Nervous breakdown: What does it mean?" *Mayo Clinic Patient Care and Health Info* (Oct. 26, 2016), accessed August 15, 2019, https://www.mayoclinic.org/diseases-conditions/depression/expert-answers/nervous-breakdown/faq-20057830.

309 **"They cannot love themselves":** *Haunted Life: Visual Culture and Black Modernity* (New Brunswick, NJ: Rutgers University Press, 2007), and *On Black Men* (New York: Columbia University Press, 2000).

311 **Elsewhere, I have written:** *Incognegro: A Memoir of Exile and Apartheid* (Boston: South End Press, 2008; Durham, NC: Duke University Press, 2015).

313 *made* **to hate yourself as White:** David Marriott, *On Black Men* (New York: Columbia University Press, 2000).

314 **"a vector through which others can accomplish themselves":** Cecilio M. Cooper and Frank B. Wilderson III, "Incommensurabilities: The Limits of Redress, Intramural Indemnity, and Extramural Auditorship," in eds. Hunter et al., "Co-presence with the Camera," *Performance Matters* (April 2020).

314 **unconscious that** *appears* **to hate you:** See "Lynching and Photography" and "Frantz Fanon's War" in David Marriott, *On Black Men* (New York: Columbia University Press, 2000).

320 **Jack and Jill conventions:** Jack and Jill of America, Inc., is a membership organization of mothers with children ages two through nineteen, dedicated to nurturing future African American leaders by strengthening children through leadership development, volunteer service, philanthropic giving, and civic duty. Accessed June 28, 2019, https://jackandjillinc.org/about-us/.

327 **that civil society was a murderous juggernaut:** *Red, White & Black: Cinema and the Structure of U.S. Antagonisms* (Durham, NC: Duke University Press, 2010).

327 **"The slave is the object or the ground that":** Saidiya Hartman, *Scenes of Subjection: Terror, Slavery, and Self-Making in Nineteenth-Century America* (New York: Oxford University Press, 1997), 62.

330 **"there are only two Black homeowners in Kenwood":** After a few years of cajoling, my parents convinced another Black family to try to buy a house in Kenwood. They bought one across the street from us in 1968—it wasn't easy.

330 **"the uniqueness of Kenwood":** "Open Letter: Closed Minds in Kenwood?" *Minneapolis StarTribune*, April 10, 1968.

334 **When my first book came out:** *Incognegro: A Memoir of Exile and Apartheid* (Boston: South End Press, 2008; Durham, NC: Duke University Press, 2015).

ABOUT THE AUTHOR

Frank B. Wilderson III is professor and chair of African American Studies, and a core faculty member of the Culture & Theory Ph.D. Program at UC Irvine. He spent five and a half years in South Africa, where he was one of two Americans to hold elected office in the African National Congress during the apartheid era. He also was a cadre in the underground. His books include *Incognegro: A Memoir of Exile and Apartheid* and *Red, White & Black: Cinema and the Structure of U.S. Antagonisms*. His creative writing has received a National Endowment for the Arts Literature Fellowship; the Maya Angelou Award for Best Fiction Portraying the Black Experience in America; the American Book Award; and the Zora Neale Hurston / Richard Wright Legacy Award for Nonfiction.

To inquire about booking Frank B. Wilderson III for a speaking engagement, please contact Evil Twin Booking at https://eviltwinbooking.org. His critical documentary, *Reparations . . . Now*, is available for educational screenings on Vimeo: https://vimeo.com/73991006.